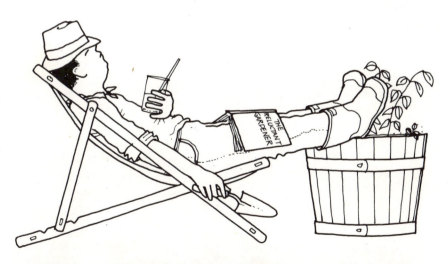

GARDENER

Windward

b35

First published 1983
Text © 1983 by Leslie Godfrey
Illustrations © 1983 by Whittet Books Ltd

Produced by Whittet Books Ltd, The Oil Mills, Weybridge, Surrey

Published by Windward
an imprint owned by WH Smith & Son Limited
Registered No 237811 England
Trading as WHS Distributors,
St John's House, East Street, Leicester, LE1 6NE

British Library Cataloguing in Publication Data

Godfrey, Leslie
   The reluctant gardener.
   1. Gardening
   I. Title
   635   SB450.97

ISBN 0-7112-0329-6

Printed and bound in Great Britain
at The Pitman Press, Bath

THE RELUCTANT GARDENER

LESLIE GODFREY

with illustrations by Ian Layzell

THE RELUCTANT

CONTENTS

The measurements in this book

After a great deal of deliberation we have decided to use old fashioned measurements and not the new metric ones. Old fashioned measurements have one great advantage to the reluctant gardener. They are expressed in inches and feet and although we may not always have a tape measure with us we do usually have feet. If you are lucky like me your foot will measure a foot – or rather your shoe will if you take size nine. The spread of my outstretched fingers from tip of big finger to tip of thumb is nine inches. So I can measure most things in the garden with bits of my body. Why not measure bits of yours and choose the easy to remember ones? It saves a lot of bother.

If your brain has been converted to metric measurements, here is a conversion chart:

Multiply number of		by	to obtain equivalent number of	Multiply number of	by	to obtain equivalent number of
Inches (in)	{	25·4	millimetres (mm)	Millimetres	0·03937	inches
		2·54	centimetres (cm)	Centimetres	0·3937	inches
Feet (ft)	{	30·48	centimetres	Metres	39·3701	inches
		0·3048	metres (m)		3·2808	feet
Yard (yd)		0·9144	} metres		1·0936	yards
Fathoms (6ft)		1·8288			0·54681	fathoms

LET US LOOK AT THE PROBLEM

The problem is time, money and inclination. Or a bit of each.

I would love to be able to offer you emerald green lawns, beautiful flowers and shrubs, limpid pools and fountains, trained climbers and stately trees, luscious fruits and fresh vegetables all in season with no work at all. I'd love them for myself. But I am afraid it's not on. If you want *all* those things you have either got to be rich and pay someone else to produce them or you have got to spend most of your spare time with mud on your hands.

But there is no reason why you should not have just some of them and still have time for other things.

First let us look the problem fairly and squarely in the face. Gardening is different from most other pursuits in one important respect. You can put the golf-clubs in the cupboard and forget about them, you can close the kitchen door and go out for a meal instead of cooking it, you can lock up the car in the garage and pretend you don't own one. But you can't do that with a garden. You can't lock it up, it won't go away and worst of all it won't even stand still. Every moment of the day it is in a state of change – flowers are blooming, fading and dying, the lawn is getting like a hayfield, moss is covering the paths and nettles, dandelions, docks and thistles are slowly but relentlessly marching across the beds and borders.

There is another way in which being a reluctant gardener is different from other reluctances. You can't hide it away. You can't keep it private. It is a public matter. Neighbours can put their heads over the fence and see what you haven't done in the back garden and passers-by can see what you haven't done in the front garden. There is no hiding your successes or your failures.

A COUPLE OF RULES

To make gardening tolerable, or even enjoyable, you must follow a couple of rules – rules of attitude.

The first is that your garden is yours and no one else's. So don't let anyone give you a conscience about it. Provided you don't annoy the neighbours by smoking them out with your bonfire on a summer's day or letting clouds of weed seeds drift across their land it is your garden to do with as you please – provided you don't cause a nuisance. If you want to have your garden all roses you have it all roses, if you want it all rhubarb you have it all rhubarb, or if you want it all tarmac you have it all tarmac – no, on second thoughts if all the extra rainwater drained on to next door's plot that might be classed as a nuisance, but you know what I mean. Do what will give you or your family and friends the most pleasure.

The second rule that I would suggest is 'Never tell anyone but your nearest and dearest what you are going to do with the garden – what you intend to achieve.' It is so easy in our mind's eye to turn a battlefield of brick bats, mud and old beer cans that the builder has left us into a tranquillity of colour and delight that we forget it might take more than a few weeks to accomplish. In practice it takes a little longer so it is best to say nothing and then if you haven't got around to doing anything by this time next year it

.... AND PROMISE TO TELL YOU WHAT I WILL DO WITH THE GARDEN.....

doesn't matter and if you have then everyone will be impressed. 'Do good by stealth and blush to find it fame.'

There isn't, of course, one neat and tidy plan to suit everyone. Some of you will have small gardens, others will have large ones. Some gardens will be fresh from the builder's care decorated with half-bricks like a spotted dick or given the cosmetic treatment with turf to hide the blemishes. A few builders will do you proud and leave you some genuine soil. Some gardens will be on good rich loam and others on sand, gravel, chalk, peat or heavy clay. So first we must look at the soil.

1 THE SOIL

Soil is the most significant factor in determining the success of your gardening efforts. Even if you just intend to pave over it it is important to consider what type of soil you have. No matter how precious your time may be please do give a little of it to take stock of your soil before you do anything else at all. It will save you time, trouble and tears in the long run.

If you lay paving on deep rich loam the activity of the living organisms in the soil will soon turn your paving into the Rocky Mountains. On the other hand if the builder has been mean enough to leave you with just solid clay subsoil it might make a good foundation for your paving but it will break your heart and strain your back if you try to cultivate it.

So no matter how keen you are to turn your plot into an easy to maintain garden in the shortest possible time pause a while and investigate your soil. This still holds good if you take over an established garden. Good soil is a living city of millions and millions of minute creatures ranging from micro-organisms to earthworms existing on living, dead or decaying matter mixed with the pulverized sands and powders of the original rocks. As leaves fall from the trees and plants and creatures die they rot down and nourish the top layer of soil to enable it to support a new cycle of life. If we stop the process by destroying our leaves and lawn mowings and putting nothing back our soil will slowly and surely deteriorate.

You can, of course, dig out the whole lot and replace it with new soil but that is an expensive process. You could, however, introduce just pockets of soil in selected areas to suit certain types of plants, or if your soil is poor and starved it can certainly be improved. First of all recognize what kind of soil you have – what you have to deal with. Let us look at the terminology, the words used when talking about soil.

TOPSOIL

This is the darker layer of soil at the top – hence its name. It can be anything from a mere two or three inches deep to almost a couple of feet in very well cultivated gardens but the normal is 9 in to a foot – about a spade's depth. It contains the living organisms necessary to healthy plant growth. If you take over a newly built house do ensure that you have adequate topsoil. Sometimes builders are careless when digging out foundations and bury some of the topsoil under the subsoil. It has been known for a builder to remove most of the topsoil from the site altogether – it fetches a good market price – and spread just a thin layer of topsoil over the subsoil when he has finished building. So find a place where the plot has not been disturbed by the building operations to see what the soil should be like. If you have any doubts dig a trench across part of the area to see if the topsoil has got buried. If so it is worth all the effort to get the topsoil back on top again. Even if you intend to have just a lawn and nothing else get that topsoil back where it belongs or your lawn will be a poor troublesome thing. It may look as if I'm creating work for you but believe me it will save you a lot of work in the long run. Do avoid mixing the topsoil with the subsoil especially if the latter is sticky clay or chalk.

When excavating for paths, walls or for other operations treat the topsoil as precious and stack it on one side ready for use where the plants and lawns are to be.

SUBSOIL

This is usually lighter in colour than the topsoil and as the name implies lies beneath it. It is generally pretty useless for good growth and should stay where it is down below. It may be sand, gravel, chalk, clay or rock depending on where you live.

HUMUS

This is the miracle matter in the soil. Humus is a jelly-like substance, the end product of the process of decay, that coats the minute particles of soil. It benefits the soil in many ways. It helps it hold a larger amount of nutrients and make them available to the plants. It gives the soil a good 'crumb structure' which will help to retain moisture in light soils and yet open up the soil to aid drainage in heavy ones. It makes light coloured soils darker and helps them retain heat. It enables the soil to crumble down into a good seed bed. It makes the soil easier to work and it encourages good root growth. It is truly the wonder substance in the soil that turns infertile ground into good crumbly loam.

We do not add humus as such to the soil – we add well-rotted compost, leafmould or manure which nature turns into humus. The process is called humification.

ACID OR ALKALINE

Some plants like an acid soil and others an alkaline one but most plants like a soil that is just between the two – nearly neutral. Chalk and lime make a soil alkaline while the constant addition of compost, peat, leafmould or manure tends to make it acid. It is therefore easier to make soils more alkaline than it is to make them more acid – by just sprinkling them with lime.

The level of acidity or alkalinity in the soil is usually referred to as the pH factor. Literally the term pH means 'the negative decimal logarithm of hydrogen ion concentration in the soil measured in moles per litre'. Use that definition to impress others if you will, otherwise just think of the pH factor as a way of expressing how acid or alkaline the soil is.

Most garden centres or suppliers sell testing kits which are fairly easy to use. If you don't want to bother to test the pH of your soil don't worry too much because many plants will grow in it anyway and you will find out in time which ones do best. But you may be depressed by your inability to grow plants when the problem isn't you but the acid level of the soil. So testing the pH level can save some time in the long run. If you have a very big garden it may even be worthwhile taking soil samples from a few different places. pH 7 is neutral, readings less than pH 7 indicate an increasing level of acidity in the soil while readings greater than pH 7 indicate greater alkalinity.

SOIL TYPES

Most of us don't have any choice in the matter and our gardens have topsoils of many different kinds. We have to do the best with the soil we have got and continually aim to improve it.

Soils don't come parcelled into exact groups. Most are somewhere between one type and another but let us have a look at the main soil types.

Sandy soils

As you would expect these have a high level of sand in them. They are loose to the touch and if you pick up a moist handful and squeeze it together it will crumble apart again when you drop it whereas its exact opposite, clay, will stay in one lump. Being loose sandy soils have a poor water-holding ability and dry out easily but they warm up quickly in the spring so are good for early plants and crops. They are nice and easy to work. Nutrients vital to the growth of plants are easily washed out of them so they need liberal additions of humus-making material – composts and manures – all the time you are growing things in them.

Silt

Silty soils are often found in river plains. They are rather like sandy soils but the particles are smaller. They are usually deep and fertile and because the soil spaces are smaller than in sandy soils they hold water better. They are marvellous soils for reluctant gardeners.

Clay soils

There is a lot to be said for clay soils and most of it is rude. Clay sticks to your boots and your spade and the effort of trying to get it raked down into a fine seedbed will send most reluctant gardeners back to their deck chairs. If you walk on clay when it is wet it will pan down and when it dries out it can be like rock. Because clay has finer particles than other soils it can retain a higher level of water. When it is wet clay swells up and if you have the energy to bend down and pick up a handful you will find it sticky to the touch. If you squeeze the handful it will stay squeezed and will probably stain your hand.

Although clay soils are certainly not the ideal ones for reluctant gardeners they do have one great point in their favour. They are almost always rich in nutrients and will grow a wide range of plants. It is a question of improving their texture to make them easier to deal with.

Dig them in the autumn and incorporate all the compost, leafmould, peat or manure you can get. If the soil is really sticky stuff don't dig deeply but incorporate that organic matter within the top six inches to make the soil easier to work in the spring. Leave the soil rough dug for the winter. Don't attempt to break down the lumps – the frosts will break them down for you. And at all costs keep off the ground when it is wet. If for some reason you just have to walk on it put a plank down first and walk along that.

I would suggest that before you buy a house you quietly pick up a handful of the garden on a damp day and squeeze it in the hand. If it feels sticky and stays in a solid lump when you let go hand it politely back to the owner and ask what good labour-saving devices the house has to make up for the time you are going to have to spend in the garden.

Stony soils

People get worried about stony soils but they are usually very fertile. Seed falling on stony ground can do very well indeed. Stony soils may be based on clay and the less fertile ones on sand. The stones can, of course, be a bit of a nuisance in a seedbed but they are handy to throw at marauding pigeons and they aid drainage by keeping the soil open. Remove the big stones if you wish and be grateful that you haven't got heavy clay or chalk.

Chalky soils

These contain large quantities of calcium and so are very alkaline with a high pH reading. They are certainly not the ideal soils for reluctant gardeners as they need a lot of love and care. They tend to become sticky when wet, and free-draining when dry. They are usually shallow and because they have a low nutrient holding capacity plants can suffer from what is called 'lime induced chlorosis'. They don't grow well and their leaves turn yellow.

If your soil is chalky dig in as much organic material as you can lay your hands on – compost, manure, peat or leafmould and add a compound such as sequestrine which you can buy from garden shops, which will help release the nutrients in the soil locked up by the lime. As you will probably have surmised chalky soils need no lime on them.

Peaty soils

Peaty soils are just the opposite to chalk in that they are very acid with a low pH reading. They occur in parts of Lincolnshire, Cheshire, Lancashire, Somerset and in Scotland and Ireland as well as other areas. They are dark soils with a high content of ancient dead plant matter that has stopped completely decaying through the exclusion of air by waterlogging and the build-up of acids. In some areas they will need to be drained and in other areas they will not – so be guided by local conditions. They can be low in potash and phosphates and usually need the addition of a compound fertilizer in April or May.

I would say a peaty soil is ideal for the reluctant gardener. You can grow acid-loving plants in the flower garden – heathers, azaleas, rhododendrons and many other shrubs. You will find that only the finer, slower growing grasses will grow in the lawn, which must be a benefit, and you will get a reasonable return from the vegetable garden if you spread lime in late winter or early spring. Your cabbages may not be too brilliant but there are more things to life than cabbages.

I'D MUCH RATHER HAVE CHRISTMAS PUDDING

Loam

A magic word to the enthusiastic gardener and even the reluctant one should show a little interest in the word. It is used to describe those soils which are the ultimate fertile mix of sand, silt and clay with a good content of humus. Usually dark in colour loam is to plants what Christmas pudding is to a hungry boy, except that it is much more crumbly than most Christmas puddings I have met. If you are blessed with a dark loamy soil there is a distinct danger that given time you will be transformed from a reluctant gardener into an eager one.

MAJOR PLANT NUTRIENTS

Plants need the energy from sunlight to build up complex substances from water and carbon dioxide. So most of them need to be grown right out in the open, although some have adapted to varying degrees of shade. Plants also need potassium, nitrogen, phosphorus, calcium, magnesium and traces of other chemical substances. Some of these substances occur naturally in the soil while others are supplied from manure or compost. The three major plant foods are potassium, nitrogen and phosphorus. They each have a complex and interrelated part to play in the growth of plants. Do make sure that your plants get their proper requirements of all three.

You should do a detailed analysis of your soil with one of the soil-testing kits that are obtainable from most plant centres. This would tell you how much of each major plant food you should apply but if you can't get around to it the simplest way to avoid plant starvation is to make sure your garden gets a full ration of compost each year and then a top up with a general purpose fertilizer like National Growmore. Sprinkle it over the whole garden in April or May. The grass will be grateful for some as well as the plants so sprinkle it over lawns, flowerbeds, shrubs, and the vegetable garden (quantity per square metre as directed). The plants will grow better, the lawns will be greener and the flower colours will be brighter.

2 COMPOST AND HUMUS– IS IT WORTH IT?

'Compost' is confusing: there is 'potting compost' used for bringing on seedlings or for potting up plants in flower pots; there is also the product of the compost heap. I'm now talking about the latter.

To some people it is a slimy, smelly, half-rotted heap of nastiness that has festered in a dank untidy pile in a corner of the garden and is unlovely enough to put anyone off gardening for ever. To others it is a sweet-smelling, dark, crumbly substance that is pleasant to handle and which is a miracle worker in the soil. That is the kind you want. The point about compost to the reluctant gardener is this – if you will take the trouble to build some proper compost boxes in the first place you will save yourself so much time and trouble in the long run that gardening may even become a pleasure. If you want easy gardening you must have proper compost and proper compost either comes from proper compost boxes or must be bought.

Proper compost boxes are not difficult to build – they may look a bit complex on the drawings (see pp 16-19) but they are not when you come to build them – and they produce a beautiful friable magic matter that makes gardening so much easier. Plants grow well, they withstand attacks from pests and diseases, the soil is easier to work, it smells good, weeds come out more easily, sandy soils more easily retain water and heavy soils have better drainage. I know that sounds like a contradiction but it is true.

My task is surely not just to make life easier for you for *one* year but to make it a bit easier for you for every single year until the eternal reaper comes for you. And compost is the main key to your life of ease. So put your feet up for a moment and join with me in contemplating compost.

The stark cold truth is that tens of thousands of town gardens and some country ones as well have got thin, disease-ridden soil in which poor, sickly plants struggle to survive for lack of compost. Many years ago when the houses were built most of those gardens produced strong colourful plants, green lawns and excellent vegetables. But over the years the gardens have slowly and surely deteriorated and produced poorer and poorer plants until many of the owners have given up trying and have let the weeds take over.

Let us have a look at nature for a moment. In uncultivated areas of the world nature continuously replaces the humus and nutrient content of the soil by the natural cycle of growth and decay. Animal and vegetable life continuously grows and dies and forms a natural layer of composting material on the surface of the soil. The earthworms and other insects take this compost down into the soil which enriches it for further plant growth. Even where the ground is cropped by grazing herds and the fruits, leaves and nuts eaten by other animals, dung is left behind to replace what has been eaten. When they die their bodies also return to mother earth – often by a complex chain of smaller animal life – so that nothing is wasted. The earth supports life and life then enriches the earth to support more life. There is a continuous cycle of growth, decay and growth. Sometimes a calamity like a forest fire, or a major change of climate, may upset that balance with far-reaching results. The great Sahara desert, for instance, was once covered with vegetation.

Compare the life cycle of nature with what happens in some gardens. If the lawn mowings and dead plants are put on the rubbish tip, the leaves swept up every year and burnt and no compost is put back into the soil then it will just get poorer and poorer. Soils must have organic material continually put back into them. Large areas of America, India and South Africa were ruined by a continual process of cropping with no replacement of humus. Artificials were used by the planters and farmers to stimulate plant growth but the humus content of the soil slowly but surely disappeared leaving the earth thin and at the mercy of the wind. It blew away.

The thin earth in some of our gardens has not blown away but it is a poor medium in which to grow plants. And don't ignore the lawn, because what is a lawn but plants – hopefully mostly grass plants rather than moss, clover and dandelions. The soil is often lacking in both humus and plant nutrients. To put matters right such gardens need to have *more* organic matter put back into them each year than is taken out by the plants until in a few years the soil is once again a rich, loamy earth instead of a thin sand or hard clay.

Sometimes people are misled by city soil – when it is wet it can look so nice and dark but that darkness *may* be caused by deposits from coal smoke. Our cities are very different places from fifty years ago when the air was a constant haze of smoke from thousands of chimneys. The deposits from the smoke darkened the soil – and the buildings – but did little good apart from keeping black spot disease off the roses.

The darkness we need in our soil is not from soot but from compost, manure or leafmould. One popular and much advertised organic material is peat; if used just by itself it will not supply the balanced minerals, enzymes and food for the millions of bacteria and fungi that should be working in the soil to keep it in the right condition for healthy plant growth, but it will improve the soil texture and help to give the right conditions for ericaceous plants like heathers. You can also buy organic manures based on spent hops or seaweed but these tend to be expensive. Another much advertised material is Forest Bark. This makes a good mulch to keep down weeds but must not be dug into the soil as it has not been composted and will deplete the soil of nutriments while it is rotting – which will take many years. So if you do use it, just spread it on the surface.

So, dear reluctant gardener, it *will* take you just a little time and effort to replace or retain the humus in your soil. You can, of course, ignore the rest of this chapter and go straight on to Chapter 3 but, unless you have a really tiny back garden with no room for compost, do stay with me awhile because a good understanding and use of compost and manure will save you a lot of work and disappointment in the long run.

THE MAGIC OF MUCK

Polite gardeners call it farmyard manure, but farmers call it muck. It is usually cow manure mixed up with bedding straw but it may well contain pig or poultry manure as well. There's nothing wrong with that. These days, because few farmers keep horses in any numbers, horse manure usually comes from riding stables. Good manure is expensive and not always easy to obtain. It can vary greatly in the amount of plant foods it contains depending on how the animals have been kept and how the manure has been stored.

Animal urine is a valuable ingredient of manure but if the manure has been stored in the open the urine may well have been washed out by the rain.

Don't use it raw

Manure must be well rotted before it is used in the garden. In its raw state it contains acids harmful to plants. Young seedlings will turn up their toes and die if you tuck it up against them. So, if in doubt, stack any new manure in the garden for a few months covered over with a couple of inches of soil or some kind of temporary roof to keep the rain off it until it has mellowed.

Buying manure by the bag is very expensive, although if you have only a tiny plot it may be the sensible way. If you need any quantity it is best to buy a load from a manure merchant, riding stables or farm, although many farmers are now coming round to putting the muck back on their own land.

HUNGRY LAND WILL NEED WELL FEEDING

If the soil in your garden is really poor then there is a lot of organic material and plant nutrients to be replaced. If your total plot measures 40 ft by 40 ft or thereabouts you could invest in at least one ton of manure to give your garden a good meal to start it on the road to recovery and if it's twice that size get two tons. That is like giving a hungry boy one good meal, so don't just leave it at that but keep your garden topped up each year with compost made from your own kitchen and garden waste. You can, of course, get rid of all the plant refuse from your garden in the dustbin or on the bonfire and buy in manure each year but that is an expensive way of doing it and you save little effort because you've still got the job of distributing the manure, the trouble of smoky bonfires and the bother of trying to get your dustmen to take away your garden rubbish.

So be reluctant about other aspects of gardening if you must, but please don't be reluctant about compost.

HOW TO USE THE MANURE

With land that has to be dug (see p. 25) – either new flower borders or the vegetable garden – the manure will normally be dug in as you go. With existing flower borders or rose beds, spread it on top – ideally in a 1 inch layer, but you never will get it exactly even. Use it on very light sandy soils as a top mulch.

The best way to return organic material to the soil is via the compost heap. You could, of course, ignore the compost heap and put fresh material such as shredded plants, grass cuttings, kitchen waste or straw straight back into the soil but during decomposition the activity of micro-organisms in the material would use up nitrogen (an essential plant food) and then extract further nitrogen from the soil. Once decomposition was completed the nitrogen would be returned to the soil but in the meantime your plants would feel quite poorly. They would show the typical telltale signs of nitrogen deficiency – small pale leaves and stunted growth. So do rot down any animal and plant waste in a compost heap before you return it to the soil.

THE ROTTING PROCESS

Successful compost making depends on a number of things.
A mixed diet – Heaps made from just one material such as lawn mowings will give a poor result.
Moisture – Dry material should be watered but not made sodden.
Air – Those micro-organisms that break down the plant material need air. The air flow should, ideally, be provided from underneath the heap to rise up through it.
Shelter – The bacterial activity heats up the heap and this has the useful function of killing weed seeds and perennial roots like dandelions and couch grass. Rain and snow could lower the temperature, slow down the rate of decomposition and stop this useful work.
An activator – This is not necessary in the spring and early summer when plenty of nitrogen will be supplied from lawn mowings and young weeds but useful in the autumn and winter to feed the bacteria with nitrogen when they have tougher material to digest. Animal manure or urine – human urine if you like – is an excellent activator. Add what you can get. Otherwise sprinkle a

handful of fishmeal, hoof and horn or dried blood to every alternate 9 in layer of a heap that is, say, 3 ft by 3 ft. You can use proprietary inorganic activators but the organic ones release their nitrogen more slowly over a longer period.

A little lime – The material will not rot down completely in excessive acid conditions. So add about 4 oz of lime mixed with a couple of shovelfuls of topsoil to the layers that do not receive the activator. But don't add any lime if you are going to use the compost on lime-hating plants like heathers or rhododendrons.

A top blanket – This is to keep in the heat in winter and the moisture in summer. But it needs to be porous to keep the air flowing through the heap. You could use sacking or an old piece of carpet, or an opened-out thick plastic sack – the latter two with holes 1 in in diameter and 9 in apart in each direction.

MATERIALS TO INCLUDE IN THE COMPOST HEAP

Include all vegetable and animal matter from the kitchen and garden that will rot down quickly. Don't include wood, sawdust, bones or anything greasy or badly diseased such as rose leaves heavy with black-spot or the roots of the cabbage family which may have club-root disease. The cabbage stalks can go on but bash them up first.

Don't include large quantities of tree leaves. They take too long to rot down. Add just a few by all means but if you have large quantities rot them down separately to make leafmould. Give evergreens a miss – they are very slow rotters.

The best rotters are:

All weeds. But don't include perennial roots or weed-seeds if you plan to have only a makeshift compost heap.

Lawn mowings. Alternate these with the other materials. By themselves lawn mowings will not rot well.

Spent plants. Everything from the vegetable and flower garden.

Prunings and clippings. Just the young and tender ones from shrubs and hedges.

Tree leaves. Up to 10% of the total material in the heap.

Torn up newspaper. Again only up to 10% of the total. Tear it up small and soak for 24 hours first. Don't use glossy or coloured paper.

Droppings. Any organic material from rabbits, poultry, guinea pigs, pigeons and human urine if you wish

Kitchen waste. All kitchen fruit and vegetable waste and crushed-up egg shells. Throw in the tea leaves and coffee grounds if you wish but there won't be much goodness left in them.

Feathers and flock. Feathers make good compost whether from an old pillow or a new bird. If you want to stop them flying everywhere – as is their custom – wet them first. Cotton flock may be added in small quantities. Do not add man-made materials or fibre.

Mixing

Good mixing is important. It allows proper ventilation and ensures an even spread of micro-organisms to break down the tougher stuff.

The base

The base of the heap should be raised off the ground with bricks and weldmesh, or built on brushwood to allow air to circulate.

CHOOSE YOUR METHOD

Compost can, like our own food, be highly nutritious or just adequate. If you are very reluctant to build proper compost boxes – they can save a lot of time and energy in the long run – then go in for bought plastic compost bins, 'better than nothing compost' or 'the press box'.

Plastic compost bins

The advertisements say that you put in raw material at the top and shovel out rich compost at the bottom. They are no doubt useful in very small gardens and will make a reasonable product if the instructions are followed; they have a tendency to blow away (particularly the lids). I prefer compost boxes.

'Better than nothing compost'

If I can't tempt you to make proper compost boxes then a compost heap in the corner of the garden is certainly much better than nothing. Put some brushwood at the base so the air can get through. Start with a base about 3 ft by 3 ft and then build up the heap in layers of about 9 in to a total height of 3–4 ft with sloping sides to about 2 ft square at the top so that the heap doesn't topple over. Cover the whole heap with plastic sheeting with holes in or with sacking. (Start a second heap leaving the first one to mature.)

     The heap will shrink as the material rots down. When the centre of the heap has rotted (up to 3 months in summer and 6 months in winter) strip it down and rebuild it with the unrotten outer material in the centre and the well-rotted stuff on the outside and leave it to carry on rotting under its blanket. Or you can use the well-rotted centre and add the partly-rotted stuff to your second heap.

     Don't use this 'better than nothing compost' as a mulch as it will probably contain lots of live weed seeds. Use it to dig in in the autumn so that it will have further time to break down.

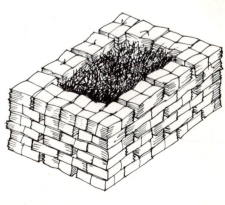

The press box

There is no doubt whatever that if you want to save time and energy in the long run you should build proper compost boxes but it is also a reasonable bet that some reluctant gardeners will also be reluctant handymen or handywomen. They will say don't bother with the long-term easy way, just give us the short-term easy way. So I will. I call it 'the press box'.

     Beg, borrow and save as many newspapers as you can. The tabloids are just as good as the large upper-crust ones. In some ways more meaty. Neatly bundle up the papers into building blocks approximately 9 × 13 × 4 in high tied up with string. This means, of course, that the tabloids will be folded in half and the bigger newspapers into quarters.

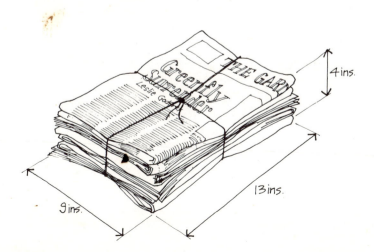

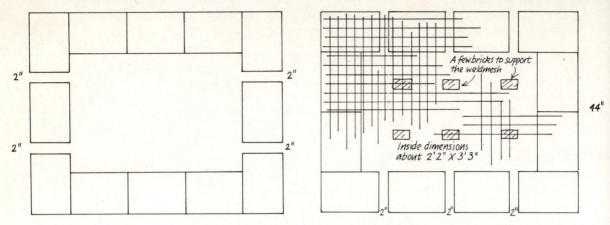

Now prepare a level site of bare earth. Set out 12 bundles of newspapers to form a rectangle about 57 by 44 in. Leave the 2 in gaps as shown to both allow air to enter the heap and to have the right dimensions to marry up with the next course. Cover this first course with a sheet of strong weldmesh (or planks of wood with gaps between) and lay the next course in the following pattern to build up the outer wall of the compost bin. Build up the course of newspaper blocks as you fill the box, laying each course alternately to form a good bond and give a firm box. This type of structure will give the compost the necessary supply of air from underneath. Fill the press box with the same layers as for the compost heap on p. 16.

When the press box is 2 ft or more high and nicely loaded with rotting material cover it over with a sheet of sacking or a piece of plastic or old carpet (with 1 in holes cut every 9 in to let the gases escape but to keep the rain out) weighed down with a few stones. Leave the heap to rot. The compost will shrink as it decomposes and in a couple of weeks or so you will be able to recover the top layer of bundles to use in your next box and a few weeks later another layer. After from two to six months – depending on the time of year and the quality of the ingredients – you should have a very reasonable load of compost. The newspaper blocks will, of course, have started to turn into compost themselves but many may be reusable for subsequent boxes.

The aim should be to have at least one box in the rotting stage and another in the building stage. The newspaper blocks act as very good insulators to keep a good high temperature in the heap and you should get good results from this method, especially if you include a good mixed diet well chopped up.

With a little ingenuity it is possible to build smaller heaps than the dimensions I have given but you won't get good results if you make the heaps too small. You can, of course, save on newspapers by making the lower layer under the weldmesh of bricks, building blocks, kerbs or timber.

Connoisseur's compost

On the other hand you may be a reluctant gardener but a keen handyman. If so you can build some compost boxes that will give you the finest possible product and make handling your compost so much easier that compost making will become a pleasure. Even if you are not a brilliant artisan you won't find compost boxes too difficult to construct.

Top quality, five-star compost is made in one fell swoop by having enough material to fill a box in one go. The heap then reaches a temperature of 60°C (140°F) and literally cooks to death any weed seeds or perennial roots and disease spores to give a crumbly, sweet-smelling product that can be used as a mulch or dug in in the normal way.

Method. The material should be chopped up with a spade or put through one of the compost machines that are now on the market and then dampened.

Lightly fork over the earth at the bottom of the box, put in the weldmesh floor and then load the box layer by layer with any coarse material first to keep open the air supply using an activator on alternate 9 in layers and a mixture of lime and earth on the others until the heap ends up 1 ft higher than the height of the box itself. This will allow for settlement. Cover with sacking or the plastic blanket with holes in and if you can put on a roof to keep out the weather so much the better.

Within a week in the summertime steam will be seen coming from the heap if the blanket is lifted back and a temperature of over 60°C will have been reached. Two weeks later as the heap just starts to cool down fork the material into another box with the unrotted outer stuff to the centre and cover over again with the blanket. If this operation is timed before the temperature falls too far there will be enough energy left in the heap to bring the temperature back to 60°C to complete the weed destruction.

Two weeks later the heap will have shrunk to half the size and the worms will have moved in. Two weeks after that it can be dug in or used as a mulch. If it is to be used near very young plants leave it yet another couple of weeks as any remaining traces of ammonia could damage the plants.

That's the recipe for top quality compost – what about the boxes?

CONSTRUCTING COMPOST BOXES

Compost boxes should be snugly built side by side to keep in the heat and make it easier to shovel the contents from one box to another. Make the boxes with three fixed sides and removable fronts so that they are easy to load and unload. There should be a roof to keep off the sun, the rain and the snow and an air supply coming up from underneath so build the heap on brushwood or on well-spaced loose boards on bricks, or strong weldmesh resting on bricks.

The build it from what you can get box

Traditionally boxes were made from timber but new wood is now very expensive so build your boxes from whatever you can get. This could be concrete blocks, bricks, breeze blocks, railway sleepers, old kerbs, old timber, packing cases, corrugated iron sheets or, if you live in the country, bales of straw. They are excellent at retaining heat and after a while they rot down and become compost themselves. If you put on a roof leave about a couple of feet clear above the top of the boxes to make them easy to load or unload – or make the roof removable.

The purpose built box

If you are a reluctant gardener but a keen handyman, you may well like to have a go at building the Godfrey Box detailed in Appendix B. This takes time to build but makes top quality compost and saves time in the long run.

FILLING THE BOXES

Remember the best compost is made if you have enough material to fill the box in one go. If not, follow the other rules we have already discussed and you can still end up with a four-star product. First a layer of coarse material to keep the air supply open. Then an evenly spread layer of material about 9 in deep. If dry make it moist but not sodden. Scatter activator over the layer to feed the bacteria. Put in another layer of material and then scatter this with about 4 oz of lime mixed with a couple of spadefuls of soil.

Repeat the process until the box is more than full – to allow for shrinkage. Cover with a top blanket of old compost, plastic sheeting or sacking.

...B,BUT I THOUGHT IT WAS SALAD IN THE COLANDER...

COMPOST COLANDER COLLECTION

To ensure that you become a compulsive compost collector with the minimum of effort have a colander right by the kitchen sink to collect all compostable kitchen refuse. Empty it once a day into a plastic bucket (preferably with lid) outside the kitchen door and empty the bucket on the compost heap once a week or when you feel like it.

LEAFMOULD

Large quantities of autumn leaves should be stacked separately to make leafmould. They will take up to two years to rot down. It is a shocking waste of time and compost to burn them.

Make a cage by driving four posts or lengths of angle iron into the ground as uprights and fixing wire netting or weldmesh to form the cage: 4 ft square by 4 ft high is a good size. Pile in the leaves and tread them down, adding some water if they are very dry. In about two years the heap will have shrunk to half its height and be ready for use as a mulch or for digging in.

Have two cages so that you have an empty one to fill each autumn.

3 THE GARDEN ENVIRONMENT

One of the essential rules in reluctant gardening is to grow only those things that will survive and flourish with little attention.

The fact that some plants will do well in your garden and others will not may have nothing to do with your skill as a gardener but be a direct result of local conditions – of the environment in which the plants are growing.

Very few of our garden plants are truly indigenous – our ancestors discovered them over a span of thousands of years in quite different parts of the world, yet we wish to grow them side by side in one small plot in Croydon, Coventry or Carlisle. Would it not be reasonable to assume that they would need quite different conditions in which to flourish? Well of course they do; but don't be too alarmed – man, with his ingenuity, has over the centuries been breeding and selecting strains and varieties that will flourish in our climate.

From a gardener's point of view our climate is truly marvellous. We live on an emerald isle set in a silver sea watered by the rain clouds coming in from the Atlantic and warmed by the Gulf Stream to give us a climate in which to grow a wider variety of plants than perhaps anywhere else in the world. But there are limitations and different plants like different conditions. As a reluctant gardener it will pay you to select those things that like your own local conditions.

GENERAL LOCAL CONDITIONS

You could put off gardening for a bit and carry out a scientific survey of your specific locality, taking into account your latitude, your height above or below sea level, the distance from the sea, the direction of the prevailing wind, the analysis of the local soil and the annual rainfall. Or you could take a more simple course and just wander round your locality to see what does well in other people's gardens. Having a good look at other people's plots and finding out about their successes and failures is a good way of getting a general idea of what will do well in your neighbourhood without too much effort. You may gather a few free plants and cuttings (see p. 136) into the bargain.

Find out also if your area gets any late frosts. This will give you a guide on when it is safe to put out tender plants in the spring. Frost has a tendency to flow downhill and settle at the bottom in frost hollows so try not to choose a house right at the bottom of a slope or you may find frost a problem and have to delay planting in the spring. If you are half way up the slope the frost may literally flow right past you and do no damage in your garden.

THE CONDITIONS IN YOUR VERY OWN PLOT

Having considered your general locality have a think about the specific micro climate in your very own plot. Plants need water and sunlight in order to manufacture their plant foods but different types of plants need these two basic commodities in different amounts so you would be wise to select the right plants for the right places.

HOW MUCH SUN DO YOU GET?

Lie back in a deckchair for a day in summer and study how the sun travels across the garden. Note those parts of the garden and the walls and fences that get no sunshine at all, those that get some sunshine and those that get a lot. If you stayed in the deckchair for a whole year you could study the seasonal shift of the sun's arc in the sky and see how various parts of the garden get more sunshine in summer and less in winter.

In the nothern hemisphere a garden facing south and west will be warmer than one facing north and east. If there is a distinct tilt of the land towards the south the soil will be warmer still as the sun's rays will fall more directly on to it. Generally speaking gardens facing south and west are easier to cope with than cold north-facing ones. There are some plants, however, that will do quite well in the colder parts of the garden and on the north-facing walls (see p. 140) but there will be fewer to choose from than for the sunnier parts of the garden.

There is a great deal of difference, of course, between the solid shadow cast by a large tree or a building and the dappled sunshine coming through trellis work or a loosely growing shrub. Many moderate-sized garden trees allow sunshine during some part of the day and all day long in winter when they have cast their leaves so that spring-flowering bulbs, ground cover plants, ferns and foxgloves will happily grow beneath them while in the solid shade from a wall you may be restricted to ferns and ivies and similar plants.

So study the light and shade of your garden. Decide on the all-important sitting-out or sunbathing area first. You will probably want a spot that gets plenty of sunshine, is out of sight of the neighbours, has a good view of the garden and is near enough to the kitchen for access to food and drink.

WET OR DRY?

Walls, hedges, shrubs and trees can have a very marked effect on the moisture level in different parts of the garden. The soil below north-facing walls is usually damp most of the year and suitable for plants that tolerate such conditions like musk.

Hedges, shrubs and trees not only cast shade and extract nutrients from the soil but they also take up vast quantities of water. The soil beneath large trees and thirsty hedges (privet and holly for example) can be dust dry for much of the year so you may wish to site your paths and paving to cover such arid ground.

Your type of soil will also have an effect on the moisture level – see section on Soils – also on what plants you can grow (see p. 10). Some sandy soils let water through like a sieve while heavy clays can soak it up like a sponge. Sometimes an apparently light, sandy soil may not be free draining. If the ground has been consolidated by builders' machinery or tramping feet and then other soil dumped on top of it the hard pan below may act as a barrier and not allow water through.

Rain rarely falls vertically so the leeward side of a wall or building will be drier than the windward side.

Somewhere under your garden there will be water. The level at which soils and rocks are fully saturated is called the 'water table' and its depth below ground varies from area to area. Even a sandy soil will not stay dry if there is plenty of rain and the water table is high.

A simple way to establish how your soil copes with water is to dig a hole about 2 ft deep and fill it with water. If the water disappears within 24 hours in dry weather you have a free-draining soil.

WINDY CORNERS

Walk round the garden on a moderately windy day and find out where it really cuts you to the quick. It will do the same to plants so you may wish to erect a barrier at that point. Defensive walls are expensive, fences can rot and get blown down or create a nasty draught at the base. The best answer is often a hedge which will filter the wind and reduce its velocity.

AIR POLLUTION

The air in our towns and cities is very much cleaner than it was before air pollution was controlled by law and the changes in heating systems but there is still some pollution. Heavy levels of soot, sulphur, lead and the like will kill off many plants and yet others will survive in spite of it. The plane tree of our cities is a great tolerator, as is the common holly and the periwinkles, the green forms of which are excellent ground cover plants in almost all situations.

CITIES ARE WARMER

The vast areas of paving, brickwork and glass reflect the sun's rays and the flue vents from the central heating systems in the buildings release warm gases into the atmosphere to make the large towns and cities somewhat warmer (and often more frost-free) than the surrounding countryside. A blessing in winter but not always so in summer as any city worker will tell you in a heat wave, but it allows the gardener to get his tender plants out into the garden that much earlier.

If you take time to study your local environment and the environment of your own plot you will be able to make better decisions that will save you time and effort in the long run.

4 DIGGING

Loathed by some, loved by others, digging can be a delight.

It is defined in the Oxford English Dictionary as using 'spade or pick, claws, hands or snout in excavating or turning over ground'. If you are using one of the last three it could explain your reluctance.

Take your head out of the soil, wipe your snout, wash your hands and spend a few minutes quietly contemplating whether digging is a good thing anyway.

IS IT NECESSARY?

In new gardens it obviously has to be done to get the topsoil to the top, to get the brickbats and beer cans out of the ground and to shift the soil to where you want it. But is it necessary in established gardens? Let us have a look at a few pros and cons.

A FEW THINGS IN FAVOUR

(a) It is good healthy exercise.
(b) It makes the soil look neat and tidy.
(c) It gives you a chance to clean up the garden, to get out weeds and unwanted plants and perhaps discover odd potatoes or other root crops that got left in the vegetable plot from last season.
(d) It helps drainage, stops plants getting waterlogged – and well-drained soil is warmer.
(e) It enables you to incorporate compost or manure in the soil.
(f) It ensures that air gets mixed up in the soil. Plant roots need oxygen.
(g) It loosens compacted soil – helping root growth.
(h) It helps water to travel through the soil to the plant roots.
(i) It enables you to leave the soil 'rough dug' so that the winter frosts will make it more workable in the spring for raking down into a seedbed.

AND A FEW THINGS AGAINST

(a) Unaccustomed digging done at the double may be a hazard to health. Take it slowly.
(b) Bare soil looks barren.
(c) Digging may damage plant roots.
(d) Damaged rose roots may lead to unwanted sucker growth.
(e) Digging makes soils lose moisture in hot weather.
(f) Deep digging may mix subsoil with topsoil.
(g) Nature manages without digging – why can't we?

But a garden is not nature. It is a management of nature by man for man's pleasure. (I include food as pleasure.) Left to itself nature would not produce the vast range of useful plants we find in one place in the average garden. If

you left nature to her own devices your garden would very soon be filled with the survival of the fittest – docks, dandelions, nettles, brambles and briars – not necessarily the plants you would want to survive. But there are certain circumstances where you can manage without digging as well as other circumstances where you cannot really escape it. A quick canter through the choices open to you is perhaps appropriate.

(a) **Leave it alone.** Don't dig at all.

(b) **Tickle the top.** Put the fork in a couple of inches and then twist and lift it to disturb the soil. There is little merit in this kind of digging as it just moves the weeds from one place to another and will leave some of them still living. It is much better to use a Dutch hoe – see chapter Water in the Soil and Garden Tools. But nevertheless OK for loosening the soil to make it look tidier where you may have trodden on it.

(c) **Pick it up and put it down.** Useful where there are lots of little weeds that you want to say goodbye to in part of the flower garden (mind you don't damage the roots of the flowers) or where you have cleared off one crop in the vegetable garden and want to plant another. Push in the fork, or spade, pick it up carefully with its cargo of soil and small weeds and turn it right over so that the weeds are underneath as you put it back where it came from. Work slowly, carefully and systematically so that all weeds are buried upside down and none is peeping out to romp away again when you go indoors for a well-earned rest. Don't dig in hot dry weather – it's a certain way of losing soil moisture (and personal moisture). There are several mechanical diggers on the market which make light work of this kind of digging – perhaps worthwhile if you have a really large plot.

(d) **Simple trenching.** Now we are getting on to proper digging – the kind you will certainly have to do to get a new plot shipshape and probably have to do as an annual ritual in the vegetable garden unless the soil is very light in texture.

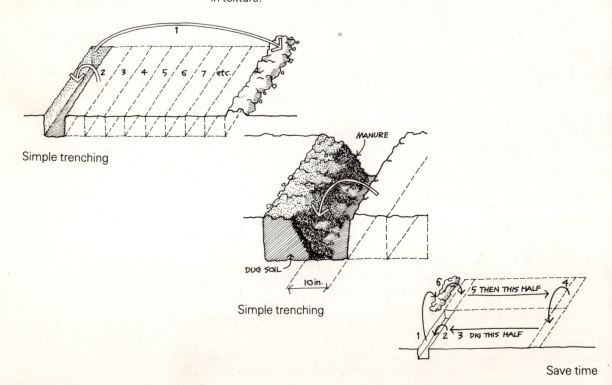

Simple trenching

Simple trenching

Save time

A trench about 10 in deep (the depth of a spade) is taken out at one end of the area to be dug. The earth is taken to the other end of the area and used to fill in the last trench at the end of the dig. Dig a 10 in wide and 10 in deep 'row' of the plot at a time. Do it in two 5 in slices if you find the spade at all heavy to lift. Push the spade in upright to its full depth. Pick up the spadeful of soil and turn it over as you throw it forward. If you are digging in the autumn or winter don't break down the lumps – the frost will do that for you. When you get to the end of each row straighten up to ease your back and admire your handiwork before you start the next 10 in slice. Manure or compost is incorporated with the soil as each trench is dug. Spread it on the sloping earth so that it is distributed throughout the depth of the top spit. Save time in trenching. If you dig the plot one half at a time like this you can save the slog of moving the earth up to the far end.

(e) **Simple trenching made easy.** If you are willing to forego some space in the vegetable plots you can completely eliminate that chore of taking out a new trench each year. Just dig the garden in one direction the first year leaving a trench at the end and then dig the garden in the opposite direction the next year ending up with the trench at the other end. Some things will even grow reasonably well in the trench so it is not necessarily wasted space.

(f) **Bastard trenching.** A more advanced system where a trench 2 ft wide is taken out to start with. As each trench is taken out the digger gets down into it to dig over the subsoil before the next row of topsoil is placed on top of it. So each *layer* of soil stays where it is but the soil is dug two spits deep in total. Manure is incorporated on top of the subsoil and within the top spit. If you go in for bastard trenching you will get very good vegetables but will have to give up your 'reluctant' status.

It is called bastard trenching because it is a variation on true trenching which is dug three spits deep – seldom done today but practised in Victorian times.

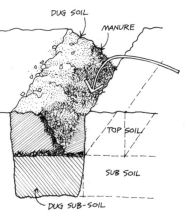

Bastard trenching

WHICH DIGGING SHOULD YOU DO WHERE AND WHEN?

Taking into account the various pros and cons and working on the basis that you will want to do the minimum possible digging I would suggest the following:

Light sandy soils. Don't dig at all – not even the vegetable garden. Keep the ground well hoed to remove weeds at all times of the year and in the spring and summer spread well-rotted compost between the rows of plants once they are well clear of the soil. Tickle the top of the soil if you must.

The rose garden. Don't dig anywhere near the plants or you may damage the roots and cause them to send up unwanted suckers. Keep the ground well hoed and put compost on top of the soil in the spring. Again tickle the top if you want to.

Shrub borders. The secret is to plan ahead for an easy life in the future by planting your shrubs the correct distance apart so that when they are fully grown they will touch each other and cover most of the soil in the growing season. Spread compost or leafmould on the soil before leaf growth starts in the spring when you can see what you are doing.

Heather beds or fuchsia beds. The same treatment as for the shrub borders but be careful not to use compost that contains lime near the heathers.

Use ground cover plants (see p. 114). Keep the soil hoed between them when they are young and then when they are fully grown they will say thank you by completely covering the ground so that no weeds can grow. Spread a bit of compost between the plants whenever you have some to spare.

Flower borders. Use the 'pick it up and put it down' system each spring to get out weeds, thin out plants and get some air into the soil. Don't dig deeply – half the depth of a border fork will do. Spread compost on top of the soil in spring or summer and let the worms take it down into the soil. Keep the Dutch hoe going in the summer. A stitch in time certainly saves nine.

The vegetable garden. In general I would recommend that you *do* dig your vegetable garden each autumn or winter – preferably by trenching – so that you can remove weeds, incorporate compost or manure and leave the plot rough dug so that the frosts can pulverize it; it will then be easy work to rake it down into a seed bed in the spring. But with the really light sandy soils it is best not to dig. Hoe and rake just before you sow any seeds and spread well-rotted compost between the rows of plants when they are a couple of inches tall. Don't let the compost touch them unles it really is very well rotted or stray traces of ammonia will kill them. If you want to use the 'no dig' method on heavier soils then you must be careful never to tread on the soil or it will become compacted. And with the no-dig method do make your vegetable beds long and thin so that they are no more than 4 ft wide so that you can do all necessary operations from either side without treading on the soil at all.

5 WEEDS

WHAT IS A WEED?

There are two definitions that appeal to me. (1) A weed is any plant in the wrong place, and (2) If you pull it up and it grows again it is a weed. Not strictly true of course but you know the feeling. The dictionary would no doubt say that a weed is a wild plant growing where it is not wanted but those first two definitions together sum up the situation for most of us.

To be able to recognize every weed that there is you would have to know every wild plant, so I will not bother you with that burden. I would suggest instead that until you begin to know one plant from another you keep life simple by putting marker sticks where you have plants, seeds or bulbs below the surface and that you treat everything else as a weed. Occasionally you will like the look of something and let it grow, only to find later on that it is not one of the chosen ones. We all do it and we all learn that way.

HEADS OFF

If you chop off the top of any weed often enough it will die as you will eventually deprive it of the essential elements of growth that have to be manufactured by the plant from sunlight on its leaves. But you have got to take off all the top and you have got to keep doing it so that leaves hardly have a chance to grow again. Many weeds will die at the first decapitation but some will not die easily and directly you stop taking off their heads they will get growing again with renewed intent to survive.

TO CHOP OR NOT TO CHOP?

I suggest the reluctant gardener regards his weeds as just two types. (1) Those that you can kill off by hoeing them and (2) Those that you need to dig up. There is no reason why you shouldn't dig up the former if you wish. The second group are those that have a root system that is capable of storing all the essential substances plants need to get growing again. But do ensure that you hoe off weeds before they flower and set seed. It is best to kill them at the seedling stage.

THE PERNICIOUS ROOTERS

There are two broad types of root systems: those that go down deep like dandelions and docks and those that travel sideways like couch grass and bindweed. With the former you must go down deep with a spade and get up all the long root and with the latter you must patiently keep digging with a fork until you have got out every last bit of root. If you don't do this the plants will grow again.

Most pernicious rooters can be killed with systemic weedkillers – the kind that are absorbed into the plant's system – but if you do use weedkillers do handle and store them with care. They will be lethal to plants as well as weeds and some can be lethal to people as well.

SOME COMMON WEEDS WITH ROOT SYSTEMS THAT NEED TO BE COMPLETELY DUG UP

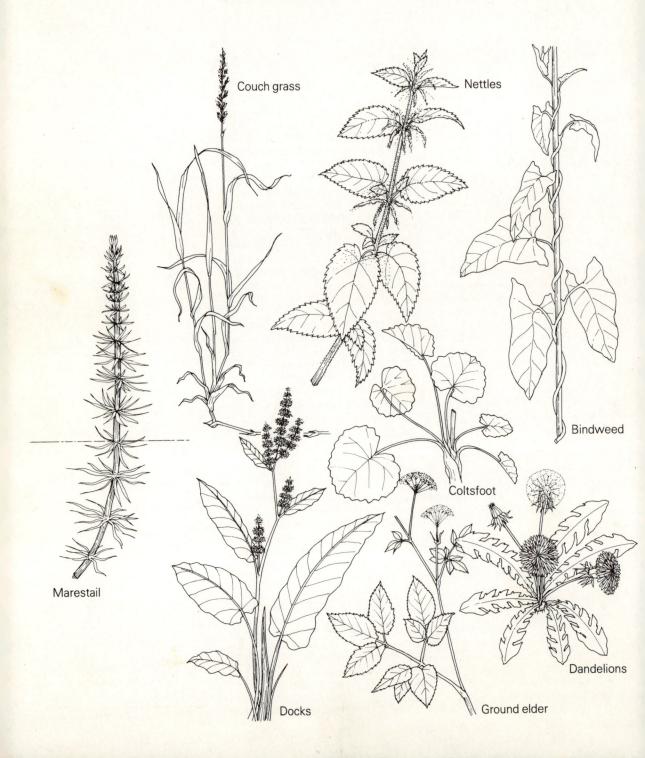

Couch grass

Nettles

Bindweed

Coltsfoot

Marestail

Dandelions

Docks

Ground elder

6 THE EASY WAY WITH PESTS AND DISEASES

The shelves of garden centres are stacked with fungicides, pesticides and insecticides to kill off almost every known plant, pest and disease, and many a reluctant gardener spends his precious time in bemused concentration trying to decide which one to use on which plant for which problem. He would do best to walk away and pretend they did not exist because even if he knew exactly which one to use for each pest and disease I doubt whether he would want to have to bother.

The whole principle of treating diseases after they have got a hold is a time-consuming affair and one in which the reluctant gardener is best not to get involved. Far better for him to take a stitch in time and so conduct his affairs that pests and diseases do not become a serious nuisance in his garden in the first place.

Let us consider a few basic principles. There is no nice simple spray that will eliminate all the pests and diseases in your gardens any more than there is one pill that will cure all our own ills. Any single spray that would get rid of all the various types of creatures in our gardens that we didn't want would be likely to get rid of all the creatures that we did want as well. Not all the creatures in our gardens are pests, not all of them are foes.

Our gardens are teeming with life from microscopic bacteria, fungi, viruses, through to insects, birds and animals and perhaps the odd frog or toad. Some we classify as pests or diseases because they do damage to the plants we wish to grow and others we regard as friends because they destroy the foes – usually by eating them up. Purely selfish of us, but there it is.

Left to its own nature will strike some sort of balance between friends and foes. Predator insects and animals that we regard as friends will, given the right conditions, keep most of the pest insects within reasonable control by eating them. They will normally not destroy them completely or that part of their diet would disappear but they will keep them within manageable proportions. In natural conditions one tends to balance the other. And that is quite an acceptable condition in our gardens. I don't mind a few greenfly, I just don't want lots of them.

In any case not all of us are happy about using pesticides based on synthetic chemical compounds – we are worried about the possibility of permanent damage to the balance of nature. I am not saying that I would never use any drastic control measures or that I would always condemn those who do. If I were farming in Africa and my entire crop was threatened by a swarm of locusts then perhaps I would reach for my spray gun, or locust-spraying aircraft, because it might be a case of all or nothing. But I would have to keep my fingers crossed that I was doing no permanent damage to the environment. With synthetic insecticides it is a question of doing just that – of keeping our fingers crossed.

I HEAR THE GRIMWADES HAVE LOCUSTS....

The manufacturers of these products take very great care, under government legislation, to make them as safe as possible and no doubt most will prove to be so. But occasionally the odd one will turn out to have unacceptable side effects – as DDT and Thalidomide did.

Some insecticides are based on natural substances which come from plants – pyrethrum, nicotine and derris for example. One should be careful in handling them, especially nicotine, but they do have the advantage that nature

I'M A HOG FOR SLUGS

DOWN AT THE SLUG PUB....

THE SLUG & PELLET FREE HOUSE

WELL – JUST ONE MORE THEN....

breaks them down into harmless substances in the soil. It cannot do this with many synthetic materials. There is a chance that some noxious substances may remain in the plant, the pest or the soil. The pests may get eaten by natural predators and the predators may get harmed by the traces of pesticide in them – either immediately or by a gradual build-up of noxious substances in their body fats.

As one example hedgehogs are great friends of the gardener. They hibernate in winter but at night time during the rest of the year they forage the garden for insects and regard slugs as very tasty titbits. If you put down poison to kill the slugs you may polish off the hedgehogs as well, whereas left to their own devices the hedgehogs will do a continuous slug-hunting job for you. So any means you use to polish off slugs should also not polish off hedgehogs.

If you haven't got any hedgehogs you can lure slugs to their doom with beer. Sink a soup plate in the ground so that its outer rim is level with the soil and fill the bowl of the plate with beer. The slugs come for a drink and drown. Use a glazed plate and not a plastic one or some of the slugs may walk out again. Have a number of these slug bars round the garden, keep them clear of leaves, clean them out and recharge with beer occasionally. You can use much the same system by burying bottles (half filled with beer) up to their rims in the soil. The slugs topple in never to come out again. You may find the resultant 'soup' is just a little bit revolting to deal with but carefully carry it to the compost heap, shut your eyes and pour it over the pile. Very nutritious.

There is one other problem and that is that if we continually use pesticides we run the risk of producing strains of pests and diseases that are resistant to these cures – like the malaria mosquitoes found in some tropical countries that are resistant to DDT.

The whole point is that for the average amateur gardener pesticides and insecticides are just not necessary and can, in the long run, do more harm than good. With a little help nature can strike quite an acceptable balance without them. I don't use any pesticides at all and people often ask me why there are so few greenfly on my roses. When I say 'because I don't spray them' they often think I have misheard them and repeat the question. The answer is that I leave the birds to do that job for me. The sparrows and blue tits eat the greenfly off the rose bushes as part of their diet. They wouldn't do that if the greenfly tasted of insecticide – they would spit them out in disgust and go elsewhere. So if I sprayed my rose bushes I would have to keep on spraying them and get no help from my feathered friends. But I prefer to let them do the job for me.

If birds are not plentiful in your garden you may need to tempt them to visit you by supplying water, fruit and other titbits in the hope they will take the greenfly as a second course. Don't give them bread in the breeding season – they tend to feed it to their nestlings and it can choke them.

Let us take these basic factors and the philosophies behind them and set them out as a set of simple rules to make it as easy as possible for the reluctant gardener to deal with pests and diseases – or rather to deal with the plants and the soil so that pests and diseases do not become a problem in the first place.

1 CHOOSE RESISTANT VARIETIES

Whenever possible obtain varieties of seeds and plants that are resistant or immune to diseases. Seedsmen and plant raisers are continually researching for varieties that are resistant to the major pests and diseases that attack them. Read the seed and plant catalogues carefully to take advantage of such research. You will for instance find varieties of lettuce that are resistant to mildew, root aphids and botrytis, potatoes that are immune to wart disease and resistant to eelworm, rose varieties that are resistant to mildew, raspberries that are resistant to virus diseases and apples to apple scab. Resistant varieties are usually no more expensive to buy than susceptible ones and, unlike pesticides, they do not, of course, pollute the environment. They will certainly play an increasingly important role in future in controlling pests and diseases in all crop plants for the commercial grower as well as the amateur.

2 NEVER PLANT A WEAKLING

Be quite ruthless when selecting plants. Avoid any that look poorly. Only accept plants and cuttings from friends if you know they come from healthy stock (the plants not the friends) and a good garden. If any plant looks sickly put it in the dustbin not in your garden.

3 PLANT IN THE RIGHT PLACE

Study the advice in the catalogues, on the plant labels and on the seed packets – and follow it. If a plant needs full sun and you put it in the shade it won't do well and, conversely, if it needs shade it won't do well in full sun. Plants that have to struggle for survival in the wrong environment are much more prone to ills and diseases. So plant in the right place.

4 ROOT OUT THE ROTTERS

If you have a plant that just will not do well in your garden dig it up and replace it with something else. Super Star is, for example, quite a pretty rose but it is prone to mildew in many gardens. If you have trouble with it then don't waste your time spraying it, just dig it up and burn it. Plant robust varieties like Fragrant Cloud or Queen Elizabeth instead. A word of warning. If you do root out a rotter avoid replacing it with the same type of plant in the same spot. There is a condition known as 'replant disease' which is not yet very well understood. Very briefly it means that roses will not do well where other roses have been and one apple tree should not replace another apple tree. They don't do well in the same spot – something gets left in the soil that affects the replacement. Some experts consider that it is no more than a lack of nutrients, others that it is a specific condition. Be on the safe side and plant something different from the type you have rooted out.

5 GROW IN GOOD SOIL

I cannot stress this strongly enough and will keep on repeating the message throughout the book. If your soil is thin and starved you will have double the work for half the results. Give it a good load of farmyard manure and keep it well topped up with good quality compost every year. It may mean one week-end's slog for you each autumn but it will save you so much time and trouble all the rest of the year. If your plants are growing in good soil they will be thriving healthy plants that will shrug off most pests. What does it matter if one leaf gets nibbled away if there are plenty of others coming along to take its place?

6 CLEAN UP

Keep your garden clean and tidy. Don't have rubbish, weeds and dead plants lying around to act as a breeding ground or hiding place for pests. Clear away all plants as soon as they start to die down and put them on the compost heap or, if they are woody, burn them or give them to the dustmen. If you can't get rid of rubbish straight away let it dry off for a few days and then store it in properly sealed plastic sacks until you can dispose of it. Keep your hedge bottoms clean and tidy. Don't push the hedge clippings under them. But don't clear away any nest-like structures on the ground – they may be winter quarters for hedgehogs.

7 HOSE OFF

Use the hose in summer to knock blackfly and greenfly off the more robust plants like roses and runner beans. If the plants need water you will be carrying out the dual task of watering and hosing off in one go.

8 ROTATE YOUR VEGETABLES

In the flower garden plants tend to stay in the same place for many years and if you root out the rotters you will be operating a selection system to ensure the survival of the fittest – certainly with the perennial plants. In the vegetable garden the lifespan of most plants is less than a year. This gives us the ability to operate a rotation system so that no plants are grown in the same place for more than one season in four. This deprives soil-borne diseases, which can stay in the soil from one year to the next, of the host plants on which they live. By the time the crops have come back to the same place again the diseases have either diminished greatly or died out. See the section on Vegetables, p. 165.

9 ROTATE THE ANNUALS

If you grow annuals like *Alyssum* and *Lobelia*, or biennials like wallflowers and Sweet Williams don't grow them in the same place two years running. Grow something different so that soil-borne diseases can diminish. Use a four-year rotation system as recommended for the vegetable garden.

7 WATER IN THE SOIL AND GARDEN TOOLS

THE CONNECTION

This may seem a strange heading but there is a close association between the two.

Most plants are over 80 per cent water. There is a continuous flow of water through them taken up by the roots and transpired from the leaves by the energy from the sun. This water brings up nutrients from the soil and also enables many plants to stand erect by distending their cells. If plants do not have a reasonable supply of water they will not grow properly and will tend to run to seed prematurely – which you certainly won't want with flowers and vegetables.

Water is, of course, flowing through those plants we don't want, as well as through those plants we do want and on a hot summer's day weeds will be taking up the moisture needed by the other plants. Moisture will also be lost directly by evaporation from the soil but that loss will be only a fraction of that transpired by the plants. A lettuce, for instance, will transpire more than half its own weight every sunny day. So our gardening techniques must be based on keeping down the weeds in the easiest possible manner and having a readily available supply of water for the other plants.

THE SOIL

Sorry to come back to this one again but a good friable soil with plenty of compost in it will hold water far better than a thin starved one and will save you so much time and energy in the long run.

ON TAP

Do make life easy for yourself by having a spare tap in the garage or outside the back door so that you can get water for the garden without being a nuisance at the kitchen sink. If the tap is out in the open make sure you have a stopcock inside so that you can empty the outside pipe in winter to save it from freezing.

THE WATERING CAN, THE BUCKET AND THE HOSE

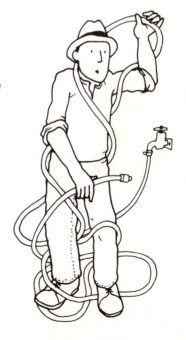

The watering can and the bucket are handy for limited watering and for emergency action when, say, container plants are gasping but when the whole garden is really short of water it will need a good continuous drenching via the hose. Getting the hose unreeled, trailed round the garden and then reeled up again after use is one of those thankless tasks most of us could do without. So why not have a permanent hose right round the perimeter of the whole garden tucked under the hedge or along the bottom of the fence? If you have to cross a path take it under ground.

Have a separate length of hose that you can plug into connecting joints at crucial points in the main hose and you will find that most of the irritations of irrigation will disappear. Watering may even become a pleasurable pastime. You will find it's a Godsend for washing the car as well as watering the garden.

STAINLESS STEEL FOR TOOLS

Buy your garden tools in stainless steel if you can afford it. It's a marvellous metal for the reluctant gardener. The tools slide through the earth with ease and stay bright and clean with so little trouble. If nothing else make sure your spade is stainless steel.

THE DUTCH HOE

Sometimes called the push hoe this is probably the most important tool for the reluctant gardener after the spade. It is used by walking backwards and pushing the hoe forward in front of you as you go to cut off any weeds at their roots and to turn the top half inch of soil into dust – what is called a dust mulch. This dust layer will help to reduce the evaporation of the water from the bare soil. Be careful to keep this dust layer as shallow as you can. If you bring damp soil up from below by hoeing too deeply it will lose its moisture and the net result will be water loss rather than retention. Deep hoeing would also cut off the roots of plants.

The great secret of making life easy for yourself with a Dutch hoe is to have a quick go round all the garden at least once a fortnight whether the soil appears to need it or not. In this way you will kill off the weed seedlings that are germinating below the soil surface before they appear. It takes very little time to do and is so much more pleasant than 'weeding'. I hate weeding and I expect you do too.

THE CULTIVATOR

This tool has got three or more vicious-looking hooked tines and is used with a chopping action to cultivate the top couple of inches of soil. It is a very useful tool for loosening up the top layer of compacted earth, especially in the vegetable garden where it may have got trodden down between rows of crops. It is often better than using a fork between growing plants as a fork may damage the roots of plants and bring too much damp soil to the surface.

There are variations on the theme of the cultivator and some have a bar fixed across the tines to chop off weeds.

THE RAKE

Get a modern rake with a light hollow metal handle rather than a heavy wooden one. You will need it for raking down the soil for a lawn or for a seedbed in the vegetable plot and for clearing up leaves and weeds.

THE SPADE AND FORK

Buy the best you can afford, preferably stainless steel. They come with different length handles so get one that suits your height. Get full-sized ones for the main digging jobs and for the vegetable plot and a smaller fork for the flower beds.

THE DRAW HOE, THE GARDEN LINE AND THE STICK

Two sticks and a length of string will make a garden line but it is worth treating yourself to the luxury of a proper metal reel – especially if you have a new garden or a vegetable plot where a line gets used a lot.

In the vegetable plot you will need a draw hoe for taking out the deeper drills for peas or perhaps earthing up potatoes but for ordinary seed drills I find it easier to use a 3 ft length of broom handle.

THE TROWEL, THE TABLESPOON AND THE DIBBER

A trowel is useful for making holes for bedding plants and for transplanting. I prefer to use an old tablespoon for the smaller plants.

The dibber is used for making holes, say for leeks. I use a handle that broke off a spade. I shaped the end and put grooves every 3 in up its length so that I know how deep I am dibbing.

THE WHEELBARROW

Think carefully about this one. Your wheelbarrow is likely to be used for carrying soil, paving slabs, rockery materials, sand, cement, concrete, bricks, manure, compost, plants, lawn mowings, leaves and a lot else. It needs to be light, leakproof, robust and easy to push and manoeuvrable.

The wooden wheelbarrows of old were beautifully made but you had to be pretty strong to push them empty, let alone full. The present day builder's barrow also calls for a good set of muscles.

For the normal gardener the choice comes down to perhaps one of three.

Ballbarrow

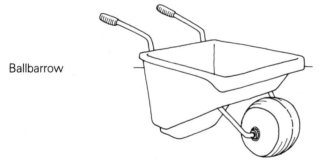

The ballbarrow

This has a large plastic ball for the front wheel, a metal frame and a plastic body. It is light to handle as the design places the load over the wheel when you are pushing it and the ball makes it easy to use over rough ground.

Galvanized

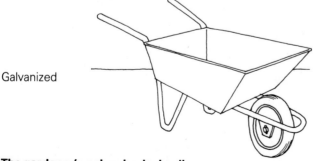

The gardener's galvanized wheelbarrow

This has one wheel at the front and a tubular steel framework supporting a galvanized metal body. As the load is distributed between your arms and the wheel it is not so light to push as the ball barrow but if you get a heavy quality one it will take an awful lot of punishment. I even light small bonfires in mine (not recommended) and it is still going strong after twenty years. This kind is fairly easy to manoeuvre round narrow paths but can leave a rut if pushed across a soft lawn. Some types now have wider wheels to minimize this risk.

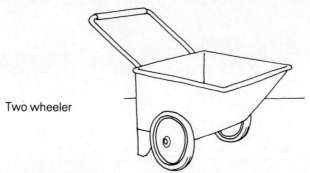

Two wheeler

The two wheeler

This kind has a wheel each side and a pram handle. The weight of the load is carried on the wheels and not your shoulders and it can be pushed or pulled with one hand instead of two – an important point for the disabled. If you opt for this kind make sure you have wide paths with negotiable corners.

8 COPING WITH SLOPES— AVOID THEM IF YOU CAN

The reluctant gardener should go for a house plot that is on the level. Most slopes cannot be totally ignored. If the slope is away from the house levelling is only absolutely necessary around the house or in a sitting-out area where you are likely to set up a table for drinks or meals. Soup and coffee do have a tendency to obey the laws of gravity.

If the ground slopes away from the back of the house it is likely to slope towards it at the front, or vice versa. The first consideration is to ensure that any flood water does not accumulate at the base of the house or drain towards the foundations so slope the land, the paths and the drive to take the rainwater away. If the house itself sits in a hollow you may need a fairly sophisticated drainage system to divert the water. It might be well to seek advice from a builder or, better still, decline to buy the house in the first place.

Apart from the practical considerations of ensuring that you don't get a garage or hall full of water there are considerations of 'time and toil' and 'the look of the thing'. Let us deal with looks first.

THE LOOK OF THE THING

A garden needs to have a look of completeness, of being a total entity and not just a slice of field or hill. A garden that slopes towards or away from the house can be more interesting than a totally flat one but if the slope is from left to right, if one side of the garden is much higher than the other, the mind does not like it. Somehow it gives the game away. The garden seems to say 'I'm not something special, I'm just a bit of something else.'

As we view our garden through the back window

this is all right	so is this	and this	but not this

 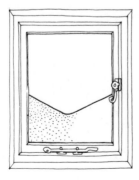  

Provided a garden is in total balance changes in level do, of course, create variety and can do quite a lot for small gardens as well as large ones. As we have already said, creating different levels is one way of adding interest at the most basic stage of a plan.

TIME AND TOIL

It will certainly take time and toil to level a slope but it may take more time and toil in the long run if you don't. Gentle slopes in a garden are no problem and can be tackled as you go along but severe ones are difficult to cope with and can even give rise to erosion of the soil by rainwater called 'land creep' or 'land slip'.

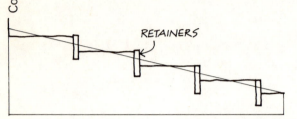

RETAINERS

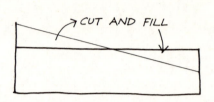

CUT AND FILL

A series of retained terraces is the usual answer. Remove the topsoil first and stack it in another part of the site. Do not make the heaps too big or you may compact that precious topsoil and spoil its structure. Level the subsoil and then replace the topsoil. It can be quite a slog but a necessary one.

The process is called 'cutting and filling' because you will need to cut soil from the top of the slope to fill in at the base of the slope. If your retaining walls are going to be constructed of bricks and mortar it is best to dig out their foundations after you have removed the topsoil and before you cut and fill the subsoil for each terrace. If the retainers are rocks then build them into the soil as you proceed, making sure they slope backwards to give strength. Tree trunks or logs can also be used as retainers and can look very fitting in the less formal parts of the garden.

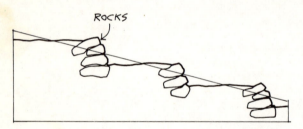

ROCKS

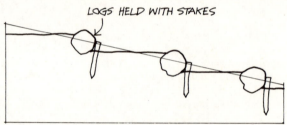

LOGS HELD WITH STAKES

Your garden will not, of course, exist in isolation and what you do with your plot may have a profound effect on the garden next door. Builders normally cope with the slopes between one house and another within the immediate vicinity of the houses and may totally level the plots if they are small ones but they normally leave the bigger ones to the owners to sort out. You have a duty not to undercut your neighbour's land so that it slides into yours nor to build up your land without retaining walls so that it falls into his. Neither should you expose the foundations of your house or his nor pile earth against the walls to cover any ventilators. Damp-proof courses should be left at least 6 in above soil or path level.

RELUCTANCY AND SLOPES

You may, as a reluctant gardener, say 'So what. I don't care about the contours of my garden. I don't give a fig if it slopes from east to west, north to south or left to right. I'll just leave it as it is.' Quite understandable. The trouble is that you have got to cope with it somehow. You have got to mow it, or put cattle on it, or pave it or dig it. So if you really feel that strongly it is best not to acquire a house on a sloping plot in the first place.

9 LAWNS

WAYS AND MEANS

It may be that you don't object to taking the mower for a walk once a week and would prefer to avoid some of the expense of paving and stonework by having a lawn. Our lawns are the envy of visitors from overseas and to be truly British you surely must have that patch of green in the garden.

There are four ways in which you may become the owner of a lawn.

You may sow seed, lay turf, convert existing meadow or get it with the house. The last one is the easiest of the lot. The other three require a little work.

CONVERTING A BIT OF MEADOW

Very few houses are built on good level meadow these days and if they are it is odds on that you would never know by the time the builder has finished with it. But it does occasionally happen that a bit of grassland is not only recognizable as such but can be converted into a lawn without too much trouble. If the grass is knee high you will first of all need to cut it with a rotary mower, shears, scythe or sickle. If it is one of the last three don't rush matters but take it gently just a bit at a time.

Gather up the hay and either feed it to a friendly cow or burn it. Now I know the latter is against my general principles of returning all plant matter to mother earth but that hay will be so full of weed seeds if it is that height that any compost you make from it will be a curse and not a blessing. Mow your new 'lawn' a couple of times a week for the first few weeks and keep it well watered in dry weather. It may look a bit pale to start with but after a month of regular mowing it will probably look quite respectable. You can now reduce the mowing to once a week. After your first flush of pride has subsided you may notice a few weeds, bumps, hollows or bald patches.

WEEDS

If it is weedy treat it with a selective weedkiller. Do make sure it is the kind intended for lawns or you could end up killing the grass as well as the weeds. Follow the instructions carefully and keep the weedkiller away from children, pets, ponds and other plants. Wash your hands after use.

BALD PATCHES

You may have bald patches where the soil has become compacted so first loosen it slightly with a garden fork by pushing it in a couple of inches and tilting it back a little all over the bald area. Now prick over the whole bald patch with the fork so that it ends up looking like a pepper pot with lots of little holes about a quarter of an inch deep. Scatter some grass seed over the area and then cover that with a light sprinkling of sand or soil – a quarter of an inch deep at the

BEFORE......   ......AFTER

very most. Gently rake it level if you wish. Keep it watered (using a sprinkler or watering can with rose) if the weather is dry and within a few weeks you will be hardly able to see the join.

BUMPS AND DENTS

Bumps and dents can be dealt with so that you would never know they had been there. Use a sharp spade to carefully cut and roll back the turf as shown. Fill the hollow with fine soil or in the case of a bump take it off and then loosen the top inch of soil with a fork. Replace the turf and pat it down with the back of a spade. Who knows – your bumps and dents may be so well matched that the surplus from one will fill the deficiency of the other. If you haven't got an amenable bit of meadowland you will have to construct your own lawn from turf or seed.

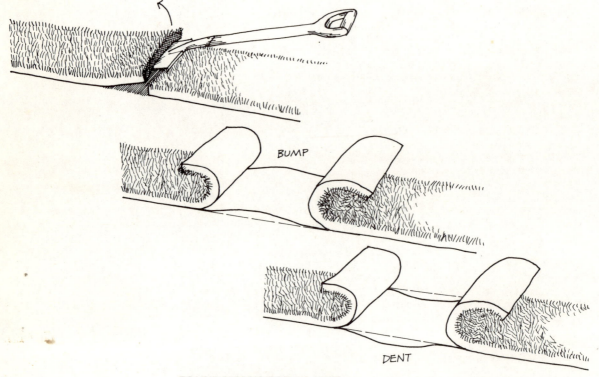

BUMP

DENT

FOUNDATIONS FOR A LAWN

You won't like me for saying so but whether you use turf or seed your lawn will need a proper foundation of good topsoil to save you trouble in future years.

It may be that you had in mind hiding all the brick ends, beer cans, subsoil and builders' rubbish under where the lawn will be. For your own sake – don't. Grass is a plant (or in the plural sense lots of plants) and it needs good growing conditions like any other plant. It will not turn into a remotely acceptable lawn if you try to grow it on builder's rubble or a slight sprinkling of topsoil over consolidated subsoil. Cracking in summer, flooding in winter and tears in between will be your reward. You will be forever levelling bumps, filling in hollows, spiking and raking, adding a little bit of this and a little bit of that to try to correct your initial transgression. For long-term ease of maintenance lay your turf or sow your seed on a full depth of proper topsoil so that it will cope with the winter rains and the summer sun and have plenty of nourishment under it to see it through the first few years of its life without too much attention while you are busy with more important matters.

It may be that you cannot avoid digging your site because the topsoil is buried under the subsoil or it is so much like the Rocky Mountains that you must dig it to level it. In that case, after you have dug it, you had better let it settle down again for as much as six months – depending on the type of soil. But if your lawn site is a good bit of topsoil, fairly weed-free and pretty level I see no sense in deeply digging it just to let it settle down again. I would suggest you need only tickle the top with a fork two or three inches deep to get out the weeds and any big stones and to enable you to get a good fine tilth all over the area. This is best done when the ground is reasonably dry and breaks down easily. After the shallow digging carefully tread all over the soil to gently consolidate it. Then rake it in both directions to level it and get out any more big stones. Tread it all over once more and then rake it again so that just the top inch is nice and fine and ready to receive the turf or grass seed. As you will appreciate this can only be done on a dry day or you will make a right mess of your boots and your soil.

..... DON'T FORGET– GREEN SIDE UP!

TURF OR GRASS SEED?

Well that depends partly on your pocket. Most turf is taken from fields of suitable grassland and can vary enormously in quality. It you are going to order a lot it may be worth your while to go and see what you are going to get. Good turf is rare and expensive. It should be reasonably weed-free, have a good colour with fine close grasses and a single turf should not fall to pieces when you pick it up. Measure the area you need and get a few quotations. When you have recovered from the shock a few calculations on a computer will tell you that seed will only be a fraction of the cost – but you will have to wait a little longer for your lawn – just a few months. The choice is yours. if you are a fairly free spender you might consider special purpose grown turves that are now available from some garden centres – but be prepared for a pretty high price. If you decide on seed you have one further decision to make.

WHICH SEED?

There are hundreds of different types of grasses and quite a few bred solely for lawns. There are fescues, bents, creeping bents, browntops, dog's tail, wavy hair grass, ryegrass and a few more. All to give you the type of lawn you need for the use to which you are going to put it. But relax. The seedsmen have made the choice quite easy for reluctant types. All you have to decide is whether you want (1) a hard-wearing lawn for the kids to play on, (2) a posh lawn to impress the neighbours or say (3) one for shady places. Look in any good garden seed catalogue and you will find a mixture for your purpose.

SOWING THE GRASS SEED

This has got to be done with a bit of care on a day when there is very little wind otherwise you will have a very patchy lawn and some of it may be in the flower bed. You will need 1 to 2 oz of seed per sq yd and your lawn can either be sown in September or in early spring once the weather is beginning to warm up –late March or April. To ensure that you don't run out of seed before you get to the end lay bamboo canes 1 yd apart across the site and then weigh out a handful of seed on the kitchen scales so that you can estimate how far a handful will go. Broadcast half the seed over the whole area in one direction first. Put your bamboo canes across the other way and sow the other half of the seed in the other direction. That way you will get an even spread. Take a bit of extra care round the edges so that you get a good spread of seed but not too much in the flower beds. After sowing lightly rake the surface to mix the seed with the top

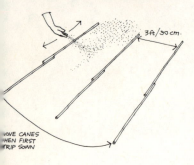

MOVE CANES
WHEN FIRST
STRIP SOWN

3ft/90 cm.

soil so that it is buried no more than ¼ in. On very light soils in dry conditions you can give the lawn a rolling with a light roller if you like but don't use a roller on heavy soils or you may find the soil and seed get stuck to the roller and ruin your good work. Sit out in the garden in a deckchair or erect a couple of scarecrows to keep off the birds. Most grass seed is now treated with bird repellent, but not all birds have been told this.

When the grass is about 3 in high give it a first light mowing to remove just 1 in of growth and to firm the grass seedlings into the ground. Use a sharp mower and only do this on a dry day or you may pull the seedlings out of the ground. Keep the grassbox on for the first few mowings.

So much for seed, what about turf?

LAYING TURF

Having decided that good turf is available and that your bank balance can stand it, ensure that the turf will be freshly cut and that your site will be ready to receive it before delivery day. The turf will come folded over or rolled up like Swiss rolls. The grass side will be inwards and if left too long like that will start to feel poorly and go yellow so be ready to lay it when it arrives. It is really a two-man job, one to fetch and carry the turves and the other to lay them. September and October are the best months for laying as it is not too dry and there is time for the roots to get established before winter. You can, of course lay them any time of the year but in dry weather you will have to keep them well watered. I should still be inclined to give the depth of winter and June, July and August a miss.

Are you ready?

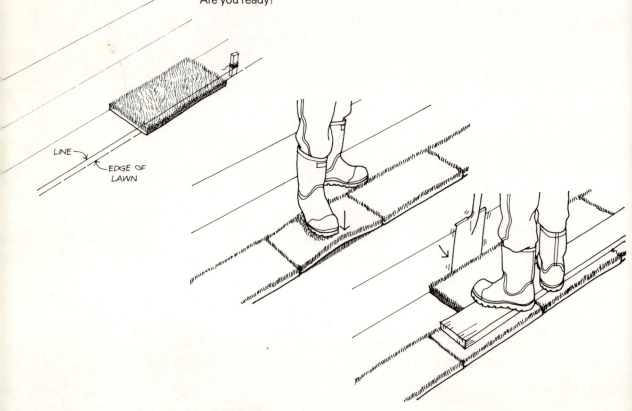

LINE

EDGE OF
LAWN

1 Put a line across the site and position the first row of turves so that they protrude an inch or so over the edge of the future lawn.

2 Tuck the turves closely up together. This is best done by leaving an occasional gap not quite long enough for a turf. Fit in the turf as shown and then gently tread on the turf to force it into place exerting lateral pressure on the adjacent turves.

3 Lay the second row of turves with staggered joints – like brickwork.

4 Firm the second row of turves against the first by tapping them with a spade to persuade them into place. Stand on a plank to do it.

5 Fill in any gaps with soil.

6 Trim the edges using the line as a guide. Make sure it is tightly stretched to give a straight line. This trimming can be done at a later date if you wish.

7 Keep the lawn well watered till established.

MOWING LAWNS

Always use a sharp mower. If your mower is the kind where you can alter the height of the cutting blades, then adjust them so that the height of cut is about $\frac{3}{4}$ in. Keep the grassbox on for the first few mowings of a new lawn and for the first and last mowings of the season but otherwise you can leave it off and let the mowings go back on the lawn – provided you cut the lawn at least once a week. The short mowings will rot down and help the soil to retain its nutrients. If you let the grass grow long then use a grassbox and put the mowings on the compost heap.

AN AUTUMN SCRATCH

In late autumn summon up enough energy to use a lawn rake to clear up any leaves, scatter any worm casts, remove any dead grass and moss and allow

AUTUMN SCRATCH......

... RAKING IN BOTH DIRECTIONS

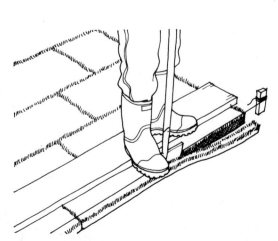

rain to drain through the grass and not be caught on the surface causing conditions for disease. Do the raking in both directions so that the lawn has no itchy places left and put the rakings on the compost heap. Rest well afterwards.

MOWERS

Rotary mowers have a rotating blade: one kind works on the hovercraft principle and the other kind has wheels. They leave the mowings on the lawn. They can cope with sloping banks, awkward corners and long grass. Some are driven by electricity – needing a handy power supply – and others by petrol.

Cylinder mowers come in two types – roller mowers and side-wheel mowers. Roller mowers are usually power driven, cut right up to the edge of the lawn, are easier to handle but can't cope too well with grass over 3 in tall. Side-wheel mowers can cope with taller grass than this, are either hand or petrol driven, usually cheaper but can't cut right up to the edge of a lawn.

There are now all kinds of variations on these three main types, including battery-driven models. If you have just a small area of grass near the house then a small cylinder or side-wheel model driven by electricity would suit. If you have tall grass in an orchard I expect you'll want a big petrol-driven rotary mower and if you want your middle-sized lawn to look posh for the neighbours you'll opt for a good quality petrol-driven cylinder mower.

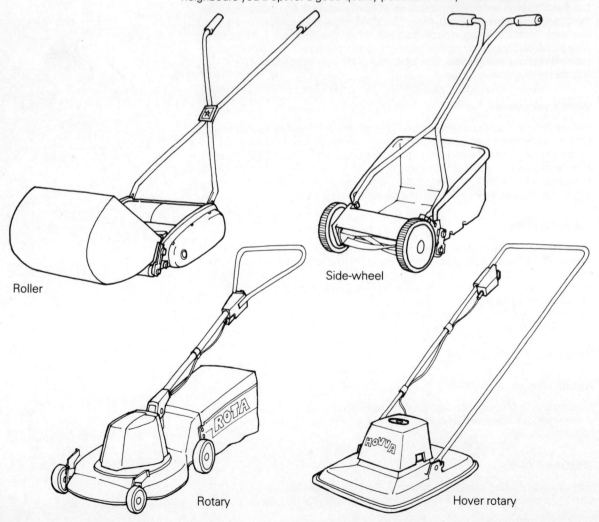

Roller

Side-wheel

Rotary

Hover rotary

10 GARDEN PLANS

A FEW CONSIDERATIONS

It isn't possible for me to propose a plan that will exactly suit *your* garden. I don't know its shape, size, aspect, location or soil or just how reluctant you are to get mud on your hands. So I'll concentrate on basic ideas and leave you to select and modify those that are nearest to your needs and dreams.

Put it on paper

Some people with a wide knowledge of plants, plenty of time to ponder and the ability to clearly visualize distances, shapes and sizes can completely plan their garden in the mind's eye. Most of us find it easier to do our first planning on paper – preferably graph paper to make measuring easier. It is also easier to alter a plan on paper than on the ground and an overall plan is easier to assimilate on a smaller scale. See later sections on particular plants for suggestions of what to grow.

What's your view

But remember that you will never see your garden from the same angle as the plan. You will never look directly down on it unless you hover over it in a helicopter. So as you develop your ideas put your plan flat on the table and then kneel down so that you can look along it. This will give you a better idea of how the plan will look, say, from the house. Gardens look longer and narrower on paper than they do when viewed from ground level.

Topsoil is shifty

Whatever plans you choose for your plot do remember that the topsoil is an ever-changing world of living organisms and if you propose to lay any kind of paving you will need to remove the topsoil and build the paving on the inert subsoil, or preferably on ash or sharp sand. All brickwork should be built on proper concrete foundations. Otherwise the changes in the soil will create movement, settlement, tilting and cracking.

The precious topsoil should be kept for the lawns, beds and borders and if it's double depth because you have added the topsoil from the areas to be paved so much the better.

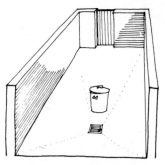

The bare yard

A plain start

Bearing in mind our original rule 'do what you like as long as you don't annoy the neighbours' there will be some people who will want no garden at all. So let's start there.

THE BARE YARD

This could be paving, tarmac or concrete. Or if you wanted to be really dashing, coloured concrete. The simple rules are, remove the topsoil and give it

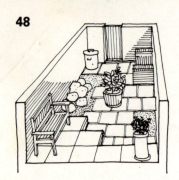

The better yard

to a friend, treat any weeds with weedkiller – if you don't you will find that the strong ones like dandelions will push their way up through tarmac – put a proper base of hardcore, ash or sharp sand as required and slope the site to a drain or to a point where water naturally drains away. Make sure this is on your own territory.

THE BETTER YARD

The bare yard effect can be relieved with a classy statue, a bird bath, an interestingly shaped rock or two, a tree, or areas of gravel – which could solve the drainage problem if strategically placed. This landscaped yard treatment is ideal for very tiny gardens.

THE CONTAINER GARDEN

Developing the theme you can add 'containers' to your yard – planted out in summer with colourful but simple subjects like geraniums that don't need to be watered too often. The bigger the containers the less often you will need to get out the watering can. Make sure the containers have drainage holes in the base – plants can't stand being waterlogged – and if you are really kind refill the containers with good loam or potting compost each year.

Containers are very useful in town gardens where the soil may be sour and acid through ages of pollution from domestic and industrial chimneys where, before the clean air acts, airborne chemical substances turned the rain into weak acids and solutions of nasty salts. In some soils there is almost no worm activity and little organic matter. Although in most cases this can be put right by correcting the acid level with lime and building up the organic content with compost, peat or manure there are occasions where a garden is completely locked in by other buildings and transporting ripe cow dung across the Wilton carpet can present a problem.

Plants in tubs, boxes and pots are particularly useful in these situations because each one can be grown in the soil that suits it. The containers can be moved around like furniture and an acid-loving plant can rub shoulders with a lime-loving one – hardly possible if they are both in the same bed.

And when you are tired of one layout you can pick up the furniture and move it around.

A FOCAL POINT

Study your plot from those positions where it will be seen most – the living-room window, the kitchen window and the sitting-out area. No matter how simple your design try to add a focal point, a point of interest, from each viewing place. Don't make it the dustbin, the shed or the compost heap but rather the bird table, bird bath, an archway or a piece of sculpture. Sometimes one can complement the other. A statue of a comely maiden gazing towards the bird table will take the viewers' gaze there also.

CHANGING LEVELS

To give more interest you could build a lily pond, change levels, have a table and chairs for the summer. Plants in containers and ground-hugging plants set in gaps in the paving would soften the effect. Dig the pool first so that, if it's suitable, you can use the spoil to build up the other areas.

Leave small spaces between the paving – 6 in square will do – for ground-hugging plants like thyme which will soften the prospect and only need a 5-minute haircut once a year after their flowers have faded.

Leave enough space to walk comfortably round all features including the pool. Make sure the site slopes very gently from all directions towards a drainage point and that there is an overflow for the pond. If the paving slopes the wrong way you could end up with pools you never intended.

Where the door
is opposite the steps

THE BASEMENT GARDEN

In towns and cities a basement garden may be all you have and because it is
overshadowed and small it is better treated as a small courtyard rather than a
garden. Grass and sun-loving plants are not likely to flourish and standard
paving slabs may look drab. So, spend a little money and make a mosaic of
coloured bricks and cobble stone with a few plants that will tolerate the shade
to soften the total effect. But try to avoid cobbles as part of the pathway to the
door. They can be a little uncomfortable to walk on continually. The bricks must
be waterproof – what are classified as 'hard' or engineering bricks so that frost
will not damage them – or granite sets will do nicely.

Sometimes a basement garden is part of a larger front garden area in
one of those tall Victorian houses where the front door is up an imposing flight

Where the door is
the other side
from the steps

of steps and originally the kitchens and servants were down below – but
perhaps now there is a separate household below stairs (see p. 52).

If the gate is right in the middle of the front garden wall and the front
door set off to one side the trick is to get from the gate to the door without
putting a thin diagonal path slap across the garden which would have the effect
of slicing the garden in two.

Any treatment of the garden must be in accordance with the dignity of
the house so materials should match or harmonize with those of which the
house is built.

There may or may not be a lower door, or it may be tucked under the
steps to the front door.

The textured concrete areas could all be on the same level if the garden
is flat, or each one stepped up from the other if there is a slope. Again, make
sure all bricks are 'hard' or engineering bricks – sometimes called blue bricks.

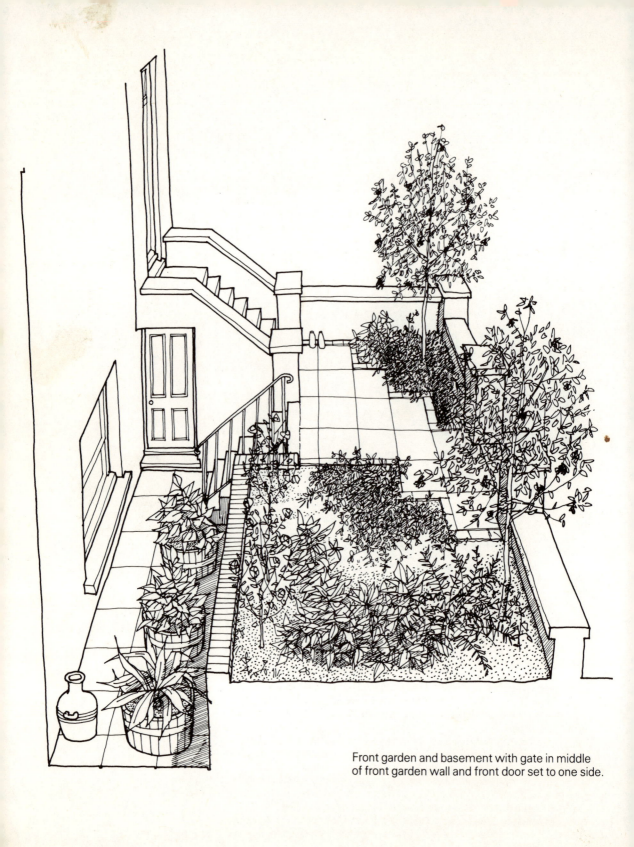

Front garden and basement with gate in middle
of front garden wall and front door set to one side.

RAISED BEDS WITH PAVING BETWEEN

If you are disabled or find stooping difficult or just want an easy way of gardening you might like to change levels quite dramatically to bring the soil surfaces up to a comfortable working height. This can be done using a variety of shapes and materials to suit your style and your pocket. The raised beds can be used for fruit and vegetables as well as shrubs and flowers.

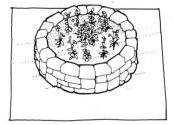

Circular beds of natural or reconstituted stone, or hard brick

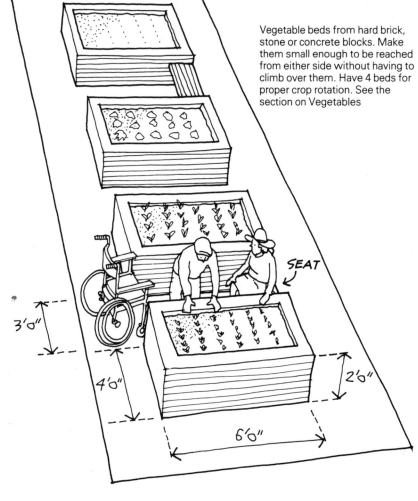

Vegetable beds from hard brick, stone or concrete blocks. Make them small enough to be reached from either side without having to climb over them. Have 4 beds for proper crop rotation. See the section on Vegetables

SEAT

3'0"

4'0"

2'0"

6'0"

Concrete sewer pipes of varying heights for a floral display

An old beer barrel for a small tree or shrub

The beds could be arranged at the right distance apart for a wheelchair to negotiate between them or close enough together to give a disabled person, not in a wheelchair, support all round the garden. A few sitting places would no doubt be much appreciated. Pave or tarmac between all the beds for ease of maintenance.

If you have a blind person in the household put some plants with interesting leaf textures or pleasant perfumes at hand or head height. Herbs give plenty of scope in this way.

Avoid steps, overgrown paths, thorny subjects, glass or anything else that could be classed as a hazard. The same principle of raised beds with paving between for ease of maintenance can be extended to larger gardens. If these are carefully planned the topsoil removed from the paved areas can be just the right amount to fill the raised beds and borders.

There would be a lot of initial work and outlay to establish a garden like this but very little work to maintain it.

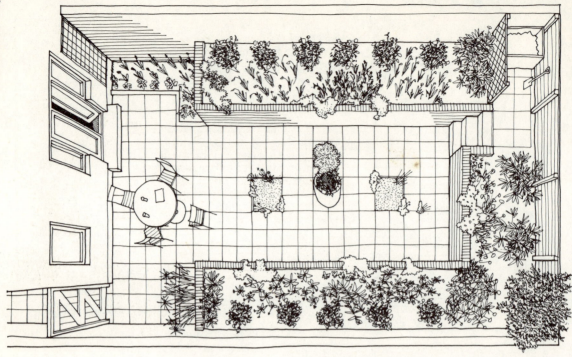

Stone or brick walls – with a fence built on top of the outer walls with, say, concrete uprights built into the walls – or the outer walls themselves built up to 'fence' height.

This layout has been planned so that the raised beds are roughly the same total area as the paved areas giving enough spare topsoil to fill the beds. The construction sequence would be to dig out the foundations for the walls taking out enough soil to give comfortable room to work, to build all the walls and then to move the soil from the areas to be paved into the raised beds. Last of all lay the paving.

This garden is somewhat severe with its straight lines and right angles so let's soften it on the next plan.

THE SOFTER PLAN

The curved line of the end wall with the circular statue, or bird bath, and circular pond will give a much softer and more harmonious effect. The softness can be enhanced with plants in containers, areas of gravel and creeping plants like thyme planted among the paving – just leave out the odd small paving slab, swap the subsoil underneath for a little topsoil and pop in a plant.

Follow the same construction sequence as before. First check the depth of the topsoil, measure the site and then draw a plan on graph paper. Peg out the site with sticks at salient points so that you can have an idea of what your plan will look like and that it is what you want.

First dig out and put in the foundations for the walls, then build the walls themselves, transfer the topsoil to the beds, construct the pool (see p. 141) 00) and then finish with the paving, gravel and cobblestones. Plant the shrubs and roses, put clusters of various types of bulbs between and around them and then put in some ground cover plants. You can think up all kinds of variations on this general theme to suit different sites. Once constructed this garden will be very easy to look after.

The height of the walls will depend on the slope of the site and the amount of topsoil available. If this were a level site, the dimensions were as shown and the topsoil about 9 in deep, the far end shrub bed would need to be

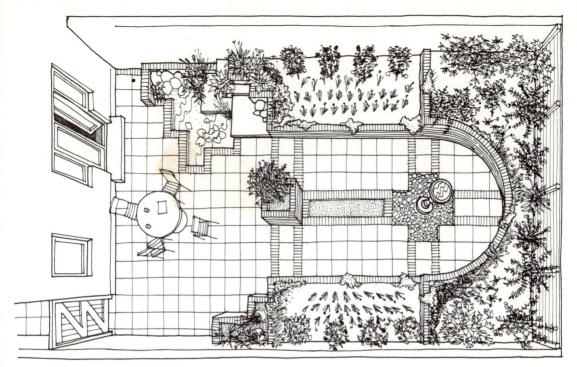

about 2 ft high and the rose borders at least 1 ft high to accommodate all the soil.

If you draw a plan on graph paper you will find it fairly easy to estimate the amount of soil you will have to dispose of and therefore the height of the borders.

With small shrubs chosen to flower throughout the year, roses and a wide variety of bulbs you can have a long season of interest and display with the minimum of effort

PAVING IS PRICY – SO WHAT ABOUT GRASS?

The plans so far will cut maintenance to a minimum once they are established but they will require a lot of initial work to construct yourself; a high outlay of cash for bricks, stone, concrete, mortar and paving materials, and an even higher outlay if you get a contractor to do it.

If you are even more of a reluctant handyman than a reluctant gardener you may wish to avoid a lot of that initial work and opt instead for a lawn as part of your plan. Grass is cheaper than paving and less work at the outset. It is also, of course, more comfortable to lie on or play on in the summer and acts as a pleasant foil to plants and flowers.

But as we all know grass means work once it is established, design your plot to reduce this ongoing work to a minimum.

PLAN FOR EASY LAWN MAINTENANCE

Edges. If you like cutting lawn edges arm yourself with a pair of edging shears – the long-handled variety – and enjoy the exercise once a week. Or go in for more sophisticated equipment worked by push or power. If you are a very reluctant edge trimmer the best way to avoid that chore is to have your lawn butting up to paths or paving wherever possible.

Make sure the lawn is just a little higher than the paving (up to an inch – and remember to allow for settlement) so that you can run the mower over both grass and paving without damaging the blades. The grass will, of course,

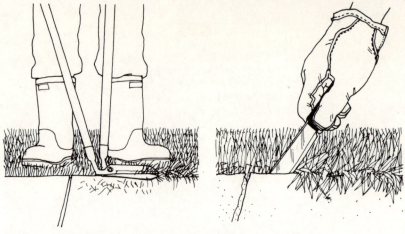

grow over the paving so you will have to cut the edges occasionally but this may be as seldom as twice a year.

You can do it with shears or with a sharp knife slipped down between grass and paving. This can be hard work so do it when the soil is moist and wear a glove to avoid blisters.

Avoid irritations. Don't have grass growing right up to walls or it will be awkward to mow and there will be a lot of shear work to do.

Don't have it growing right up to tree trunks either or to hedges or to other obstructions.

Put a border or a path in between and avoid problems.

If you have a statue or a bird bath put it on a paving slab or on a plinth just below lawn level so that you can mow round it with ease.

Don't use grass paths where there is a lot of traffic such as in vegetable gardens – they'll get messy and muddy in bad weather. Use paving slabs instead.

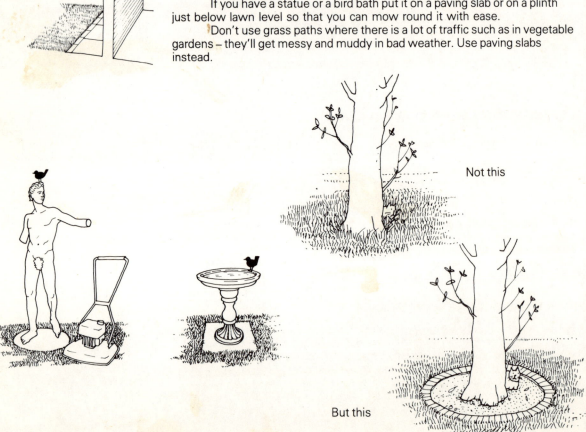

Not this

But this

Square lawns will cause you to pause with the mower at each corner to change direction, or if you are mowing in strips you will need to turn the mower right round at the end of each one. Whereas if your lawn is laid out as a circle or oval you can start with the mower at the outer perimeter and keep going round and round and round without stopping at all until you come to the centre. Then it is best to stop before you disappear without trace.

        Circular or oval lawns may not always be easy to accommodate but you can always use the basic principles when planning by smoothing off corners in your design. It is quicker to mow a shape like this ◯ than this. ☐

It is also quicker to mow a complex lawn layout like this

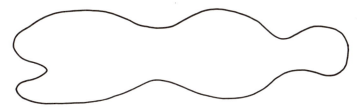

than this

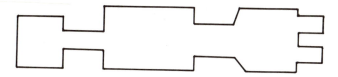

simply by going round and round and round with the mower.

So cut the corners in your planning and you will be able to cut them in your mowing.

THE STANDARD SMALL GARDEN

Many small back gardens are laid out with a patio by the house, a square lawn and flower borders on three sides. It seems the simplest answer and may be all you wish to do but it is a little uninspiring and may even present a few problems of maintenance. The two top corners of the lawn will make it difficult to manoeuvre the mower without damaging the plants in the borders or treading on them and the lawn leading straight off the patio is rather dull. So round off the two top corners, extend the border by the terrace, add a feature like a statue or bird bath and you will have a little more style with no more work. Or you could be slightly more daring and use a shape like an artist's palette with a small round bed where the thumb hole of the palette would be.

        These simple designs with the flower borders going out to the boundaries are fine if you are surrounded by fences but they have some serious drawbacks if the garden is surrounded by hedges. The hedges send their roots straight into the flower borders to deprive them of the water and nourishment that your plants need, the hedge growth gets tangled up with the shrubs and flowers and you need to trample over the borders to cut it back. You can solve these problems by putting a path right round the plot and you will then be able to cut the hedges in comfort. Round off the lawn to make it easy to mow and put a little path to give you a short cut to the compost heap. If you curve this little path you can make it less obvious.

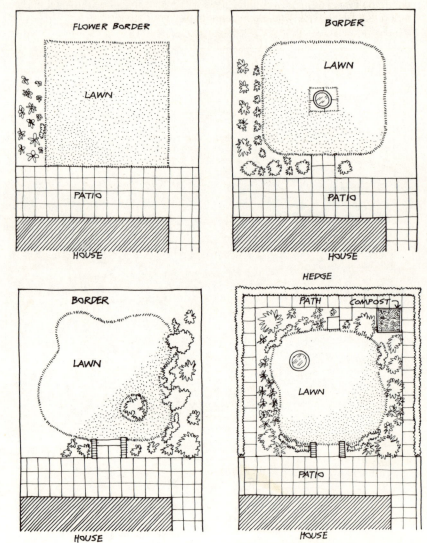

TAKE IT EASY

If you want to reduce maintenance of a plot like this to the bare minimum but want a bit of colour, fill the borders with flowering shrubs, plant daffodils between and in front of them and add some ground cover plants between the shrubs. Don't bother with any edge to the lawn but just let it merge into the border at the same level.

Keep the weeds hoed off between the shrubs for the first couple of years till the plants have taken over.

As it is good gardening practice to avoid cutting daffodils down until the leaves have died – it helps to conserve their strength for following years – you have the perfect excuse for just mowing up to them and not bothering to trim the edges. Just let the grass grow among the daffodils and leave the whole border to fend for itself once the ground cover plants have grown. But, once the bulbs have died down, mow the grass once a week to show that you care. Or you could have a more formal design based on a perfect circle. This design will need some care to establish but it will be easy to maintain. For the best effect make sure the circle really is a true one. Take care to find the exact centre point and then draw out the circle with sticks and string, keeping the string taut all the time. Use graph paper to plan your garden.

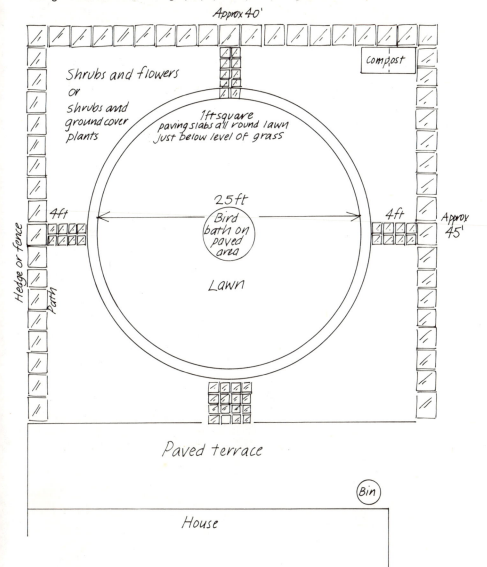

Approx 40'

Shrubs and flowers
or
shrubs and ground cover plants

Compost

1ft square paving slabs all round lawn just below level of grass

Hedge or fence

Path

4ft

25ft
Bird bath on paved area

4ft

Approx 45'

Lawn

Paved terrace

Bin

House

A LITTLE MYSTERY

The plans we have seen so far have everything on view. We don't have to wonder what is there because we can see it all. There is no mystery.

Mystery adds interest to a garden. We like to wonder what is round a corner or the other side of an archway and will probably wander out into such a garden to see. When we get there it may be nothing more than the vegetable patch but it will have been fun finding out.

There is much more scope for this approach with oddly shaped gardens and with long ones than there is with small square ones. A wedge-shaped site, for instance, might look like the illustration. (Note that the irregularly shaped pond, if you are making it yourself, would be tricky: you might prefer a simple rectangular one.) In each case the sitting-out or sunbathing areas are facing the sun and have a focal point of interest to look at.

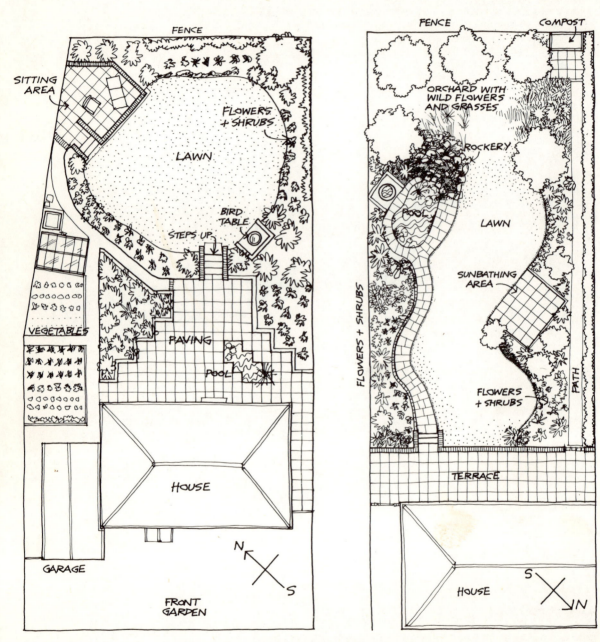

FENCE

SITTING AREA

FLOWERS + SHRUBS

LAWN

BIRD TABLE

STEPS UP

VEGETABLES

PAVING

POOL

HOUSE

GARAGE

FRONT GARDEN

N
S

FENCE   COMPOST

ORCHARD WITH WILD FLOWERS AND GRASSES

ROCKERY

POOL

LAWN

SUNBATHING AREA

FLOWERS + SHRUBS

FLOWERS + SHRUBS

PATH

HEDGE

TERRACE

HOUSE

S
N

As more heathland and wild places fall to the plough to increase our food supply there is growing concern among conservationists for the populations of native birds, butterflies and small mammals which need these natural habitats.

As a reluctant gardener you might well be doing your duty to let part of your long garden go back to nature in a controlled kind of way. That area in the orchard in the last plan would lend itself nicely to a semi-wild garden where you need only cut the grass twice a year. Your children would certainly love it and might even give more care to the tidy parts of the garden if they can let rip a little in the wild one.

But do it properly. Don't just let the nettles, thistles and docks run riot to annoy your neighbours. Dig over the ground properly, rake it level and in April or September sow it with a mixture of meadow grases, herbs and wild flowers – the kind that were in sweet hay meadows before the second world war (John Chambers, 15 Westleigh Road, Barton Seagrave, Kettering, Northants can supply them).

If you cut the grass once in July and again in Sept/Oct each year you will keep it from becoming a jungle and the annual wild flowers will have time to set seeds for next year so that you will have a perpetual sweet hay meadow. You may have to do this cutting with a sickle, scythe or shears if you can't get a suitable mechanical mower to tackle long grass.

Rake up the grass and compost it separately from the rest. It will be fairly full of seeds so return it whence it came to the wild garden. If you use it elsewhere you will have wild flowers where you don't want them and you will probably then call them weeds.

THE PLAIN MAN'S PLOT

If you cannot bother with focal points, bird baths, statues or pools but just want to meet the basic needs of your family with no frills I suggest that first of all you think about those needs in detail, list them in some order of importance and then translate them into a plan by playing around in pencil on graph paper until you get the best answer you can. Graph paper is so much better than plain paper because by treating each small square as, say, 1 ft you can get the details in proper proportion to each other.

Draw in the fixed essentials first, such as a path all round the plot if it is surrounded by hedges. A typical list of needs might be:
1   A path all round the plot.
2   Space for growing vegetables. (Four areas for proper rotation – see the section on Vegetables)
3   Two compost bins
4   The maximum length of lawn for ball games.
5   Somewhere to dry the clothes near to the house.
6   A paved area at the back of the house.
7   A sunbathing area facing south.
8   Shrubs and flowers.

Of course, you may not wish to have these exact features. It may be that you don't want to bother with vegetables but would like a play area instead. The important thing is to plan your garden to suit yourself. So just list what you do want and plan accordingly. You could translate your needs into a Plan A (p. 62) But it is rather dull and uninspiring and will give the garden a narrow look by fragmenting it into strips. On the other hand you could use much about the same space for each item on your list but end up with a Plan B (p. 62) which is which is still basically simple and easy to look after but which treats the garden as one entity and gives a more interesting view from almost any part of the garden or house.

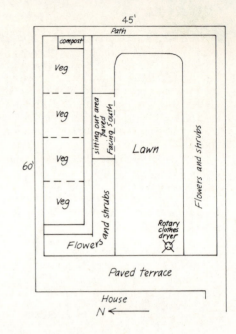

Plan A

45'

Path

compost

Veg

Veg

Veg

Veg

sitting out area
Paved
Facing south

Lawn

Flowers and shrubs

60'

Flowers and shrubs

Rotary
clothes
dryer

Flowers and shrubs

Paved terrace

House

N ←

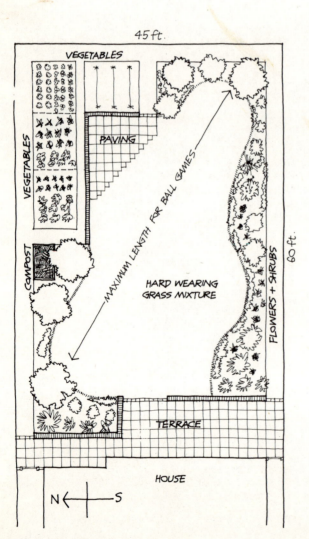

45 ft.

VEGETABLES

VEGETABLES

VEGETABLES

PAVING

COMPOST

MAXIMUM LENGTH FOR BALL GAMES

HARD WEARING
GRASS MIXTURE

Plan B

60 ft.

FLOWERS + SHRUBS

TERRACE

HOUSE

N ← + → S

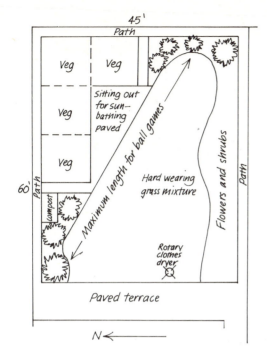

45'

60'

Path

Veg | Veg

Sitting out
for sun—
bathing
paved

Veg

Maximum length for ball games

Veg

Hard wearing
grass mixture

Compost

Flowers and shrubs

Path

Rotary
clothes
dryer

Paved terrace

N ←

The same ideas in a longer and narrower garden.

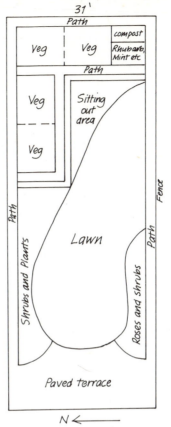

31'

Path

Veg | Veg

compost

Rhubarb,
Mint etc

Path

Veg

Sitting
out
area

Veg

Shrubs and Plants

Path

Lawn

Roses and shrubs

Path

Fence

Paved terrace

N ←

THE LARGE PLOTS

If your horticultural reluctancy ever wanes and gardening gets such a grip on you that you take on half an acre or more – or if you bought one without thinking of the work – you would still be wise to follow the same basic philosophies that we have discussed for the smaller plots so that your finished plan gives you what you want but does not involve you in time-consuming chores.

Your list of needs might now include:

1 A path all round the plot.
2 Enough space in the front garden to park two or more cars.
3 A vegetable garden to feed a family of four for most of the year.
4 Soft fruits – raspberries, gooseberries, currants, etc.
5 Cordon or espalier apples and pears.
6 Four or more compost bins.
7 A glasshouse for tomatoes and cucumbers.
8 Garden frames for bringing on tender plants.
9 A wide range of shrubs, roses, dwarf trees, heathers, fuschias and bulbs but not too many time-consuming herbaceous plants.
10 A garden pool with fish, frogs, water irises, lilies and a fountain.
11 Somewhere near the house to dry the clothes.
12 A paved area at the back of the house.
13 A sunbathing area facing south.
14 Bird baths, bird tables and a few choice statues.
15 Places for rhubarb, mint and other herbs.
*16 Somewhere to practise your putting if you are a golfer.
17 A hose laid all round the garden to make watering easy.

A garden to meet this list of needs might take ten years or more to mature so it is worth spending a little time on planning. Opposite is one possible plan for a plot of just under half an acre (again using graph paper).
And much the same plan scaled down for a plot of one seventh of an acre.

*A good golf game for any number of players. Put the hole in a suitable spot – the middle of the pool lawn will do nicely – and clock golf numbers round the lawns. If the ball goes into any flower bed the offender must retrieve it and place the ball six inches on to the lawn where it went off and add one stroke to his score. This rule will protect your prize plants from inconsiderate swipers. If the ball goes into the pool just pushing the offender in will probably serve the same purpose. As always the lowest score wins.

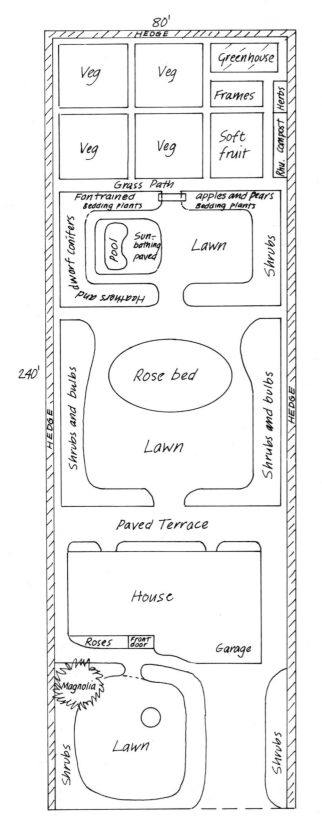
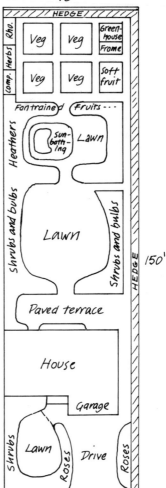

11 THE NAME GAME OR WHAT'S THE DIFFERENCE

Some people call a spade a shovel but, of course, there is a difference. If you specifically need a spade a shovel won't do. It pays to use the right name. The same with plants.

PLANT NAMES

You could be forgiven for thinking that many plants have been given long, complicated and unpronounceable Latin names just to confuse the amateur. The feeling is understandable but untrue.

The range of plants is immense. Some 'common' names are quite specific but many are local and of limited value and not all plants have them – or perhaps have more than one. Some Latin names have come into common usage and present no problem. Most of us now regard names like antirrhinum, delphinium, geum, nasturtium and asparagus as 'English' rather than Latin.

I have used common names in this book where I think there will be no confusion, but to be able to distinguish between one plant and another there is often no alternative to using the 'proper' name. Plant knowledge comes with experience – a bit at a time – and most of us are still learning.

THIS YEAR, NEXT YEAR OR FOREVER

Plants have different life spans like 'annual', 'biennial' and 'perennial'. The words are often connected with descriptions, such as 'hardy', 'half hardy', 'tender', 'bedding' or 'herbaceous'.

Perhaps a few words on the generally accepted meaning of these phrases would help.

Hardy. Hardy plants will put up with our climate in normal winters. They can be left in the open all the year round and need no protection from normal frosts.

Half hardy. Plants that are designated half hardy are quite happy outdoors until the frosts come. Some will stand no frosts at all but others will survive mild frosts but not severe ones.

Tender. Gets easily hurt. Will give up the ghost at even a mild frost. Tender subjects should not be planted outdoors until all danger of frost is past – about the last week of May in the south or near the coast and the first week of June for the rest of us. But be guided by the weather conditions at the time.

An annual is a plant that germinates, grows, flowers, seeds and dies within one calendar year. A 'hardy' annual is one that can do this in our own climate and many will come up each year from the self-sown seed of the previous year.

A biennial germinates and partly grows one year then completes its growth and flowers the next. So the seed sowing has to be done one season ahead of the flowering. A bit of a bind for reluctant gardeners but worth the effort. Wallflowers and sweet williams are well-known examples.

A perennial plant lasts for more than two years – usually many more. How long exactly depends on several factors – plant type, weather, soil conditions, disease and habit of growth. Some stay roughly the same size while others expand their root system and their territory. The latter usually need to be divided (see p. 128) every few years to retain their vigour. Some perennials are best replaced with new plants every few years while others seem to keep going for ever.

Herbaceous. Strictly speaking any plant which is not woody and which dies down to ground level at the end of the growing season is herbaceous but the word is normally used for herbaceous perennials. So a herbaceous border is a flower bed that is mainly, or wholly, planted out with perennials.

Bedding. Again strictly speaking a bedding plant is any plant that is suitable for a garden bed but the word is normally used to describe the process of planting a flower bed with plants just for one season. In fact in some very posh parks and gardens bedding displays of, say, pansies or polyanthus are used for the spring or early summer and then dug up to make way for other bedding displays for the summer and autumn. This gives a long season of display. Hardly a 'reluctant' practice.

The pretenders. I'm sure you won't worry too much about this point but quite a few plants which we treat as half hardy annuals are in fact perennials which can't survive severe winters. Antirrhinums are a case in point. It the winters are mild many varieties of antirrhinums will survive from year to year but as they can get a bit tatty they are usually replanted afresh each year. My advice to you, dear reluctant reader, is to leave such perennials where they are. They will often do very nicely indeed the second year, or even the third, without the bother of putting in new plants.

A FEW PROS AND CONS

Annuals are cheap because you grow them straight in the soil from seed, but you have the bother of sowing them afresh every year. They are good for bare patches not yet planted up.

Biennials are even more bother still if you grow them from seed, but you can buy plants, of, say, wallflowers and sweet williams in the autumn raised by your nurseryman, which will give very early displays of colour in the spring.

Perennials cost the most, but they will come up and give a good display year after year, so they may well not be expensive in the long run, especially if you can win a lot of them from friends whose plants need dividing up.

12 PLANTING AND SOWING

Success is the sweetener. Fame is the spur. Whatever we do in life we need to get it right often enough to encourage us to go on to do it again. Whether it is baking a cake, throwing a dart, making a speech or getting a little seed to grow into a big healthy plant we certainly need to get it right more often than we get it wrong.

And when it comes to planting plants and sowing seeds there is sometimes a danger of a little too much failure. Seeds sometimes sulk and stay in the ground rather than vigorously thrust their way through mother earth to gallop into abundant growth. Some plants that are put in with such high hopes and loving care sometimes stay still, shrink a little and then slowly and miserably pass away.

Such happenings do not engender confidence. If repeated too often they can lead to muttered incantations and mysterious talk of 'green fingers', as if some selected humans had magic powers not possessed by others. Forgive me if I offend but I must dissent from such quaint conclusions. Continued success comes to those people who have taken the trouble to acquire the simple basic rules of sowing and planting and there is no reason why you should not be one of them.

So before we go on to consider Flowers and Vegetables let us briefly look at a few rules and wrinkles regarding sowing and planting so that we can ensure good germination, sure and certain growth and the sweet smell of success.

OF MICE AND MEN, CATS AND KIDS, SLUGS, SNAILS AND BIRDS

I know I have discussed pests and diseases elsewhere in this book but a few more cautionary words are, I think, apposite in this section.

Slugs and snails

I have a friend, a good-looking vegetarian lady, who sometimes sadly sighs that fortune does not favour her garden as much as it does mine. She feels that there must be something wrong with the seed she buys, something lacking in her soil and in her touch, that she must surely sow at the wrong phase of the moon because any seeds she sows never seems to even germinate, let alone grow into healthy plants.

...WOULD YOU LIKE THE MENU ?

Her seeds germinate all right and when she is asleep at night they are busy thrusting their way through the soil towards the stars. But as they do so from all the dark and shady corners of her garden, from cranny and crevice, from under hedges, from piles of old bricks, logs and junk slowly but relentlessly glides a multitude of slugs and snails. A veritable army of gastropods sedately slime their way across her garden when she is in the land of sweet sleep and munch their way through almost every little seedling in sight. What they miss one night will be on the menu the next night.

One night I took her by the hand, and with a torch to light the way, showed her the death scene of her seedlings.

'What could she do? What should she do? However could she cope?' I explained that one way she could cope would be by using slug pellets to polish them off but that it was a painful death and a cruel end for one of nature's creatures and that I advocated one smart blow from a heavy hammer or a housebrick to hasten each slug or snail to heaven.

'But I couldn't do that', she cried. 'It's too cruel.' And she didn't. And she still won't. But she still goes on about how difficult life is in her garden, how her seeds never do as well as mine, because the truth is too difficult for her to face. So she doesn't have her own crisp fresh lettuce but buys rather limp ones from the greengrocer and dares not dwell on what other men have done to make them free of slugs.

So before you blame your seed or your soil do please clean up all piles of junk to give such pests no hiding place and with a heavy housebrick in your hand stamp out the slugs and snails. Or you may prefer to down them in drink (see p. 32).

Men, kids and cats

These can also lead to seed sowing failure. Whenever you sow some seeds, do tell the family where they are so that they know where not to put their feet. The family won't remember of course and you may well forget yourself so it pays to mark the spot. In the dark winter days when there is nothing else to do get out your saw and chopper and make some firewood sticks 6 to 9 in long, paint them with white emulsion and you will have made some good cheap marker sticks which are easy to see and on which you can write the names of plants or seeds. If you are planning to grow quite a few of your own vegetables it is worth making a hundred or more of such sticks.

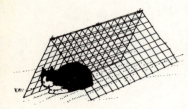

Cats are lighter on their feet than the family but they don't always do as they are told and they can quickly tread a good seedbed into a compacted cat pathway and ruin your seed-sowing efforts. Cats may also, of course, use your nicely raked seedbed as an earth closet. They may have to be deterred by physical barriers. Tent-shaped structures made from wire netting are easy and cheap to make and can be moved from place to place.

Dogs

If dogs don't treat the garden as they should you may have to send their owners on a training course.

Mice

Mice can be deterred by a cat of course. Or you may prefer to deny that you have ever had mice in the garden – and you may well be right. But if your peas have ever completely failed to appear or your tulips have all disappeared you may well have been visited by tiny feet and teeth.

You can protect peas from mice and other pests by soaking them in paraffin for an hour before sowing them. It doesn't damage the peas but it gives them a flavour the mice aren't too fond of. Some country people, and town people too for all I know, sprinkle holly leaves among newly-sown peas before they cover them with soil to act as an uncomfortable defence barrier.

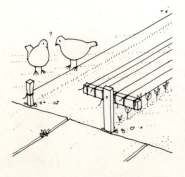

Birds

Do by all means welcome the birds to the garden as they do such a good job in eating up a number of pests, but if the birds become pests themselves by having dust baths in your newly raked soil or by pecking at seedlings use either the wire netting barriers to keep them off (see Cats above) or stretch lengths of black cotton 1–2 in above the soil where the seeds are. The birds don't easily see the cotton and are deterred by the unwelcome feel on their legs. A single strand is often enough to protect a row of seedlings until they get going.

So much for some common causes of failure, now let's look on the bright side and see what positive measures we can take to ensure success.

Use fresh seed

Don't use old seed. Some seed will, it is true, last for years, especially if it is stored in foil and kept in a cool dry place like the bottom of a refrigerator but with other seed the lifespan is short. After all the work of preparation I don't think it is worth taking the risk of a failed crop by using old seed. So buy fresh seed each year.

Don't sow too deeply

A lot of seed gets sown too deeply. The finer the seed the shallower it should be sown. See what it says on the packet and sow no deeper than that.

By sowing depth I mean the depth of soil that finally ends up over the seed. If the instructions say sow one inch deep don't make it two inches for luck. You won't get much luck that way. In nature, of course, a lot of seed just lands on the surface of the soil. It doesn't get put into drills but enough of it manages to survive. Putting it into drills of the right depth will certainly improve its germination rate but don't kill it with kindness by burying it too deeply.

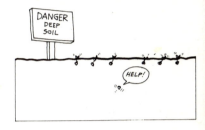

See your seeds

Many seeds are the colour of the soil which makes it difficult to see how thickly you are sowing them. A little talcum powder or lime shaken up with the seeds in the packet will help you to see them against the soil.

State of the soil

Don't try to sow seeds when the soil is wet and sticky. Seeds won't germinate in cold wet conditions and you will only spoil the structure of the soil if you walk on it when it is wet. Wait till the wind and sun have dried the soil so that it doesn't stick to your hands or boots and is in a nice easily crumbled condition – what gardeners call 'friable'.

Prepare the ground

If you rough dug the soil before the winter frosts the top few inches should have weathered down to a nice crumbly structure. On a fine dry day rake the soil backwards and forwards until you have broken up the lumps. Remove any large stones. Lightly firm the soil by shuffling across it with boots or wellingtons on until it is trodden down – but don't stamp on it or jump on it. Now rake it again until it is a fine tilth and no particle of soil is bigger than a pea and most are smaller than grains of wheat. If you do this when the ground is wet you will ruin the structure of the soil and when it dries out it will be like concrete so do wait until the soil is dry and crumbly before you do the shuffle dance. If you have a sandy soil it will, of course, dry out much more quickly than a heavy one.

Sowing times

These will vary depending on which part of the country you live in, the type of soil you have, which way your garden faces and whether spring is early or late. The instructions on the seed packet will give you a good general guide. With spring sown seeds it is usually better to err on the side of sowing a little later rather than a little earlier. If you can cover the seeds with cloches you will be able to sow a few weeks earlier. Be guided by local conditions and, in time, your own experience.

Taking out the drills

The word 'drill' has several meanings. In gardening terms it is a small furrow – a deep scratch in the soil if you like. The basic aim in all seed sowing is the same – to take out a drill or a hole, put in the seed, cover with soil and gently firm again so that the soil is in contact with the seed. What size drill or hole you make depends on the size of the seed.

The standard drill. This is used for most kinds of seeds. If it is in the vegetable garden you will almost certainly decide on a straight row. Peg out a line – a length of string stretched between two stout sticks will do – and take out a drill using the corner of a draw hoe, the angle of a rake, or the end of a stick. I prefer the latter and have used a 3 ft length of broomstick for many a long year. If you are sowing a small quantity of seed in the flower garden you won't need a line but just the stick to take out a few short drills.

The watered drill. If you wish to sow seed when the soil is dust dry in the height of summer trickle some water along the bottom of the drill *before* you sow the seed. Cover the seed with the dry soil and do not be tempted to water again until the seed has come up.

The pea or bean drill. This is a flat-bottomed drill rather like a very shallow trench which you can take out with a draw hoe or a narrow spade – a strong seaside one is ideal – and a line to ensure that it is straight.

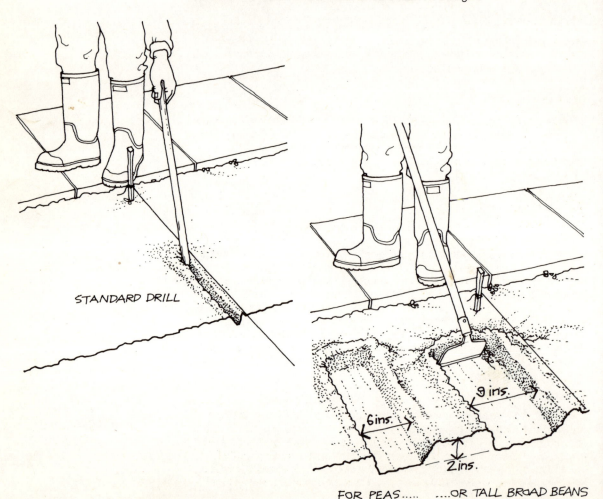

STANDARD DRILL

9 ins.

6 ins.

2 ins.

FOR PEAS..... .....OR TALL BROAD BEANS

The potato drill. This is like a bigger version of the standard drill and you can dig it out with a spade or use a strong draw hoe. Or you can make a separate hole with a trowel or spade for each potato.

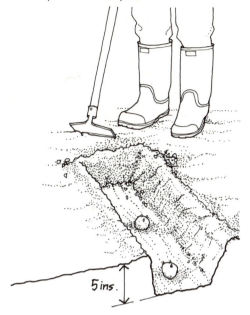

5 ins.

Bulbs

A trowel is ideal if you are planting just one bulb. If you are planting in a lawn you will find it less tiring to use a bulb-planting tool that takes out a core of soil. If you are planting groups of bulbs in a border take out an area the right depth with a spade, incorporate some compost, set out the bulbs, cover with soil and mark the place with some sticks. Avoid planting bulbs in straight lines – they just don't look right. Plant them in clusters.

Planting shallots

Use a small trowel or old dessertspoon to take out small holes about 1 in deep and 9 in apart. Put each shallot in its hole so that it is only half buried. Don't press the bulb down or you will compact the soil under the shallot and make it difficult for the roots to penetrate. Just pull the soil around each bulb and gently firm. Blackbirds sometimes pull out the shallots to see if there are any insects underneath so protect them with black cotton.

Bulb planting tool

Planting onion sets

You can plant them individually but I think you will find it easier to take out a 1 in deep drill with your stout stick using a line as a guide. Plant the onion sets upright 4 to 6 in apart in the drill and replace the soil so that just the tips of the sets are showing above the soil. You will have to fiddle about a bit as the sets tend to be different sizes. Or you can take out one drill for the bigger ones and a shallower drill for the smaller ones. Firm the earth around each bulb after planting and keep the birds off with black cotton.

Sowing marrows, cucumbers and sunflowers

If you wish to sow the big flat seeds like marrows, courgettes, cucumbers or giant sunflowers out in the open take out a hole about 4 in deep and 6 in square where each plant is to be and fill with compost. Plant two seeds on their edges in each such station about ¾ in deep. If both seeds come up remove the poorer one. Or you can sow the seeds in pots in the greenhouse a couple of weeks earlier than you would outdoors.

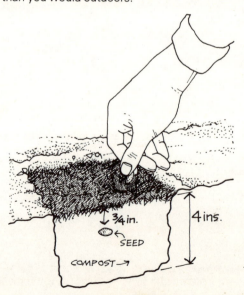

The actual sowing

This is where you can do yourself a good turn or a bad turn. You can do it all in a rush and put in far too much seed so that the seedlings come up like a little hedge with each plant fighting its neighbour for moisture and nutriment with their roots all tangled up together and then a few weeks later you can spend hours trying to thin them out. Or you can take just a bit more time at the sowing stage and save yourself a good deal of hassle later on – as well as giving your seedlings a better start in life.

     So slow down, take a deep breath and relax. Take all the time in the world so that your seeds end up nice and thinly spaced with no more than two seeds to the inch. If they all come up they will, of course, still be too close together so you will need to continually pull out the weaker plants as they grow so that they never touch each other and ultimately only the best are left at the correct spacing for the particular variety – when a little contact is quite in order. You will find this type of thinning quite pleasant and not like the frustrating chore of trying to thin out a seedling hedge.

Sowing thinly isn't easy

I'd like to say that sowing seeds thinly is nice and easy but it isn't. It requires a bit of practice but that practice is well worth it in the long run. One of the problems of sowing is that seeds not only come in different sizes they come in different shapes. Some are round, some are like flat discs, others are long annd thin, some are smooth, some are knobbly. Although there are several gadgets on the market that claim to make seed spacing easy I think there is nothing to equal the dextrous use of hands and fingers.

The very big ones

Well, there is no problem with the very big ones like broad beans or runner beans. They are easy to sow. Just put them in at the spacings recommended with a few spares at the end of the row for transplanting later into any gaps.

The fairly big ones

The fairly big ones like lupins and the flat disc ones like parsnips are, I think, best sown singly by tipping some seeds into the palm of one hand and sowing them with the fingers of the other.

Sowing from the packet

Most seeds can be sown straight from the packet. As this requires a little patience and skill you may want to practise first on a strip of cloth laid out on the garage floor. At least if they all come out in one go you can gather them all together, put them back in the packet and start again. It is a bit more difficult to do that if it happens in the garden. But it is reasonably possible to avoid this calamity altogether.

     Cut off the end of the seed packet with a pair of scissors so that you have a clean straight edge at the end and not a torn one. Open the packet and make a crease about 1 in long in the middle of one side. Relax and take your time. Hold the packet between the thumb and big finger and tap it on the edge with the index finger. The seeds will roll down towards the opening but the crease in the packet will cause them to queue up and just a few will come out at a time. As they do you will need to move the packet along the row. After a big of practice it is possible to get them to come out one at a time although occasionally too many will try to escape and you will have to show them who is boss – tilt them all back into the bottom of the packet and start again.

TAP, TAP!

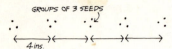

GROUPS OF 3 SEEDS

4 ins.

Station sowing

This takes the theory of 'saving time in the long run' one stage further. Instead of sowing a continuous row of seeds and wasting time thinning them later on just two or three seeds are sown at 'stations' the same distance apart that you want the final plants to be and when they come up they are then thinned down to one per station. In practice it is best to sow at half stations to allow for the slugs or birds seeing the seedlings before you do. So if you want your parsnips 8 in apart put three seeds every 4 in – about $\frac{1}{2}$ in apart – and ultimately thin to 8 in apart.

Cluster seeds

Several plants produce cluster seeds. What looks like one seed does in fact have several seeds inside. Beetroot is perhaps the best known example. Each seed will send up several seedlings which have to be thinned down to one. Sow a single seed at half stations, say 4 in, and finally thin to the full distance – say 8 in. However, to make life more easy for you some varieties of beetroot are now being bred with 'mono' seeds which produce just one seedling from each cluster.

Sowing in pots or boxes

If the conditions in your garden are really difficult – perhaps the soil is sticky clay, the slugs invade the place no matter what you do, perhaps you can't be bothered with wire netting or black cotton and you get backache every time you bend over – you may elect to start off some of your plants in pots, boxes or seed trays in a greenhouse or perhaps indoors.

You may also wish to use this method to start off plants that could be killed by a late spring frost if sown too early outdoors. It is the accepted way of raising half hardy plants to give them a quicker start than if you had to wait to sow them outdoors.

The usual practice is to sow the seeds in one container and then when the seedlings are just big enough to be able to hold them individually by their small first leaves (or cotyledons) to transfer them to plant trays or pots at the correct spacings for the variety. The tiny plants will be about 1 in tall and this transference is called 'pricking out' – I suppose because the little holes into which they will go have been pricked out in the compost.

MARG

Plastic margarine tubs make quite good starting off pots. Make several drainage holes in the bottom of each one – a heated skewer or other spike does quite nicely – fill with Levington seedling compost then level off and firm down so that it is $\frac{3}{4}$ full. Water with a fine rose or spray. Sow the seed thinly – no close than $\frac{1}{4}$ in apart in all directions and cover with a fine layer of sifted compost. Cover the pot with plastic film or pop it in a plastic bag and put it in the airing cupboard (not the very hot part) or other warm dark place. Inspect daily and bring into full light (but screened from direct sunlight) just as soon as the seeds come up.

If you keep the seedlings on a window sill they will turn towards the light because that is what they need. Don't send them dippy by continually turning them round to try to get them to stop leaning. Let them lean and let them enjoy the light. They will be better for it. You can always put them straight up when you plant them out.

When the seedlings are large enough to handle give them more growing space by pricking them out into plastic plant trays, boxes, flower pots or what you will. Fill the trays or pots with Levington potting compost, level off, firm down and mark the positions for the plants. The standard large size plastic seed tray is about 14 by 9 in and will take between 28 to 40 plants (4 rows of 7 plants to 8 rows of 5 plants).

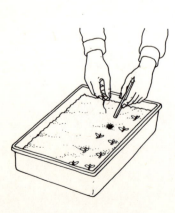

First of all water the seedlings in their growing container. Tease them out with a spoon handle being careful to always hold them by the leaves – NEVER BY THE STEM – and drop them into holes made in the seed tray with a pencil or spoonhandle so that the leaves nearly touch the compost and gently firm in. Holding the seedling by the stem would be like getting someone by the throat and stopping the vital life system – whereas a damaged leaf is nothing serious.

Water the seedlings in their new container and place in full natural light – but again keep screened from full direct sunlight. Keep them watered as necessary – damp but not sodden. When it is time to put the plants outdoors, which will depend on the variety, but will be the first week in June for most frost-shy plants, harden them off gradually by putting the trays outside by day but bringing them in at night until all danger of frost has passed (the first week in June in most places) then plant them outdoors in their final places.

But what a performance that is – although quite a rewarding one – and you may well ask how it can be made easier. A number of leading seed companies now sell seedlings of half hardy plants like bedding begonias, impatiens, petunias, salvias, and also primroses and polyanthus which are ready for planting into seed trays, so saving you the bother of the first operation. You will probably need to get your seed catalogues early and get your order in by a certain date.

The other way which most of us use for some or all of our plants is to buy the trays of plants in late May or early June all ready for planting out from local nurseries or garden centres, although it does cost a lot more than growing your own.

PLANTING OUT

If the plants have been grown in trays you will have from half a dozen to four dozen plants in each one, depending on the size of the tray and the variety of plant. The plants have now to be separated out so that each one is left with its share of compost and with its roots intact. First water the trays and let any surplus drain off. It is fairly easy to get the plants out of the small containers but not quite so easy with the big ones. The best way to deal with a big tray is to first of all hold it at an angle of about 45° to the ground and tap the end firmly on some paved area. This will cause the plants and the block of compost to move slightly to the end of the tray and will free them if they are sticking to the bottom of the tray.

Now, if you have the courage, it is possible to flip the whole block of plants out of the tray on to the paving as if it were a pancake – don't turn it over though of course. If you haven't got the courage, you'll have to slip your hand under the plants and lift them out.

Divide the block into rows of plants, then divide up each row into individual plants as you plant them. Take out holes with a trowel large enough to comfortably accommodate the rootball of each plant and deep enough so that they end up a little deeper than they were in the tray. Pull the soil round the roots with your fingers, firm down the soil and water well. The distance apart will, of course, depend on the variety, but 8 to 9 in suits many edging plants like *alyssum* or *lobelia*.

STARTING OFF RUNNERS AND OTHERS

There is a nice simple block tray system for bringing on plants right from seeds without any pricking out that is very suitable for some seeds. I use it for bringing on runner beans but it could be used for all kinds of plants.

It consists of a flat plastic base and dividing pieces that interlock to form individual plant spaces. It is easy to put together and easy to take apart so you can store it from year to year.

By locking together 6 pieces facing upwards and 6 pieces facing downwards you will get 25 compartments which you place on the flat base.

You fill the whole thing with potting compost, plant one runner bean or other seed at the recommended depth in each compartment, keep in the conditions recommended on the seed packet for the particular plants you are growing (my runner beans go in the cold greenhouse) and then when they are ready to plant out you very gently ease up and take away the uppermost layer of divisions and you can then transfer each plant in its own compost block to its growing position with almost no root disturbance. The plants get away to a really good start.

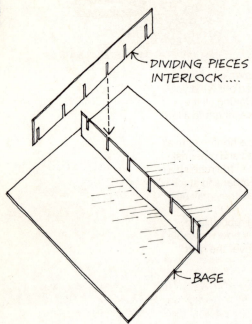

DIVIDING PIECES INTERLOCK ....

BASE

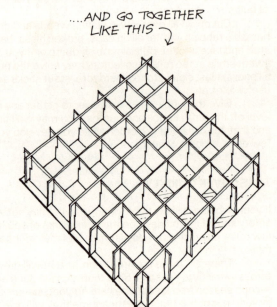

.... AND GO TOGETHER LIKE THIS

13 CLEAR OFF AND TAKE COVER

—DO HAVE A COMPLETE CLEAR UP......

If you have inherited a new plot from the builders or an overgrown site with an existing house, have a complete clear up to tidy the site and find out what you have got before you enter the planning stage. This will mean waiting till the spring to see what comes up. You may be lucky enough to have inherited a lot of bulbs.

Cut down all overgrown plants, weeds and grass, have a bonfire with all burnable rubbish, gather all tin cans, broken glass, barbed wired and other risky stuff and take it to the official rubbish dump or if you only have a little rubbish a sweet smile at the refuse collectors may solve the problem. Gather and stack all bricks, tiles, slate, stones, hardcore, stout sticks and poles as they may be useful later on.

Give the whole site a rake over to gather any remaining rubbish and level off the small lumps and bumps. You may well find that it is now mowable and that you can keep it in order while you develop your plans over the next few days, months or years.

TAKE COVER QUICKLY

If your planning is likely to be long term you may not want to look at a desolate empty site while you develop the finer points of your grand design – so go for a few quick cover shrubs and plants to fool the neighbours and give you time to think.

There are three flowering shrubs that will grow 6 ft tall and as much across within two seasons. Sow them April to June and they will flower in their second season from seed. They are not long stayers and may well deteriorate by year four or five but in the meantime they will give you quick cover and something pretty to look at in summer while other shrubs are coming along or you are still finalizing your plans. They are not completely hardy but should survive most normal winters.

The first is the tree lupin (*Lupinus arboreus*) grown in most gardens when I was a boy because it would come easily from seed, remain in leaf in winter and give a wonderful blaze of golden yellow blooms in May and June. Some plants would surprise one and come white or white and blue. After flowering carefully cut off the seed heads with secateurs or shears and you may well encourage a second flowering for September.

The lupin is a member of the pea family and so is my second suggestion Spanish broom (*Spartium junceum*), Again it can be grown from seed or you may get rooted cuttings from a garden centre. You can either let it have its head completely in which case it may grow ten feet tall within three or four years in a grotesque meandering shape or you can curb its growth by cutting it back by half in March in the first couple of seasons and then lightly pruning it each subsequent year, again in March, to keep it bushy. It won't mind if you take charge and decide its shape but don't spoil it with manure or compost – it does best on light, sandy, rather poor soils. Its bright yellow flowers are sweetly scented and will be borne from June onwards.

My third shrub suggestion is *Lavatera olbia*, a handsome bush mallow, which may attain the stature of a small tree in a few years if grown in a warm site with poor soil. If you want to keep it as a shrub rather than a tree cut it back by half or more of its height in March and tidy it up a bit in late autumn as well. The vine-like leaves are downy and the large pale rose-purple blossoms are borne from June to autumn. The variety 'rosea' is rather more richly coloured than the others. Plants from seeds will not usually come true so obtain a rooted cutting.

POTATOES AS SMOTHERERS

New potatoes straight from the garden, cooked within the hour, are a delicacy that confirm that summer has come. So if you have a bit of spare space before your plan goes into operation plant some seed potatoes in spring (see p. 169) even if you only roughly dig and don't bother to earth them up. Their haulms and leaves will smother most weeds so cleaning up the soil and you will have something sweet for your dinner plate while your grand plan is taking shape. (See the vegetable section.)

RUNNERS FOR BEANS AND BEAUTY

If you want a temporary screen for some eyesore what better than a row of runners grown up poles. They are pretty plants and a popular dish.

They need a little more care than potatoes. They don't like weeds round them so you will have to help with the hoe, they need a bit of good ground and like to be well watered in dry weather. So you will have to bother a bit, but you can get a good crop from quite a small space. (See Chapter 23.)

Now for more permanent plantings.

14 HEATHS, HEATHERS AND DWARF CONIFERS

I think that heathers were specifically designed for reluctant gardeners. Once established they smother most weeds and will stand up to hot summers and cold winters. They come in a wide range of colours. They are evergreen and as there are both summer and winter flowering varieties they grace the garden the whole year round. Some are grown just for their attractive foliage.

All they ask in return is that you understand their soil needs, that you plant them right out in the open and not under trees and that you give them a haircut once a year with a sharp pair of shears as soon as the flowers have died. Cut all the dead flowers and their stalks right off and tidy up the plant. You will need to do this operation several times a year as different varieties flower at different times.

Heathers are mostly low growing but you can add a contrasting variation of height and shape by using dwarf conifers as their companions. They too are evergreen and, like the heathers, ask no more than that you plant them out in the open and understand their soil needs.

Anyone who needs to be convinced about heathers would do well to visit the Royal Horticultural Society's gardens at Wisley near Woking or, say, the Royal Botanic Gardens at Kew and Edinburgh, the Great Park at Windsor or The Liverpool University Botanic garden at Ness in Cheshire or the Northern Horticultural Society's Garden at Harlow Car near Harrogate. These gardens show heathers on the grand scale with mass plantings of a hundred or more plants of each variety. Enjoy the spectacle and then scale down the ideas in your mind's eye to suit your own garden.

'Erica' is the botanical name for heaths. 'Calluna' is the botanical name for heather or ling. Erica has bell-shaped flowers and needle-like leaves. It is grown mainly for its flowers but there are just a few varieties grown for their foliage. Calluna on the other hand has little single or double flowers in shades of white, pink and purple, and its stubby leaves cover a range of colour through green, grey, orange and red. Quite a few varieties are grown just for their foliage. Many people do not differentiate between the species or between their other relatives Daboecia and Phyllodoce and your nurseryman will know quite well what you are talking about if you refer to them all as heather.

WHERE TO PLANT?

You can plant them as an edging to a path, as a group in a corner of a garden, as single specimens among small shrubs or in a rockery but they really do look best all together in a special garden reserved just for them – a heather garden.

One way of coping with a sloping bank that is difficult to mow is to turn it into a heather garden and save yourself the troublesome chore of cutting the grass.

WHEN TO PLANT?

As heathers are now almost always sold as container-grown plants they can be planted at any time of the year. The best times are autumn and spring when the ground is warm and moist but they can be planted in winter provided the ground is not frozen and in summer provided they are well watered both before and after planting.

THE SOIL

Like many other plants heathers have their likes and dislikes and most summer flowering varieties dislike lime. They are not too fussy as to pH. However, in most gardens the addition of plenty of peat and an occasional watering with a solution of 'Sequestrene' (available from garden centres) will allow them to be grown quite happily.

If your soil contains a fair amount of lime then stick to *Erica carnea*, *Erica darleyensis* and *Erica mediterranea*. Unless the soil is deep and well enriched with peat or other organic matter planting in soils overlying chalk will not be successful. The plants will be a pathetic sight after a year or two.

Otherwise heathers are not too fussy over soil types and will thrive in a wide range of growing conditions and even in quite poor soils.

PREPARING THE SITE

If you want to save yourself time and trouble in the long run, which must surely be the aim of every truly reluctant gardener, it is best to dig over the whole site the depth of a garden fork (single digging) and take out every perennial weed and its roots that you can find. That includes the nasty ones like dandelions, docks, bindweed and couch grass. Both the latter have trailing white roots that will spring into action again if you leave in just an inch. Get out every single weed and those white roots.

Then spread a 2 in layer of peat over the whole area. If your soil is heavy clay remove some of it and increase the depth of the peat layer to 3 in. Don't be tempted to put the remains of old growbags on the heather garden – they contain lime.

HOW TO PLANT?

I would strongly advise the reluctant gardener only to get container-grown plants – that is, those plants that have been grown in their own pots and have not been dug up from a nursery bed. The planting out can then be done at leisure and if you have a severe attack of reluctancy in the middle of the operation the plants will come to no harm in their containers as long as you keep them watered occasionally.

It will often be found that the plants are so well established in their containers that the ball of roots is quite solid. If you plant them out like that the roots may stay all tangled together and the plants will then not develop properly.

So first of all soak the whole root ball – pot and all – in a bowl of water, or even a bath if you have a lot of plants to deal with. Then remove each plant from its container prior to planting out and carefully tease the roots apart with the tines of a small hand fork or with a sharply pointed stick. If the roots are still dry give them another soaking. If they have grown through the hole in the base of the pot I think it is better to sacrifice the pot rather than the roots. Plastic pots can be cut with an old pair of secateurs, or if it is thin plastic with scissors, and clay pots can be broken with a tap from a hammer.

The depth of planting should be such that the rootball is buried just a bit lower than it was in the pot with say just an inch of soil over it. Don't plant them lower than this. Take out a hole with a trowel large enough to spread out the roots completely. Mix the soil in the bottom of the hole with a little peat and cover the roots with a mixture of soil and peat. Press down firmly round the plant with your hands and after you have put in a batch of plants water them well in. You may like to put a couple of plant labels among each variety so that if any do turn up their toes you will know what variety you need as replacements.

LAYOUT AND DESIGN

There is tremendous scope to do your own thing with heathers and have whatever design of heather garden you want. It could cover half an acre with thousands of plants and be linked with lawns, paths or stone terraces with fifty or more plants of a hundred different varieties; at the other end of the scale, you could have one little bed of, say, 6 ft by 4 ft with just three plants each of seven varieties.

Heathers are natural wild plants of moorland and hillside and although in our gardens we will need to do a little taming don't do too much. Too much tidiness with the heaths and heathers made to line up like soldiers in square formations just doesn't look right.

If you have grass paths between your heather beds there will be a problem of keeping the edges tidy, so you may decide it is better to surround each bed with strips of paving, letting the heathers grow over the paving and the paving merge in with the grass.

Put your plans on paper – square graph paper – to make planning and estimating so much easier.

I will suggest a middle-range example of a heather bed which you can, if you wish, scale up or scale down to suit your own inclinations. If you are not sure of the shape of the beds that would suit your circumstances a look at a map of the world may give you some ideas. You may like the look of Iceland, Ireland, Sicily or Sardinia for example. Personally I think that Australia, slightly rounded at the corners is quite a pleasant shape for an 'island' heather bed – one completely surrounded by paving or grass that can be viewed from all sides. I will use a size of roughly 20 ft by 16 ft.

Different kinds of heathers grow to different heights and spreads. There are tree heathers 6 ft or more tall and small heathers less than 3 in tall. Most garden varieties are between 5 and 15 in tall so those are the ones I will use. They will have different rates of growth and different spreads but to get an overall effect within three or four years I will set out the plants about 1 ft apart in each direction. (Use graph paper, making 1 square = 1 ft.)

THE PLAN

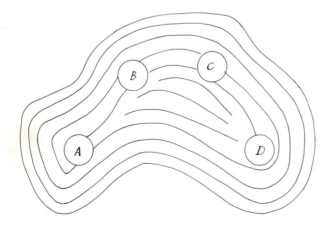

I hope Australian readers will forgive me for what I have done to the corners of their country and will accept the disappearance of Cape York in the cause of symmetry.

The outer row of heathers will be about 6 in from the edge of the bed so I have pencilled in that line and then other planting lines at about 1 ft spacings. I have also marked four circular areas about 2 ft in diameter for dwarf conifers.

On the next plan I have marked, in ink, the positions for the heathers spaced 1 ft apart along the lines so that I end up with plants roughly 1 ft apart in all directions (again using graph paper with 1 square = 1 ft).

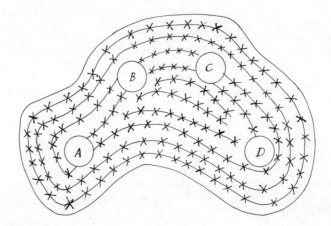

Heathers are best planted in quite large groups of the same variety to achieve a bold and natural look. If you are planting a small bed don't use less than three plants of each variety.

As I want to achieve a year round display I have used both winter and summer flowering varieties as well as some noted for their foliage. I have divided up the bed into some seventeen territories with between 8 and 12 plants in each one and marked them (W), (S) or (F) to denote Winter, Summer or Foliage and numbered the territories.

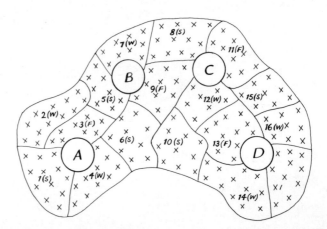

If you obtain a catalogue from one of the larger growers (like Bressingham Gardens of Diss in Norfolk) you may while away many a winter evening in an armchair round the fire deciding which varieties you might like to grow. It is a pleasant way to garden.

The varieties I have chosen are:

Specimen Dwarf Conifers

A. *Chamaecyparis obtusa Nana Gracilis* which will grow up to 3 ft tall and has dark green foliage arranged in shell-shaped sprays.
B. *Juniperus virginiana* 'Sky Rocket' which may in time reach 8 ft tall as a pencil shape. It is sky blue.
C. *Thuja occidentalis* 'Rheingold' will make a broad pyramid which is gold in summer and copper coloured in winter. May also reach 8 ft.
D. *Picea glauca* 'Albertiana Conica'. A conical dwarf spruce with bright green foliage growing to over 3 ft tall.

   If you wish to use shrubs as the four specimens instead of Dwarf Conifers I could recommend *Acer palmatum Disectum* (Japanese maple), *Leucothoe fontanesiana Nana, Menziesia ciliicalx* and *Genista anglica*.

The heaths and heathers I have chosen are:

Winter flowering

Area	Variety	Colour	Flower Time Starts	Max Height in in.
2	*Erica darleyensis* 'George Rendall'	Pink	Dec	12
4	*Erica carnea* 'Ruby Glow'	Ruby	Jan	10
7	" " 'Springwood White'	White	Feb	6
12	" " 'December Red'	Purple	Dec	7
14	" " 'Springwood Pink'	Pink	Jan	4
16	" " 'Vivelii'	Carmine	Jan	5

Summer Flowering

Area	Variety	Colour	Flower Time Starts	Max Height in in.
1	*Erica cinerea* 'C.D. Eason'	Rosy red	June	13
5	*Erica vagans* 'Mrs D F Maxwell'	Rose	July	11
6	*Calluna vulgaris* 'Alba Plena'	White	Aug	8
8	" " 'Radnor'	Reddish purple	July	10
10	" " 'County Wicklow'	Pink	July	8
15	" " 'Underwoodii'	Pink to purple	Aug	14
17	" " 'August Beauty'	White	Aug	11

For Foliage Effect

Area	Variety	Colour	Flower Time Starts	Max Height in in.
3	*Erica carnea* 'Aurea'	Green/ yellow	Dec	8
9	*Calluna vulgaris* 'Robert Chapman'	Gold/red/ yellow	Aug	10
11	" " 'Golden Feather'	Gold/green red	Aug	15
13	" " 'Rannoch'	Light green/gold/ red	July	11

You will find these foliage heathers also have quite pretty flowers though not so striking as the others.

A smaller bed

If you want a heather bed on a smaller scale you could go through the same planning and selection procedure yourself or you could use my plan on a much smaller scale with either fewer varieties or a fewer number of plants of each variety. Or if you wished to be really reluctant you could just use a part of my plan such as the six western areas rounded off a bit like this:

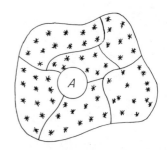

A FEW MORE WORDS ABOUT DWARF CONIFERS

I have used just four dwarf conifers in my plan but some of the larger nurserymen list well over 100 or even 200 different varieties in their catalogues. Dwarf conifers come in all shapes and sizes and quite a wide variety of colours.

The range is so big that you could plan a garden using almost nothing else but dwarf conifers. Because they need to be spaced far enough apart to display their shapes I think they are best interspersed with heathers to act as ground cover plants to stop weeds growing as well as for their beautiful colours. However, if you wished to keep down your costs you could omit using heathers and hoe between the conifers every few weeks or top dress the soil with peat or shredded bark each year to keep down the weeds. If you do use shredded or pulverized bark, ensure that it has been properly composted by the supplier and is fit for horticultural use otherwise it may damage your plants.

A REALLY RELUCTANT THOUGHT

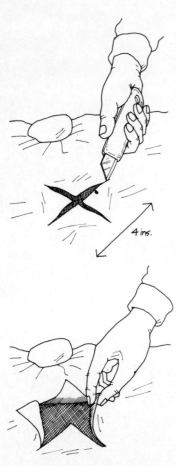

4 ins.

If the thought of weeding really does fill you with dismay you could consider an experimental system for heather beds that virtually eliminates that troublesome chore.

Plan your heather bed, dig it over and incorporate plenty of peat in the top few inches. Rake it level and water well if the soil is dry.

Now cover the whole bed with heavy-duty black plastic sheeting. Weigh down the edges with stones or fix them firmly with pegs. Then cut crossed slits about 4 in long at every point where you wish to plant. Lift up the flaps, put in the plant and neatly tuck the flaps back again. Plant at the depth that they were in the containers but make sure that you follow the instructions on p. 82 (How to Plant).

The plastic will act as a complete barrier to weeds but won't look too pretty, so when you have finished planting cover the whole area with chopped or pulverized bark (that has been properly composted) to a depth of 1 in or more so that the plastic cannot be seen. Tuck the bark carefully under the plants so that they are not buried by it. The bark should be fairly coarse, up to 1 in cubes, so that it won't get washed about by the rain. This covering of bark should hold the rain and allow it to percolate through the slits to the plant roots.

15 THE FUCHSIA GARDEN

A VERSATILE PLANT

Fuchsias are very versatile plants. They can be grown in window boxes, tubs, hanging baskets, as pot plants in the greenhouse or as border plants in the garden.

It is as the latter that I would recommend them to the reluctant gardener. Properly planted, the hardier varieties will survive some quite cruel winters to come to life each spring and give up to five months of flower in summer and autumn – or even more if you live near the sea and are free from frosts. They have the added appeal of requiring little attention.

There is something about fuchsias grown outdoors which is never captured by those grown in the glasshouse. Their leaves are a deeper green and the flowers have more intense glowing colours. And what a delight those colours can be. Nearly every variety is double coloured, the tube and sepals being one colour and the corolla another. Almost any twinning of carmine, cerise, scarlet, mauve, white, red, pink and purple can take place.

As well as a range of colours there is a wide range of heights and sizes. Some are so vigorous that they can be used as hedges like the wild fuchsias in the West Country. Those suitable for a border can range from 4 ft high like 'Mrs Popple' to the little 'Tom Thumb' only 9 in high, or the even smaller 'Alice Hoffman' at about 6 in. But if you are going to use fuchsias as hardy border plants you must only choose those varieties that will survive outside and then give them the correct initial care.

Hardy varieties that are properly planted will survive the winter in the least severe parts of the country. That includes whole areas of the Midlands and the milder parts of the North. You own micro-climate is important and frost hollows will need to be avoided – once again proving the point that the reluctant gardener must choose the site of his house with care.

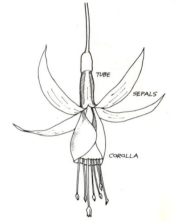

PLANT WITH CARE

Plant your fuchsias in a sunny, well drained spot. The ability of hardy fuchsias to survive the winter depends on them getting their roots right down deep into some good soil. Digging to at least the depth of the fork and incorporating plenty of compost or well-rotted manure before planting is essential. Add some sharp sand or peat if the soil is heavy.

Plant out at the end of May or early June when all fear of frosts is past. Carefully knock the plants out of their pots and plant them low enough so that the bottom part of the stem, about 4 in, is buried below ground. This will ensure that several potential growth buds are protected from winter frosts. Those buds will produce the new plant shoots for the following season.

SPECIAL CARE THE FIRST YEAR

If the summer is a dry one keep the plants well watered during their first season. Not just a surface sprinkling but a good soaking. Remember the aim is to ensure the plants have a good deep root system by the autumn to ensure survival during their first critical winter. Get them through the first winter and you will almost certainly get them through the following ones. To make assurance doubly sure heap a few inches of compost, leaf mould or some bracken round the base of the plants before the winter sets in.

SIMPLE PRUNING

Don't be tempted to tidy up when the plants have died down in the winter. Leave the dead top growth to give some protection to the lower part of the plant and then when the new shoots come up from the base in spring simply cut out all the dead wood with a sharp pair of secateurs. If the winter has been a mild one and new growth starts shooting out from last year's old stems have no mercy but cut them back to within one or two pairs of buds at the base of the plants. You will get much tidier and more vigorous plants this way. With some of the taller varieties you can leave the main stems in and cut the side branches back within two or three buds.

Hard pruning every spring is a vital operation in successful fuchsia growing to ensure new growth each spring with plenty of flowers for the summer. Just one simple operation is not a lot to ask for such a colourful reward, and as there are no thorns or prickles the pruning can be quickly and painlessly done.

SUPPORT AND TOP DRESSING

Some of the taller varieties may need some support with stout canes when they are heavy with flower. Hoe between the plants to keep down the weeds in spring, give a sprinkling of Growmore each year and a top dressing of compost whenever you have some to spare. Be careful when you are hoeing in spring that you don't cut off the new shoots.

WHICH VARIETIES FOR OUTDOORS?

The following varieties are generally regarded as among the hardiest and it is best to stick to these unless you live in the warmer parts of the country when you may be tempted to experiment with others. Those that have received awards as good garden plants from the Royal Horticultural Society after trials in their gardens at Wisley I have marked with a *.

The varieties are arranged in order of height to make planning easier as it is a little disconcerting to find one has a 4 ft high plant at the front of the border and a 9 in one hidden away at the back.

The heights can only be taken as a rough guide because your climate and soil will have an effect on the rate of growth.

The colour of the tube and sepals is given first followed by the colour of the corolla

GROUP A Up to 4 ft high
 'Edith'   Carmine/light purple
*'Madame Cornelissen'   Crimson/white
*'Magellanica Gracilis'   Crimson/purple
 'Margaret'   Carmine/purple
*'Mrs Popple'   Scarlet/purple

GROUP B Up to 3 ft high
*'Doctor Foster'   Blood red/purple
*'Graf Witte'   Carmine/purple
 'Pee Wee Rose'   Light rose/rose
*'Pixie'   Carmine/mauve
*'Ruth'   Red/purple

GROUP C Up to 2 ft high

*'Abundance'	Red/purple
*'Bashful'	Red/white
*'Blue Bonnet'	Red/violet
*'Chillerton Beauty'	Pink/purple
*'Cliff's Hardy'	Red/purple
*'Eva Boerg'	White/purple
'Florence Turner'	Pink/purple
'Glow'	Cerise/purple
*'Gracilis Variegata'	Variegated leaves with cream margins
'Howletts Hardy'	Red/purple
'Lena'	Flesh/magenta
'Margaret Brown'	Pink/rose
'Phyllis'	Rose/cerise
*'Tennessee Waltz'	Pink/mauve

GROUP D Up to 1 ft high

*'Happy'	Carmine/purple
'Princess Dollar'	Scarlet/purple
'Pumila'	Scarlet/mauve
*'Trase'	Crimson/white

GROUP E Up to 9 in high

'Alice Hoffman'	White/cerise
'Caledonia'	Cerise/violet
'Dunrobin Bedder'	Purple/scarlet
'Tom Thumb'	Crimson/mauve

My descriptions of the colours do not really do justice to them as they are often streaked and veined with other colours. The new shoots will appear in May and the plants will be a riot of colour in July and until the frosts come.

THE FUCHSIA AS A SPECIMEN OR BEDDER

These hardy fuchsias can be planted as specimens among herbaceous plants and shrubs to add summer and autumn colour to beds that may otherwise be predominantly spring or early summer flowering. It is an excellent use for them but I would suggest that their main value for the reluctant gardener is in a special 'not too much trouble to look after' bed by themselves.

You can use them either in a border with perhaps a fence behind and the tallest plants at the back or as an island bed with the tallest plants in the centre. Whichever you decide on do make due allowance for the size of the different verieties.

SOME SUGGESTED ISLAND BEDS

In general the taller the plants the more sideways room they will need so I suggest that in planning your bed or border you roughly allow:

Plants from List	A	4 ft tall to have a	2 ft 6 in diameter space
" " "	B	3 ft " " "	2 ft 0 in " "
" " "	C	2 ft " " "	1 ft 6 in " "
" " "	D	1 ft " " "	1 ft 0 in " "
" " "	E	9 in " " "	9 in " "

One could therefore plan an island bed like this (use graph paper and allow, say, 1 square = 1 ft)

Plan 1

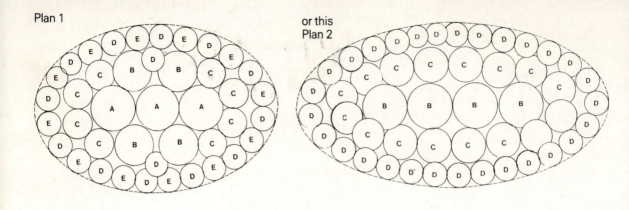

or this
Plan 2

Plants from groups
A, B, C, D & E

Plants from groups
B, C & D

Choose the plants to get the colour mix you would like. In Plan 1 the plants will rise to 4 ft high and in Plan 2 to 3 ft. To get an idea of the overall effect put canes at the height the plants will be and view the bed from all angles. If they are too high you could design something

like this
Plan 3

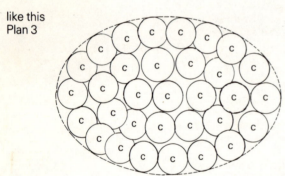

or this
Plan 4

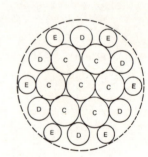

Group C only

Groups C, D & E

These lower height fuchsias are certainly easier to look after as they need little or no support.

INCREASE YOUR PLANTS AT LITTLE EFFORT AND NO COST

As a reluctant gardener you will probably prefer to buy plants rather than raise them but taking cuttings from fuchsias is so simple you may be tempted to try.

In spring or early summer cut off a young shoot, 3 to 5 in long, that has not yet flowered. Trim off the two lower pair of leaves and any stalk below them. You now have a properly prepared cutting.

For best results insert the cutting in a 3 in diameter flower pot filled with potting compost so that the next pair of leaves just touch the compost, having first dipped the cutting in hormone rooting powder or liquid. Water well and slip a small plastic bag over the top of the pot and cutting to keep in the

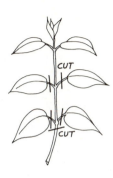

moisture. Place on a window sill away from direct sunlight until the plant has rooted and starts growing and then bring into full sunlight or plant outdoors.

That may seem such a terribly complicated task to you that you just can't be bothered. In which case you could still add to your stock by just breaking off a young shoot, make a hole in the garden with a pencil and after taking off the lower leaves slip the cutting in and press the earth gently round it. Give it a little water until it has rooted. With luck about one in four of these no-bother cuttings will root.

16 ROSES

The rose has been Britain's favourite flower since the first world war. A garden doesn't seem complete without them. The choice available is wide enough to suit everyone. They range from plants a few inches high to climbers that given support such as an old tree can scramble 30 ft or more into the sky. There are hundreds and hundreds of varieties and types, some of them ideally suited to the reluctant gardener.

ROSES FOR THE REALLY RELUCTANT

Let me first make a simple suggestion to the very reluctant gardener who may be reading this section under sufferance or from idle curiosity. Perhaps you have heard of all the budding, grafting, pruning, spraying, cutting out and tying in associated with roses and want none of them. Fair enough. You can avoid those chores and still have roses by selecting certain specimens that need no ritualized pruning and little care.

The rose 'Queen Elizabeth' is one such example. Plant it properly in good soil, keep it watered in dry weather just for the first year, give it a ration of compost dumped on top of the soil each year and it will grow into a magnificent bush up to 7 ft tall and 4 ft wide bearing beautiful pink flowers from June until winter time – provided, of course, that you have given it room to grow.

As it reaches for the sky the base of the stems near the ground may become rather bare so make sure you have planted it towards the back of a wide border so that you can hide that bareness with a few other plants. Forget all about pruning and just cut out the odd dead branch from time to time.

'Queen Elizabeth' has fine healthy foliage, lovely pink blooms, a slight fragrance and excellent qualities as a cut flower in water. It is a marvellous American bred rose named after our young Queen in the 1950s.

And 'Queen Elizabeth' is not the only rose that will give you such a good return for so little effort. The white floribunda 'Iceberg' and the hybrid tea 'Peace' can be treated in the same way – as well as a special group of roses called 'Shrub' roses which are described in more detail on page 98.

ROSES FOR THE REASONABLY RELUCTANT

Many of you may want to be just a little more venturesome and include a number of different specimens or even a bed of roses in your general garden plan. A few basic explanations are necessary so that we may understand the different types of roses that are available to us.

ROOTSTOCKS

Modern roses are not normally grown on their own roots. They are budded on to the roots of various types of wild roses to give more vigorous plants. Sometimes those wild rose roots send up growths of their own – called suckers – which have to be removed to stop the whole plant reverting to the wild one.

FORMS OF GROWTH

There is a wide range of types of growth but they can be simplified into seven main headings.

Miniature bush	1 ft 6 in or less high
Small bush	2 ft 0 in or less high
Bush	over 2 ft 0 ins
Half standard	A stem of 2 ft 6 in
Standard	A stem of 3 ft 6 in
Pillar rose	6 ft to 10 ft or more grown up a pole
Climbing or rambling rose	Grown up a wall, or along a trellis or in an old tree

MINIATURE BUSH SMALL BUSH BUSH HALF STANDARD STANDARD PILLAR ROSE CLIMBING OR RAMBLING

METHODS OF FLOWERING

Some flowers are single, others double. The flowers may be borne singly or in clusters. Sometimes the reverse of the petal is a different colour from the front. In other roses two or more colours may be striped or blended together and some cluster-flowered roses may have different coloured roses in the same cluster at the same time.

TYPES OF ROSES

Because of the great diversity there are often no clear divisions between one type of rose and another but each rose can be placed in one or more of the following classifications.

Hybrid tea roses

The most popular roses, 'hybrid' because they have evolved from mixed origins and 'tea' because some of the originals smelled like tea. Today most of them are sweetly scented. They are available in both bush and standard form. The flowers are usually double and are borne singly or with a few side shoots.

Single

Semi-double

Hybrid tea

Floribundas

Second only to hybrid teas in popularity, the flowers are borne in large trusses or clusters with many blooms open at the same time in each cluster. Floribundas can make a striking display but usually lack the scent of most hybrid teas.

Miniatures

Miniatures are popular for growing in tubs or for edging beds. Both the flowers and the leaves are small and the plant is usually under 1 ft 6 in tall and may be no more than 6 in. The flowers may be either hybrid tea, floribunda or somewhere between the two.

Climbers and ramblers

They are not climbers in the true sense of the word as they cannot climb by themselves but have to be tied to a support. They can be a magnificent sight covering a trellis or clothing a house wall but they cannot in all truth be recommended to the really reluctant gardener.

Shrub roses

A large class of bush roses that are neither hybrid teas or floribundas. There are a few modern ones but most are historic or 'old fashioned'. Some are closely related to wild roses.

Many form very large bushes which are too big for the average garden and many varieties only bloom once a year. So I cannot recommend very many to you but there are a few, just a few, which are just the ticket for the reluctant gardener. They need no pruning apart from a bit of general tidying up from time to time and the removal of any dead growth. The foliage is usually attractive as well as the flowers and many have attractive rose hips in the autumn as well.

Floribunda

RECOMMENDED VARIETIES FOR THE RELUCTANT GARDENER

We have covered the forms of growth and the various types – so which ones should we choose? Well there are literally hundreds and hundreds of different varieties and quite a few problems. Some roses suffer from black spot, others from mildew, some behave badly in wet weather with the blooms 'balling' and failing to open and yet others fade quickly in the heat of summer. Some have pretty flowers but no perfume and there are yet others where the flowers are magnificent but the plants poor. 'Papa Meilland' is a case in point. To me the dark and velvety blooms with their intense perfume are the most beautiful roses that there are but the plants are very prone to mildew and produce only a few blooms.

I have made a very careful selection of roses for you. My aim has been to avoid those that are difficult to grow or susceptible to disease and most of those that I have chosen are perfumed. Most hybrid tea and floribunda roses will flower from June till the winter frosts. If you live in a mild area you may even be able to pick a few for Christmas Day.

A word of warning. Do not believe all you read in the growers' catalogues – a grower has products to sell and may decide not to point out all the faults of his goods. If you want impartial detailed guidance on growing roses I would recommend the book by Dr D.G. Hessayon called *The Rose Expert*.

Hybrid tea

			Height
'Alec's Red'	Crimson	Very fragrant	3 ft 0 in
'Baronne E. de Rothschild'	Red/silver reverse	Very fragrant	3 ft 6 in
'Blessings'	Pink	Fragrant	3 ft 0 in
'Champion'	Gold flushed pink	Very fragrant	2 ft 6 in
'Chicago Peace'	Pink and yellow	Slightly fragrant	4 ft 6 in
'Dekorat'	Coral to pale gold	Very fragrant	3 ft 0 in
'Double Delight'	Cream edged with red	Very fragrant	3 ft 0 in
'Dutch Gold'	Gold	Very fragrant	3 ft 0 in
'Ernest H. Morse'	Rich red	Very fragrant	3 ft 0 in
'Evening Star'	White	Fragrant	3 ft 6 in
'Grandpa Dickson'	Lemon yellow	Slightly fragrant	2 ft 6 in
'Helen Traubel'	Apricot and pink	Very fragrant	3 ft 6 in
'Just Joey'	Copper orange	Fragrant	2 ft 6 in
'King's Ransom'	Yellow	Fragrant	2 ft 6 in
'Korp'	Signal red	Slightly fragrant	3 ft 0 in
'Lakeland'	Shell pink	Fragrant	2 ft 6 in
'Lolita'	Golden copper	Fragrant	3 ft 0 in
'Mme Louis Laperrière	Dark crimson	Very fragrant	2 ft 0 in
'Mullard Jubilee'	Deep pink	Fragrant	3 ft 0 in
'National Trust'	Crimson	Not fragrant	2 ft 6 in
'Pascali'	White to cream	Slightly fragrant	3 ft 0 in
'Pink Favourite'	Deep pink	Slightly fragrant	2 ft 6 in
'Red Devil'	Scarlet	Fragrant	3 ft 6 in
'Silver Jubilee'	Pink shaded peach	Fragrant	2 ft 6 in
'Summer Holiday'	Vermilion	Slightly fragrant	3 ft 0 in
'Sunblest'	Golden yellow	Slightly fragrant	3 ft 0 in
'Troika'	Deep orange bronze	Fragrant	3 ft 0 in

Floribundas

'Arthur Bell'	Golden yellow	Very fragrant	3 ft 0 in
'Allgold'	Yellow	Slightly fragrant	2 ft 0 in
'Chanelle'	Cream flushed pink	Fragrant	2 ft 6 in
'Chorus'	Crimson	Slightly fragrant	2 ft 6 in
'City of Belfast'	Orange scarlet	Slightly fragrant	2 ft 0 in
'English Miss'	Silver pink	Fragrant	2 ft 6 in
'Escapade'	Rose with a white centre	Fragrant	3 ft 0 in
'Esther Ofarim'	Vermilion with yellow base	Fragrant	1 ft 6 in
'Fragrant Delight'	Salmon with yellow base	Very fragrant	2 ft 6 in
'Iceberg'	White	Slightly fragrant	4 ft 0 in
'Korresia'	Yellow	Fragrant	2 ft 6 in
'Living Fire'	Scarlet and orange	Slightly fragrant	2 ft 6 in
'Margaret Merril'	White slightly cream	Very fragrant	3 ft 0 in
'Matangi'	Vermilion with white eye	Slightly fragrant	2 ft 6 in
'Paprika'	Geranium red	Slightly fragrant	2 ft 0 in
'Queen Elizabeth'	Pink	Slightly fragrant	5 ft 0 in
'Scherzo'	Scarlet/silver reverse	Fragrant	2 ft 6 in
'Southampton'	Orange flushed scarlet	Slightly fragrant	3 ft 0 in
'Trumpeter'	Vermilion	Slightly fragrant	1 ft 6 in
'Warrior'	Scarlet	Slightly fragrant	1 ft 6 in

Floribundas for hedges

Some floribunda roses are suitable for informal hedges. I would recommend the following. Just prune them lightly to keep the hedge in shape.

'Iceberg'	White	Slightly fragrant	4 ft 0 in
'Queen Elizabeth'	Pink	Slightly fragrant	5 ft 0 in
'Scarlet Queen Elizabeth'	Orange scarlet	Slightly fragrant	4 ft 0 in
'Yellow Queen Elizabeth'	Pale yellow	Slightly fragrant	4 ft 0 in
'Yesterday'	Mauve pink	Fragrant	3 ft 0 in

Some 'shrub' roses make even better hedges than floribundas. These are listed under shrub roses.

Miniatures

Miniature roses have a number of things to recommend them. They need no pruning – just a little tidying up with scissors. They can be used as pot plants, edging to borders or planted in their own special beds.

Keep them well watered in dry weather (they have small root systems) and if they are pot grown give them liquid fertilizer from time to time.

They are, of course, expensive as one tiny bush will cost the same as a large floribunda but they are a very useful feature especially in a small garden.

'Angela Rippon'	Carmine pink	Fragrant	12 in
'Baby Masquerade'	Yellow and pink	Slightly fragrant	15 in
'Darling Flame'	Orange vermilion	No fragrance	12 in
'Easter Morning'	White	No fragrance	12 in
'Eleanor'	Coral pink	Slightly fragrant	10 in
'Golden Angel'	Deep yellow	Fragrant	15 in
'Little Buckaroo'	Bright red/white centre	Fragrant	15 in
'Magic Carrousel'	White with red edges	Slightly fragrant	15 in
'Perla de Monserrat'	Deep pink/pale pink	No fragrance	9 in
'Pour Toi'	White/yellow	No fragrance	8 in
'Starina'	Vermilion/gold reverse	No fragrance	12 in
'Sweet Fairy'	Pale pink	Fragrant	8 in

Climbers and ramblers

No roses naturally climb – they have to be tied into place. What we mean by climbing and rambling roses is that they make enough growth to be trained to cover a wide area or a tall structure. I cannot really recommend them to the reluctant gardener as there is a lot of work training them, tying them in and pruning them. But in case the fancy takes you I had better mention a few.

Some are best used as pillar roses tied in to a stout stake 8 to 10 ft above the ground and sunk 2 ft or more in the ground to keep it steady.

'Bantry Bay'	Pink	Slightly fragrant	9 ft 0 in	Pillar
'Compassion'	Pink and apricot	Very fragrant	8 ft 0 in	Pillar
'Etoile de Hollande' Climbing	Deep red	Very fragrant	12 ft 0 in	House wall
'Galway Bay'	Pink	Slightly fragrant	8 ft 0 in	Pillar
'Golden Showers'	Golden yellow	Fragrant	7 ft o in	
'Leverkusen'	Pale yellow	Slightly fragrant	9 ft 0 in	
'Mermaid'	Primrose yellow	Fragrant	25 ft 0 in	
'Mme Alfred Carrière'	White and pink	Very fragrant	20 ft 0 in	North wall
'Sympathie'	Red	Fragrant	10 ft 0 in	North wall
'White Cockade'	White	Slightly fragrant	7 ft 0 in	Pillar

And now a mention of two climbing roses that might well interest the reluctant gardener:

Climbing 'Cécile Brunner' Pink, Slightly fragrant, 20 ft 0 in. This is a very good choice of rose for training up a tree and just letting it get on with it. Most of the flowers will appear in June with just a few flowers for the rest of the season.

Rosa filipes 'Kiftsgate'. Single creamy white flowers followed by bright red rose hips. Give it a great open space and treat it as a huge bush up to 25 ft high. Dont't bother to prune it but just cut out any dead branches as they appear. It is fragrant.

Shrub roses

They are a wide and diverse group of plants. Some are centuries old and others have been with us just a few years. I have selected some which I think you will find make good carefree shrubs. Plant them with enough space round them to grow to their full size (you could infill with annuals for the first few years), keep them well watered in dry weather the first season and then leave them to look after themselves. Those that are also good for hedges I have marked with an H. The older types of shrub rose tend to have a short flowering season and perhaps produce hips later. Modern shrub roses flower for longer. The date of introduction is included in the last column.

			High	Wide	
'Angelina'	Deep pink	Slightly fragrant	3 ft 6 in	3 ft 6 in	1975
'Ballerina'	Pale pink	Slightly fragrant	3 ft 6 in	3 ft 0 in H	1937
'Bloomfield Abundance'	Shell pink	Fragrant	6 ft 0 in	7 ft 0 in	1920
'Cécile Brunner'	Shell pink	Fragrant	2 ft 0 in	2 ft 0 in	1881
'Celestial'	Deep pink	Fragrant	6 ft 0 in	4 ft 0 in H	1780
'Chinatown'	Yellow/pink	Fragrant	5 ft 0 in	4 ft 0 in H	1963
'Felicia'	Apricot pink	Very fragrant	5 ft 0 in	6 ft 0 in H	1928
'Fountain'	Rich red	Fragrant	5 ft 0 in	3 ft 0 in	1972
'Frau Dagmar Hartopp'	Shell pink	Fragrant	4 ft 6 in	3 ft 6 in H	1914
'Fred Loads'	Vermilion	Fragrant	6 ft 0 in	4 ft 0 in	1967
'Fritz Nobis'	Salmon pink	Fragrant	5 ft 0 in	5 ft 0 in	1940
'Golden Wings'	Pale yellow	Fragrant	6 ft 0 in	5 ft 0 in	1956
'Maiden's Blush'	Blush pink	Fragrant	6 ft 0 in	5 ft 0 in	1500
'Old Blush'	Rose pink	Slightly fragrant	4 ft 0 in	4 ft 0 in	1752
'Rosa Rugosa Alba'	White	Fragrant	5 ft 0 in	5 ft 0 in H	Unknown
'Rosea Willmottiae'	Lilac pink	Fragrant	6 ft 0 in	8 ft 0 in	1904
'Roseraie de L'Hay'	Wine red	Fragrant	7 ft 0 in	7 ft 0 in H	1902
'Scabrosa'	Magenta pink	Fragrant	5 ft 0 in	5 ft 0 in H	1939
'White Bath'	White	Fragrant	4 ft 0 in	3 ft 0 in	1810

PLANTING ROSES

Roses should only be planted in good soil that has been properly dug at least one spit deep and in which compost, manure or peat has been incorporated.

Replant disease

Roses do not do well where roses have been planted before. So if you wish to replace an old rose with a new one you will have to replace the soil as well.

Plant in full sun in a well drained soil

Roses will not do well in dense shade under trees, although a few climbers can cope with a north wall. No roses will do well in waterlogged conditions.

Time of planting

Plants may either be container grown or bare root. If they are bare root they should be planted November to March – but not when the ground is frozen. November is the best time.

Container-grown plants may be planted at any time of the year but spring and autumn are preferable.

Marking out

It is best to mark out the planting positions with sticks before you dig the holes for the roses so that you can make sure they will be properly spaced.

Taking out the holes

Bare root. The common mistake is to dig a hole that is too deep and too narrow. Rose roots should be well spaced out all round the plant and the hole should be wide enough to take the maximum spread of roots and just deep enough for the grafting union to be 1 in below the soil after planting is complete.

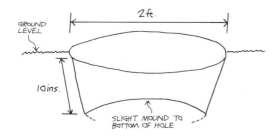

Dimensions suitable for most bush roses.

Never leave bare root roses lying in the wind or sun to dry out at planting time. Cover with wet sacking or put them in a bucket of water until ready to plant

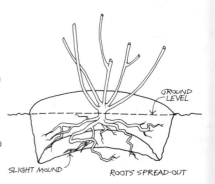

Carefully fill with good soil. Work the soil between the roots by gently shaking the bush up and down as you fill. Firm the soil by carefully treading it as you go but the aim is not to make it like rock so you should not stomp or jump on it.

Container grown plants. Make sure they have been grown in the containers and not just transferred to them from the open ground. The compost in the container will be peat based and in order to get the roots to move out of the peat into the garden soil after planting it helps to incorporate some peat into the soil round the plant. A mixture of half peat and half soil is ideal. Get some ready in the wheelbarrow. Water the plant well before removing the container. Slit the container right across the bottom. Put a 4 in depth of the soil and peat mixture in the bottom of the hole and place the container on it. Slit the sides of the container and carefully remove it. Do not disturb the compost round the roots. Fill the hole with the peat and soil mixture gently firming as you go.

Spacing

If you keep the width of the rose borders to 6 ft or less you will be able to carry out pruning and dead heading without too much treading on the soil – particularly important if you have interplanted the roses with spring flowering bulbs.

Leave at least half the planting distance between the roses and the edge of the border and stagger the planting.

Distances apart

Miniatures	1 ft 0 in
Small bush – under 2 ft 0 in high	1 ft 6 in
Medium bush – 2 ft 0 in to 3 ft 0 in high (average varieties)	2 ft 0 in
Large bush – over 3 ft 0 in high	3 ft 0 in
Small shrub ⎫ (be guided by width of plant)	5 ft 0 in or half full height
Large shrub ⎭	

Marking out

It is best to mark out the planting positions with sticks before you start planting and better still to set it out on graph paper first.

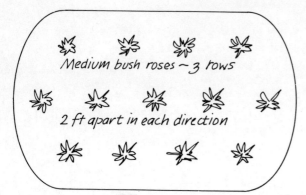

Medium bush roses ~ 3 rows

2 ft apart in each direction

Some suggested layouts

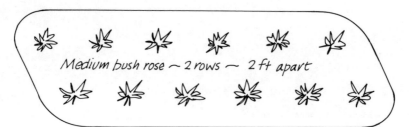

Medium bush rose ~ 2 rows ~ 2 ft apart

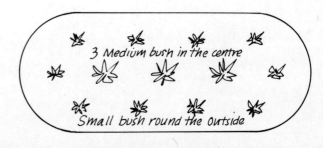

3 Medium bush in the centre

Small bush round the outside

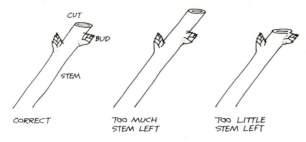

CUT
BUD
STEM
CORRECT   TOO MUCH   TOO LITTLE
             STEM LEFT   STEM LEFT

PRUNING

Hybrid tea and floribunda bush roses will need pruning each year. The purpose of pruning is to get rid of dead and exhausted wood and encourage new healthy stems each year.

In late November or December cut off the top third of any tall bushes to save them rocking about in the winter gales. Do this with secateurs or a sharp pair of shears if you like. In March or April use a good quality pair of secateurs that cut cleanly and prune in the following way.

1 Completely cut out all obviously dead and diseased wood.
2 Completely cut out all very thin stems or those that are rubbing against each other.
3 Cut out all soft or unripe stems. Test by snapping off a few thorns. If they bend or tear instead of snapping off cleanly the wood is unripe.
4 Prune the remaining healthy stems to half their length. If the winter has been severe and killed the top of the stems you must prune right back to live healthy growth. If there is a brown stain on the newly-cut stem prune again until the stain ceases to be there.
5 Prune to an outward-facing bud on each stem. Aim to produce an open-centre bush.

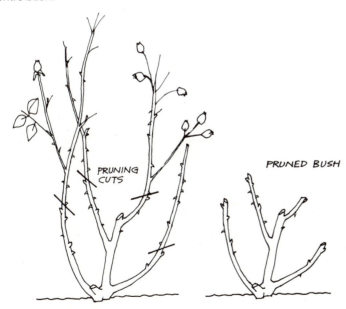

PRUNING CUTS   PRUNED BUSH

WEEDS AND SUCKERS

Weeding roses is an uncomfortable business – their thorns get your hands and clothes and digging between them is not recommended as it can damage their roots and cause suckers to grow. Suckers are shoots of the wild rose variety which form the rootstocks. If left to grow these suckers will deprive the cultivated shoots of their food supply and eventually take over. The easiest and safest way to weed roses is with a Dutch hoe. Use it, and use it often, to just skim through the top inch of soil to cut off any weeds. Never let the weeds get a hold, and if you do get any pernicious rooters like dandelions (see p. 29) dig them up carefully so as not to damage the rose roots.

Take off any suckers as soon as they are seen. You will recognize them from the other stems by the marked difference of their leaflets, their colour and their thorn pattern, but mainly by the fact that they are growing up from the roots and not from the bush. Trace any sucker back to where it is growing from the root, removing soil as necessary, tear it off right at the root and replace the soil. Cutting suckers off at ground level will only cause more to form.

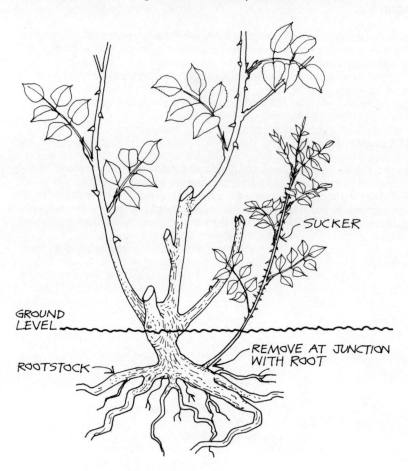

17 SPRING FLOWERING BULBS

-THE CHEERFUL BRIGHTNESS OF SPRING BULBS........

After the dark cold days of winter the cheerful brightness of spring bulbs lifts the senses and gives a welcome promise of summer. There are spring flowering bulbs to suit all gardens from the dazzling drifts of daffodils in the parks and stately homes to the pretty cluster of chionodoxa by the cottage gate.

THE CAREFREE ONES

From the reluctant viewpoint flowering bulbs can be divided into two categories – the troublesome ones that have to be dug up each year, dried off and replanted the next and the carefree ones that can be left where they are to come up again year after year and, if the conditions are reasonable, they will divide and multiply just where they are. I suggest we concern ourselves with the latter.

Although as I've said before gardening has a nasty habit of only giving you back what you put into it, what you put into it can sometimes be a bit tiresome and at other times pretty easy. I am pleased to say the 'carefree' kind of bulbs are pretty easy and only ask for a little understanding and attention. The right planting depth is, for instance, very important so I have mentioned it in each case.

BULBS OR CORMS – DOES IT MATTER?

I am including corms as well as bulbs in my selection as they are treated in much the same way. A corm is a fleshy underground stem and differs from a bulb in several respects, the main one being that a new corm forms each year just above the old one. A bulb is composed of fleshy scales enclosing an embryo bud but I don't think we need concern ourselves with the botanical niceties between them. For our purpose we can regard them all as bulbs.

BULBS CAN HAVE A LONG LIFE

A bulb is a storehouse of food and the embryo parts of the new plant. After it has flowered a bulb needs to go through a recovery period to build up these embryo parts and replenish its store of food so that it can be ready to flower again the next year or divide and multiply as many bulbs do.

To do this it needs three basic things: water, a nourishing soil and the action of sunlight on the leaves. Green plants must have that energy from sunlight to build up complex and necessary substances from water and carbon dioxide. They do this through their leaves and if you cut off the leaves just after the plant has flowered, or if you grow them in poor soil or in bone dry conditions they will not be able to recharge themselves and as a result they may either become blind and fail to flower or they may give up the ghost altogether and never grow again.

HOW TO TREAT THEM

The treatment is simple. Feed your bulbs by giving them a yearly ration of compost spread on top of the soil and a yearly sprinkling of National Growmore when they are in bud or just coming into flower so that it is there to be taken up after flowering to rebuild the bulb. The other essential thing is to leave the foliage on the plants for at least six weeks after the flowers have faded. You needn't remove it at all if you don't want to but at the end of six weeks you may remove it if you wish without seriously depriving the bulbs. I am afraid you can't get round the problem as some people try to do by tying the leaves into tidy little bundles. That is just as bad as taking them off altogether as the sunshine can't get at them when they are bunched up like that.

If you are growing naturalized bulbs in grass you have the perfect excuse for not cutting the grass for six weeks after the bulbs have flowered. In most years there is plenty of rain in spring and early summer to keep the soil moist but if the soil is very dry during that six-week period do ensure the plants get a proper soaking with the hose – not just a surface sprinkling.

GOOD COMPANIONS

Spring flowering bulbs are the perfect companions for deciduous shrubs and trees. Because they grow early they get their ration of sunlight before the leaves on the trees cast a dense shade over them. They are also the ideal bedmates for growing with hardy fuchsias and roses. Roses don't like their roots damaged by digging and you won't be digging if you have got bulbs there. In most parts of the country the roses and fuchsias don't flower till June so the bulbs can add their cheerfulness to the early part of the year for you. Just very shallow use of the Dutch hoe is all the cultivation that is required.

MARK THEM WELL

Few of us have either the time or money to plant all the bulbs we want in one fell swoop so we tend to add a few each autumn. There will be nothing to show where the existing bulbs are and a little frustration can be avoided if you have had the foresight to mark their positions with a stick or two.

A NATURAL EFFECT

Spring bulbs don't look right planted singly or in small groups of just two or three bulbs – they look lonely. Nor do they look right set out like soldiers in straight rows. So put them in groups or drifts of at least half a dozen bulbs and give them room to divide and multiply.

The same applies to bulbs naturalized in grass. It is better to throw a bucketful of bulbs over the grass and plant them where they fall than set them out in rows.

MY CAREFREE SELECTION

I can't give you a completely carefree start as it will be quite hard work to dig over the beds, remove all the weeds, incorporate plenty of compost, leafmould or well-rotted manure and get the bulbs planted. But once that initial slog is completed you will have beautiful flowers to delight the eye with very little ongoing work to depress the spirit if you choose from the following carefree varieties.

Chionodoxa

The exquisite little blue and white flowers will bloom in late winter and early spring. They are sometimes called Glory of the Snow. They are easy to grow, will do well in almost any garden soil and can be used for naturalizing in grass as well as in the flower beds or shrub borders. From 4 to 6 in high, they should be planted 1 in deep and about 3 in apart in the autumn.

Muscari Botryoides (grape hyacinth)

These popular blue grape hyacinths will increase readily if planted in good, well-drained soil and left undisturbed. They should be planted about 4 in apart and 2 in deep and will grow to about 6 in tall flowering in late winter and early spring.

Crocus

They give a striking effect naturalized in lawns and as drifts or edgings to beds and borders. They seem to thrive in almost any soil and will multiply rapidly if left undisturbed. Plant about 1 to 2 in deep – no more or they may fail to flower.

There are two main groups and many colours and types in each group. The crocus species (the types from the wild) are winter flowering and come out with a rush once the worst weather is past. The more common large flowered crocus follow in late winter and early spring.

Galanthus (snowdrop)

They like a cool shady place better than a dry sunny one and can be planted in groups in the flower bed or naturalized in areas of the lawn.

Plant them in late summer 3 in deep and about 4 in apart; they will flower in the middle of winter. Sometimes they can be a bit difficult to establish from dormant bulbs. If you have a friend who can spare a few established ones transplant them when they are in flower with some earth still round the roots.

Hardy cyclamen

These are the ones that grow outside and not the greenhouse variety. They are delightful plants about 5 in high with pretty pink flowers and handsome foliage. They like a peaty soil in a shady spot and will do well under trees or naturalized in the open garden.

To get the best effect ten or more corms should be set in a group 6 in apart and 3 in deep. Some varieties are autumn flowering. *Cyclamen repandum* will flower in April and May, *C. neapolitanum* in Sept and Oct, *C. cilicium* in October to December and *C. coum* in December to March.

Puschkinia

Pretty little plants about 6 in high flowering in March and April. The white flowers are sometimes striped pale blue. They should be planted 1 to 2 in deep and about 4 in apart.

Tulips

A very large group of plants of many colours, types and sizes. The ones I would recommend for the reluctant gardener are the tulip species. They are sometimes called the botanical tulips and are the wild ones native to Asia Minor. They come in a wide range of types, some having several flowers on each stem. Most of them are smaller than the more common bedding tulips and range from 4 to 10 in tall, so they rarely get damaged by the wind. They flower in March, April and May and many a passerby will pause to admire their striking beauty.

Plant them in October or November in groups of three or more of the same kind about 4 in deep and 6 in apart. If your soil is heavy put a handful of sand under the bulbs. These species tulips can be left in the ground from year to year although they will sometimes succumb to various ills or get eaten by mice. If mine disappear I simply plant another group in a different place. The correct treatment is to dig them up when the leaves die, dry them off and replant each autumn – but I don't bother.

Fritillaria meleagris

These elegant flowers that hang their beautiful heads in modesty are usually called snakeshead fritillarias. They are especially suitable for planting in groups in shady borders or on banks in grass. They vary in colour from creamy white through rose and lilac to purple and grow up to 1 ft high, flowering in April. Plant them 3 to 4 in deep in autumn about 5 in apart.

Scilla siberica (Siberian bluebell)

The Siberian bluebell is a miniature. It is a brilliant sapphire blue about 4 in tall. It flowers in early spring and is excellent for naturalizing in grass. Plant in groups about 2 in deep and 3 in apart.

Scilla campanulata (Spanish bluebell)

The Spanish bluebell can now be obtained in pink, white or blue varieties. It is best not used in the flower border as it gets difficult to weed between and looks a bit untidy after flowering, as of course do many of the others, but it is excellent for naturalizing among trees and shrubs and on rough grass banks. It grows up to 12 in tall and should be planted in groups or drifts about 4 in apart and 2 in deep.

Daffodils and narcissi

What is the difference? For all practical purposes none. Once upon a time the trumpet-shaped ones were daffodils and all the rest narcissi but that distinction has gone the way of the wind as different types have come along to give no clear dividing line between the two.

    They are a wonderful group of plants for the reluctant gardener. They will grow in beds and borders and many of them are excellent for naturalizing in grass. But do plant them where their leaves can be left intact for 6 weeks after flowering to build up the bulbs for the following year.

    I must say I have a predilection for the miniature and wild forms, especially for the front of borders but they all have their place. Many are excellent for planting among shrubs and in rose borders or fuchsia beds to give colour in the early part of the year.

    Don't mix the varieties but plant at least 6 bulbs of any one variety in a group or drift. Plant from early autumn to December in good soil. The distance apart will depend on the size of the variety, the very large bulb varieties 1 ft apart with 6 in of soil over the top of the bulb, the medium ones 9 in and 4 in of soil and the smaller ones 6 in apart with just 1½ in of soil over the neck of the bulb.

A ROSE AND BULB BORDER

A border planted with medium sized rose bushes planted 2 ft apart (R) with small daffodils (D), species tulips (T) and *chionodoxa* (C). Depending on the varieties you have chosen the bulbs will be in flower in March, April and May before the roses start to bloom in June. (Use graph paper to translate this into your garden plan.)

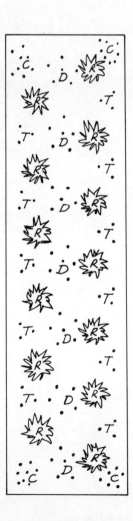

18 TREES AND SHRUBS

WHAT'S THE DIFFERENCE?

A dwarf conifer might be regarded as a shrub but one 200 ft tall would certainly be classed as a tree. So when does a shrub attain the status of a tree? There is, of course, no clearcut dividing line but the usual definition depends on structure and not height. A perennial woody plant with a single stem is usually classed as a tree and one with a number of stems emanating from near the ground is called a shrub. So a bonsai tree is still a tree even though it may be only 9 in high.

THE VALUE OF TREES AND SHRUBS TO THE RELUCTANT GARDENER

Shrubs and trees are very important to all gardeners. Some of them come nearer than any other plants to satisfying the needs of the reluctant gardener for something that will fill the garden with greenery and grandeur with the least possible work.

     If asked for the attributes he or she needed in a plant the reluctant gardener might well reply, 'Give me something that:

    Needs no clipping, training or pruning.
    Is easy to plant.
    Will grow in any type of soil and is not fussed about it being acid or alkaline.
    Quickly attains the required size.
    Has a long season of pretty flowers and leaves.
    Is able to survive hot summers and cold winters.
    Has attractive fruit, hips, berries and bark.
    Never drops its leaves so that there are never any to sweep up.'

If you find a shrub or tree that meets all those conditions I would certainly like to hear about it. But as the word 'attractive' is open to personal interpretation we might still not agree that you had found the ultimate plant.

     But there are trees and shrubs that meet quite a few of those conditions and, if you have enough room, it is possible to have a garden full of trees and shrubs that in one way or another meet nearly all of them.

GET THE SIZE RIGHT

Very many gardens have got shrubs or trees that are way beyond a suitable size for their allotted space and cause endless trouble by robbing almost everything else of light, water and nutrients and have to be kept within some sort of bounds by pruning that is so severe it borders on mutilation. Many of us have made the error of planting something quite unsuitable in size, or put up with a tree or shrub because it was there, or even nurtured a self-sown forest seedling only to regret it in later years when eventually we have had to cut it down and start again.

     One tree that became popular in small gardens some years ago was the large weeping willow (*Salix chrysocoma*), but as the years passed it was the owners who were weeping as they tried to contain the size of these vigorous

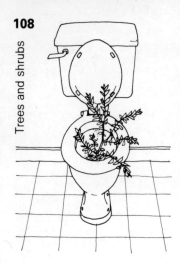

trees by first pruning and then sawing off whole branches. What should have been magnificent trees became emasculated monstrosities and eventually most of them were dug up. This species of willow makes a very handsome tree if it is left to attain its full shape and size – perhaps 30 ft across – but it is a sad sight when it has been hacked about to try to make it fit into a small space.

So the most important rule of all is to plan your planting according to the *ultimate* height and size of your chosen trees and shrubs. On no account plant or nurture large forest trees in small gardens. Apart from doing a takeover bid on space and light their roots may well do damage to the foundations of the house and many a thirsty root has wormed its way into a succulent sewer pipe and stopped up the whole works.

SOIL AND ASPECT

You must also consider the nature of your soil. Is it acid or alkaline, damp or dry and is the aspect sunny or shaded or a bit of each? There are suitable trees and shrubs for almost all conditions.

A LONG DISPLAY

If you have planned your garden in detail you may have a pretty good idea of the sizes and shapes of trees and shrubs you need and where you wish to plant them. If not it is well worth while drawing a plan on graph paper. You may also want to consider whether you wish to have a long season of interest or would be happy to have just one blaze of glory.

Most of us prefer the longer display so that we have something of interest to see at all seasons – an evergreen to cheer the dull winter days, something flowering early, something late, some late summer interest with hips, haws or fruit, trees with interesting bark and the startling beauty of autumn foliage so that there is something of interest the whole year round.

SOME TECHNICAL TERMS

I am afraid I must now talk technicalities. You will need to know a few terms that are used in describing shrubs and trees, mainly the latter, so that you can talk to the nurseryman in his own language. Forgive me if I start with the simple stuff.

Evergreen A shrub or tree which bears leaves at all times of the year, such as holly. Evergreens do in fact shed their leaves but never all in one go.

Deciduous One which drops all of its leaves in autumn such as a cherry.

Conifer A tree which bears cones. Most conifers have needle-shaped leaves and some, such as the larch, are deciduous but most are evergreen.

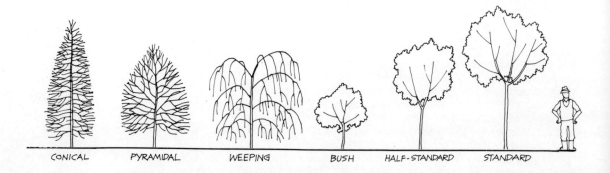

CONICAL   PYRAMIDAL   WEEPING   BUSH   HALF-STANDARD   STANDARD

Conical Shaped like a cone – normally, as far as plants are concerned, with the point upwards.

Pyramidal Shaped like a pyramid. Often not much different from conical.

Weeping With the branches hanging down.

Grafting Many trees and shrubs have the top part of the plant grafted on to a different root system to control the habit of growth. This may be because the chosen cultivar (variety) would produce too weak a plant on its own roots, or conversely because it would produce too large a plant. Roses are grafted on to wild rose rootstocks to give bigger bushes and most fruit trees are grafted on to special dwarfing rootstocks to produce smaller trees.

The grafting may be carried out using either a 'scion' or a 'bud' of the chosen variety.

Scion (pronounced sy-on). A dormant one-year old shoot of the cultivar which is grafted on to the rootstock.

Bud A single bud with its surrounding young bark which is inserted into the bark of the rootstock to produce the new tree or shrub.

Top worked Where the graft has been made some distance from the ground, such as a standard rose.

Bottom worked Where the graft has been made just above the ground.

Maiden tree A tree with just one year's growth from a bud or graft.

Bush tree One that is shaped like a bush but with a clear trunk about 2 ft tall from which the branches come. Fruit trees are often trained in this way by cutting the central shoot when the tree is young to induce branching. Bush trees are sometimes planted on lawns but they are not really suitable as they are rather difficult to mow under.

Half standard A tree with a trunk about 4 ft tall from the ground to the first branches.

Standard A tree with a trunk of 5$\frac{1}{2}$ ft – or, of course, much more. Also applies to roses which are budded about 3 ft or more above ground level.

Head The collection of branches of a standard or half-standard tree. The measurement of a tree is often given as the total height followed by the total width of the head. A tree described as 30 × 20 ft would be 30 ft high and 20 ft maximum width.

Leader The main leading shoot of a tree.

Lateral A branch growing sideways from the main leader or main branches. Espalier fruit trees are trained with horizontal laterals.

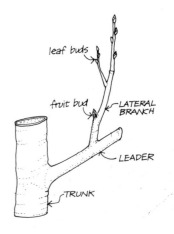

A LITTLE PLANNING SAVES A LOT OF WORK

If you plant the right kind and number of shrubs and trees in your garden they will save you endless work in the long run compared with herbaceous, annual or bedding plants. Choose the right varieties, give them the right conditions, the right places in or out of the sun, a little love in the first few years by keeping the weeds at bay till they are well established and they will then repay your labour by smothering the weeds themselves and giving you beauty and interest the whole year round.

But if you just buy shrubs and trees in a haphazard way and pop them in anywhere as the fancy takes you you will end up with a second-rate show. It won't be a complete failure because nature will take over on the basis of the survival of the fittest and there will be 'something' pleasant to look at but you will do so much better with a little simple planning to start with so that everything has room to develop properly.

Planning is the secret weapon of the idle man. It saves a great deal of work in the long run.

We have already agreed that you need a garden that, as far as possible, will look after itself once you have got it established. Trees and shrubs tend to have a long life – they may be around for longer than some of us – and they don't take too kindly to being dug up and replanted every time they outgrow their space, or being overshadowed by their neighbour if they like the sun, or sitting in the blazing heat if they like the shade.

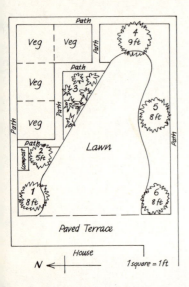

So in deciding on what trees and shrubs to have put a plan on paper if you haven't already done so. Mark out all the main areas of the garden including the paths, beds, lawn and fences. Now decide if you want any specimen trees, where you want them and how much room they will take up when fully grown. Make your selection carefully, especially if you want something of interest at all seasons of the year. Mark in the trees with their ultimate width.

Your plan might look like this having decided on five specimen trees and a bed of roses to start with. In this plan the *prunus* will be in flower in April, the *caragana* in May and the *oxydendrum* in July and August. The latter does, by the way, need a lime-free soil. All five trees have handsome foliage, especially the *acer* and the holly (*ilex*) which will also cheer the winter days with its bright berries. In deciding where to put the trees imagine how they will look from the house as well as from the garden and give them enough space to develop properly. Also bear in mind where they will cast their shadows – you won't want any dense shadows over the vegetable garden – or over you. (Use graph paper for accuracy.)

1   *Prunus persica* 'Aurora' (cherry)
2   *Caragana arborescens* 'Pendula'
3   Roses
4   *Ilex aquifolium* 'Handsworth New Silver' (holly)
5   *Acer palmatum* 'Atropurpureum' (Japanese maple)
6   *Oxydendrum arboreum* (sorrel tree)

Now it is easier to see just what space there is left for shrubs. Mark in the shrubs you want being ready to alter your plan if it doesn't work out as you want it to the first time – or the second time.

A SELECTION OF TREES AND SHRUBS

There are literally thousands of varieties of trees and shrubs which you could plant in your garden and selection is very much a matter of personal taste. Visits to parks, gardens and nurseries are strongly recommended so that you may form a personal judgement of what appeals to you but do view the plants in relation to their backdrop of space. Many trees and shrubs that look fine in a large garden would completely dominate a small one.

I will start with trees and suggest a few which may be planted as specimens in the small garden – but remember this is just a personal selection.

The distance apart will depend on the type and size. I would suggest that you make it a minimum of 15 ft or the maximum spread of the head of the tree if that is greater.

The sizes of the trees listed are the ultimate height of the tree in average conditions followed by the maximum width of the head.

SOME SPECIAL EVERGREEN TREES

Arbutus unedo – the strawberry tree. Slow growing with dark green leaves, pinkish white flowers and red fruits in autumn and winter. The fruits are edible but not very palatable, 20 × 15 ft. A fairly big tree.

Ilex – the holly. Don't give precious garden room to just any old holly but go for a choice specimen and if you want berries make sure you choose a female plant. One very pretty one that has gold margins to its green leaves is *Ilex altaclarensis* 'Golden King' – which is a strange name for a female, 10 × 10 ft.

Ilex aquifolium 'Argenteomarginata' has white margins to its leaves and plenty of berries. So does *Ilex aquifolium* 'Handsworth New Silver'. Both will grow to 12 × 9 ft.

If you want a holly with few spines on the leaves choose *Ilex aquifolium* 'Pyramidalis' which grows to about 15 × 8 ft.

Two handsome weeping varieties of holly, both well berried, are *Ilex aquifolium* 'Pendula' which has green leaves and *Ilex aquifolium* 'Argenteomarginata Pendula' with its white margined leaves. Both 15 × 15 ft.

Ligustrum lucidum (tree privet) is another pretty evergreen for the larger garden, being 20 × 20 ft. It has dark green glossy leaves and long panicles of white flowers in late summer.

Evergreen conifers

Some special evergreen conifers of medium size suitable for the small garden would include:

Chamaecyparis lawsoniana (Lawson's cyprus) 'Columnaris'. Tall and narrow with blue-green leaves, 15 × 4 ft.
C. I 'Lutea' with yellow foliage, 15 × 8 ft.
C. I 'Pembury Blue' with silver blue foliage, 15 × 9 ft.
C. I 'Wisselii' with blue-green foliage, 15 × 6 ft.
Cupressus (cyprus) macrocarpa 'Goldcrest' with golden foliage, 15 × 4 ft.
Cupressus obtusa 'Crippsii' with fern-like golden foliage, 18 × 9 ft.
Juniperus virginiana 'Skyrocket' (Pencil cedar). Very slim with blue-grey foliage, 15 × 2 ft.

DECIDUOUS FLOWERING TREES

First of all you may want to consider whether you would like the very pleasurable returns that can be got from normal fruit trees. Most of them have very pretty flowers in the spring as well as the visual pleasures of the crop itself. There is something very seductive about fruit hanging from a tree as a young gentleman found out very many years ago. If you are tempted turn to the section on Fruit Growing.

If you are not tempted and prefer to opt for beauty without edible fruit the following is a small selection from the many beautiful flowering trees that are now available for the smaller garden.

Caragana arborescens (pea tree). 'Pendula'. A very hardy small weeping tree that has yellow, pea-shaped flowers in May, 10 × 5 ft.

Cercis siliquastrum (Judas tree). It has purple, pea-shaped flowers in April and May, 15 × 10 ft.

Cornus kousa (Japanese dogwood). In June it has masses of white bracts that look like flowers. These are followed by strawberry-shaped fruits and then deep red autumn leaves. Can be grown as a bush, 15 × 10 ft.

Cornus mas (Cornelian cherry). Often has more than one trunk. It has small yellow flowers in February followed by edible fruits, 18 × 12 ft.

Genista aetnensis (broom). In July it has yellow flowers on graceful drooping branches, 15 × 12 ft.

Laburnocytisus adamii. It has the fascination of having two kinds of flowers on the same tree which appear in May. Some look like yellow laburnum flowers and othes like purple broom flowers, 15 × 10 ft.

Magnolia. There are several types of magnolia but most grow too big for the small garden so I have chosen just two rather special ones.

Magnolia × loebneri, 'Leonard Messel'. In April and May it has pink flowers with white centres, 15 × 8 ft.

Magnolia salicifolia has fragrant flowers on leafless branches in April followed by attractive green leaves, 15 × 8 ft.

Malus (the flowering crab apple tree). There are many of them and they make interesting and colourful trees. I have chosen seven for you to think about.

Malus coronaria, 'Charlottae'. Large pink flowers in late May followed by highly coloured autumn foliage, 15 × 8 ft.q

Malus 'Hillieri'. In May the crimson buds open into semi-double pink flowers, 15 × 10 ft.

Malus floribunda. Densely covered in carmine buds which change to 1 in wide single flowers in May. Followed by yellow fruit, 15 × 15 ft.

Malus 'Lady Northcliffe'. Covered in pale pink flowers in May which develop into small yellowish brown fruits, 15 × 10 ft.

Malus 'Neville Copeman'. The leaves have a purple tinge. The large soft pink flowers in April develop into orangey red fruits, 15 × 10 ft.

Malus 'Royalty'. This one also has purple leaves which have a gloss on them.

The large pink flowers in April develop into bright red fruits, 15 × 10 ft.

Malus sargentii. The smallest of the crab apple trees, it is sometimes more like a bush. Its very pretty white flowers in May are followed by cherry-like small red fruits, 10 × 8 ft.

Prunus. This is a large group of stone fruit trees (almonds, cherries, peaches and plums) some varieties of which are grown purely for their blossoms and general decorative effect. I have chosen eight flowering prunus suitable for the small garden.

Prunus 'Amanogawa'. A small tapering tree, ideal for front gardens or formal positions. Large pale pink flowers in April and May, 15 × 3 ft.

Prunus amygdalo-persica 'Pollardii'. Has large pink flowers in March, 15 × 8 ft.

Prunus × blireana. Large double pink flowers in April. Coppery purple leaves, 12 × 10 ft.

Prunus davidiana 'Alba'. Single white flowers from January to March, 15 × 10 ft.

Prunus incisa. White flowers with a pink tinge in March. Good autumn colour, 10 × 10 ft.

Prunus persica 'Aurorà'. Dense clusters of rose pink flowers in April, 12 × 8 ft.

Prunus persica 'Iceberg'. Large semi-double pure white flowers in April, 12 × 8 ft.

Prunus 'Shimidsu Sakura' is a square-shaped tree with a flattish top. Very pretty pink tinted buds open to pure white double flowers in April and May, 12 × 12 ft.

DECIDUOUS TREES WITH COLOURED FOLIAGE, BERRIES OR BARK

Some trees have fairly insignificant flowers but are very pretty in other ways. Here are some from which you can choose.

Acer (maple) *ginnala* is a small maple whose leaves turn to orange and deep crimson in autumn, 12 × 12 ft.

Acer griseum is a very pretty maple with bark that flakes off like paper to reveal the cinnamon-coloured underbark. The leaves turn to red and scarlet in autumn, 18 × 9 ft.

Acer grosseri is one of the 'snake bark' maples with a green and silver striated or fluted trunk and main branches and red leaves in autumn, 18 × 10 ft.

Acer japonicum 'Aconitifolium' has deeply lobed leaves which turn a rich ruby red in autumn, 15 × 15 ft.

Acer palmatum 'Atropurpureum' is perhaps the most popular 'Japanese maple'. The leaves are bronzy crimson throughout the summer, 12 × 8 ft.

Acer pseudoplatanus 'Brilliantissimum' has pink leaves in spring which gradually change to bronze yellow and then green, 12 × 8 ft.

Acer palmatum 'Senkaki' is a slow-growing erect maple with coral-red branches and soft yellow-coloured leaves in autumn, 15 × 10 ft.

Crataegus orientalis. A round-headed hawthorn with deeply cut, silver-grey leaves and orange yellow berries in autumn, 15 × 10 ft.

Oxydendrum arboreum is only suitable for lime-free soils. It is rarely seen but is a very pretty tree with racemes of white flowers in July and August followed by beautiful autumn colouring of crimson and yellow, 12 × 8 ft.

Photinia villosa. A small broad-headed tree with hawthorn-like flowers in May and brilliant scarlet and gold leaves in autumn, 15 × 10 ft.

Sorbus (rowan) *cashmiriana* has soft pink flowers in May and dropping clusters of shining white marble-like fruits in autumn which stay on the tree after the leaves have fallen, 15 × 8 ft.

Sorbus vilmorinii is a beautiful tree with green fern-like leaves which change to purple and red in autumn. The drooping clusters of fruits are rose-red at first then slowly change through pink to white flushed with rose, 15 × 10 ft.

Stewartia pseudocamellia requires a lime-free soil. It has flaking bark revealing a smooth light brown trunk, cup-shaped white flowers in summer and yellow and red foliage in autumn, 15 × 10 ft.

Robinia pseudoacacia 'Frisia'. A round-headed tree with erect branches which has bright yellow flowers in the spring and coppery coloured autumn foliage with bright red thorns. Good in cities, 18 × 12 ft.

GROUND COVER SHRUBS AND PLANTS

Before we go on to look at hardy shrubs let us consider those that can offer you help in your quest for an easy life.

Many shrubs are low growing and have not only adapted their life style to cover the ground quickly but quite a few of them will flourish in either full sun or the semi-shade of other shrubs and trees. They are called ground cover plants and many can be planted close enough together in groups to keep the ground completely carpeted covering the bare soil and smothering the weeds that might otherwise take over between the larger shrubs and trees.

This situation is quite natural in the wild, of course, where the plants most suited to a particular environment will flourish and smother weaker competitors. The only difference is that in the garden we can select the plants that we wish to grow and survive. We will almost certainly want plants that are hardy and have enough vigour to cover the ground in the first few seasons. They should form a dense low-growing cover, preferably be evergreen, and be attractive in their own right. We will also want them to be low in maintenance requirements with perhaps just an annual sprinkling of Growmore fertilizer and an occasional clip with the shears to keep the more vigorous ones within bounds. If they require more attention than this they defeat the object of the exercise.

But to ensure that it is they who survive and flourish and not the weeds, ground cover plants do need to be looked after and kept clear of weeds in the early stages. It is particularly important to remove perennial weeds such as ground elder, couch grass and bindweed before you do any planting as they are almost impossible to control once the ground cover plants have started to cover the soil. Then keep the annual weeds under control until the ground cover plants have established their dominance.

The shrubs listed below are particularly effective at this important job. You will find further details about them under the following section on Hardy Shrubs.

	Approx. height*	Planting distance
Berberis thunbergii 'Atropurpurea Nana'	2 ft	1 ft
Cotoneaster congestus	9 in	3 ft
Cotoneaster dammeri	6 in	2 ft
Cotoneaster dammeri 'Coral Beauty'	6 in	3 ft
Cotoneaster horizontalis	1½ ft	3 ft
Cotoneaster microphyllus	1½ ft	3 ft
Cotoneaster salicifolius 'Repens'	1 ft	2 ft
*when grown along the ground as opposed to up a wall.		
Euonymus (spindle) *fortunei* varieties	1 ft	1½ ft
Gaultheria procumbens (for lime-free soil)	6 in	1 ft
Hebe pinguifolia 'Pagei'	6 in	1 ft
Hedera (ivy) *colchica* 'Dentata Variegata'	6 in	2 ft
Hedera helix 'Hibernica'	6 in	2 ft
Hedera helix 'Imp'	6 in	1½ ft

Hypericum (St John's wort) *calycinum*	1 ft	1½ ft
Pachysandra terminalis	6 in	1 ft
Rubus tricolor	6 in	3 ft
Sarcococca humulis	1 ft	1½ ft
Vinca (periwinkle) varieties	1 ft	2 ft

Other good ground cover plants for open sunny situations are heaths and heathers (see p. 81) and some deciduous plants which are not classed as shrubs include the following. They will tolerate shade as indicated.

Epimedium × versicolor. Pretty foliage, pink and yellow flowers. Deep shade. Medium growth.	9 in	9 in
Euphorbia (poinsettia) *robbiae*. Deep green foliage, greenish yellow flowers. Deep shade. Medium growth.	1 ft	1½ ft
Galeobdolon argentatum. Pretty marbled foliage and yellow flowers. Deep shade. Rampant growth, so good under trees or shrubs but not where there are small flowers.	6 in	2½ ft
Geranium phaeum. Maroon to white flowers. Deep shade. Medium growth.	1 ft	1½ ft
Geranium sylvaticum. Lavender blue to white flowers. Seeds freely. Medium growth. Deep shade.	1 ft	1½ ft
Prunella (self-heal) *grandiflora*. The variety 'Loveliness' has pink flowers. Medium growth. Medium shade. Not on very dry soils.	6 in	1 ft
Pulmonaria (lungwort). Almost all the species and hybrids are good ground-cover plants. Medium growth. Deep shade.	6 in	1 ft
Symphytum grandiflorum. Different varieties with yellow, pink or blue flowers. Rapid growth. Deep shade.	6 in	1 ft
Tellima grandiflora 'Purpurea'. Pink flowers, green foliage turning purple in winter. Medium growth. Deep shade.	6 in	1 ft

Don't use ground cover plants where you wish to grow other small plants as they may well smother them.

A SELECTION OF HARDY SHRUBS

My selection is a small offering from the thousands available. But it is a special selection. It avoids those beauties that are demanding of too much attention – they are best left to those with the inclination to pamper. But it embraces all those who will reward you with their good looks but will not be too demanding of your time. In the main I have selected the smaller types and varieties. They will make their presence felt but will not dominate the scene.

  Because foliage is such an essential part of the garden I have included some that are grown mainly for their handsome leafage to give form and colour, the deciduous ones for at least half the year and the evergreens the whole year.

  Soil type, the area of the country, weather conditions, in fact the total environment of the planting positions in your garden has such an effect on the growth of shrubs and the times of flowering that the information I give can only be taken as a general guide – but, I hope, a useful one.

Information and symbols

With the very small shrubs I have indicated the approximate number needed to fill a square yard and with the larger ones their approximate height. In most cases this can be taken as their spread as well.

The flowering period is shown in months – 6-8 means June/August. Their liking for sun or shade is shown as ○ needs full sun, ◑ needs partial shade, ● needs full shade. If there is no sun symbol it means the plant is tolerant of either a sunny or shady position.

E = Evergreen. F/P = Flowering period. S/S = Sun or shade. H = Height in ft. D = Density or number per sq yd.

	E	F/P	S/S	H	D
Abelia × grandiflora. Pink and white flowers and dark green glossy leaves.		7/9		4	
Berberis stenophylla 'Corallina Compacta'. Showy orange flowers and dark green leaves	E	5		$1\frac{1}{2}$	4
Berberis thunbergii 'Atropurpurea Nana'. Compact habit, orange yellow flowers and copper purple leaves.		4/5		2	4
Berberis thunbergii 'Baggatelle'. An ideal foliage plant for the small garden with coppery red leaves.		4/5		1	4
Berberis thunbergii 'Rose Glow'. Most striking. Young silver pink shoots turn to rose then to purple.				3	1
Cotoneaster congestus. Neat creeping habit with small leaves, white flowers and red berries. Ground cover.		6/7		$\frac{3}{4}$	4
Cotoneaster dammeri. Ground hugging. Glossy green leaves, white flowers and red berries. Ground cover.		6/7		$\frac{1}{2}$	2
Cotoneaster dammeri 'Coral Beauty'. Striking form not quite so flat as *dammeri* but similar. Ground cover.		6/7		$\frac{1}{2}$	1
Cotonoeaster horizontalis. Very popular with herring-bone pattern branches. Will grow along the ground or up a wall. Small green leaves, pink flowers, red berries. Will grow 6 ft or more up a wall.		6/7		$1\frac{1}{2}$	1
Cotoneaster microphyllus. Much the same as *horizontalis* but evergreen. Ground cover or up a wall.	E	6/7		$1\frac{1}{2}$	1
Cotoneaster salicifolius 'Gnome'. Ideal ground cover for restricted areas. Evergreen carpeting. Red berries.	E	6/7		1	2
Euonymus (spindle) *fortunei* 'Emerald Gaiety'. Good evergreen ground cover. Grey-green leaves with cream margin.	E			1	3
Euonymus fortunei 'Emerald 'n Gold'. Green, gold and pink-tinged leaves. A very good foliage plant.	E			1	3
Garrya eliptica. Majestic evergreen shrub. Green leathery leaves. Long silvery green catkins adorn branches in Jan. to March. Grows well against north or east wall.				6	
Gaultheria procumbens. Creeping evergreen ground cover for lime-free soils. White flowers. Red berries in autumn.	E	4/5		$\frac{1}{2}$	5
Genista (broom) *lydia*. Graceful sprays of canary-yellow flowers. An outstanding dwarf shrub.		5/7	○	2	3
Hebe 'Carl Teschner'. Dwarf evergreen shrub with small violet flowers.	E	7/8	○◑	2	4
Hebe ochracea 'James Stirling'. Bright green in summer turning to burnished bronze in winter	E		○◑	1	4
Hebe pinguifolia 'Pagei'. Blue grey foliage. White flowers in May. Excellent shrub or ground cover.	E	5	○◑	$\frac{1}{2}$	6
Hebe vernicosa. Compact. Bright green leaves. White flowers in June. Nice shrub.	E	6	○◑	1	4
Hedera (ivy) *colchica* 'Dentata Variegata'. Bright green leaves and yellow margins. Good climber or ground cover.	E			$\frac{1}{2}$	2
Hedera helix 'Hibernica'. The Irish ivy is very vigorous and makes excellent ground cover with large dark green leaves. Good for shade.	E			$\frac{1}{2}$	2

Plant					
Hedera helix 'Imp'. An American variety. Outstanding for ground cover with veined green leaves.	E			$\frac{1}{2}$	4
Hydrangea serrata acuminata 'Preziosa'. A very handsome shrub. Attractive deep green foliage turns to bronze. A succession of rich salmon-red flowers in late summer. Do not let it dry out		7/9	◐	$2\frac{1}{2}$	1
Hypericum (St John's wort) *calycinum*. Rather invasive but useful as ground cover in a difficult warm place. Golden-yellow flowers	E	6/7	◐	1	4
Mahonia aquifolium 'Apollo'. Glossy green serrated leaves. Large clusters of yellow flowers in early spring followed by blue black berries.	E	4			4
Pachysandra terminalis. Excellent non-invasive ground cover for quite deep shade. Diamond-shaped green leaves and greenish-white flowers in Feb. and March.	E	2/3	●●	$\frac{1}{2}$	5
Photinia × fraseri 'Red Robin'. Brilliant foliage shrub. New bright red growth turns to green. Pruning will encourage new flushes of colour throughout year. White flowers.	E	5/6		7	
Physocarpus opulifolius 'Dart's Gold'. A good foliage shrub. Leaves golden-yellow in summer make good contrast with other plants. White flowers in June.		6		2	1
Pieris 'Forest Flame'. *Pieris* need a lime-free peaty soil. New foliage shoots are brilliant red in spring turning pink, cream and then green. Very effective.	E			7	
Pieris taiwanensis. Beautiful shrub with lily of the valley type flowers followed by bright red foliage which turns bright green. Needs lime-free soil.	E	3/4		6	
Potentilla fruticosa 'Abbotswood'. Very free-flowering. Greyish leaves and white flowers. Excellent shrub.		5/10		3	2
Potentilla fruticosa 'Beverly Surprise'. Large orange pink flowers.		5/10		2	3
Potentilla fruticosa 'Goldfinger'. Bushy shrub with large deep yellow flowers.		6/9		$2\frac{1}{2}$	1
Pyracantha 'Mohave'. A new 'Firethorn' from the USA. White flowers followed by very large bright red berries in autumn set off by dense green foliage.	E	5/6		6	
Pyracantha 'Tiny Tim'. A dwarf firethorn. Small and neat. Cinnamon-coloured berries and green foliage.	E	6/7		3	1
Rubus tricolor. Glossy evergreen ground cover. Large white flowers on furry trailing stems sometimes followed by edible red fruits. Sun or dense shade.	E	6/7		$\frac{1}{2}$	1
Santolina virens. Emerald-green bushes with golden-yellow flowers for places in the sun.	E	6/8	○	2	3
Sarcococca humilis. Excellent ground cover dwarf shrub. Small white flowers in late winter. Glossy leaves.	E	2/3		1	4
Spirea bumalda 'Goldflame'. A foliage plant with golden spring leaves turning to yellow and crimson flowers in late summer.		7/8		2	
Spirea japonica 'Alpina'. Superb dwarf shrub forming a compact mound. Tiny rose pink flowers and small leaves.		7/8		1	3
Spirea japonica 'Little Princess'. Rose crimson flowers on a dwarf compact shrub.		7/8		2	1
Symphoricarpus (snowberry) *doorenbosii* 'Magic Berry'. Easy growing shrub with insignificant flowers followed by attractive rose-pink berries lasting into winter.		6/7		3	
Vinca (periwinkle) *major* 'Variegata'. Easy to grow trailing evergreen ground cover plants. Any fertile soil. Sun or shade. Shiny leaves splashed and edged white. Blue flowers.	E	4/6		1	3
Vinca minor. Smaller leaves than major and plain green foliage. Blue flowers.	E	4/6		$\frac{1}{2}$	4

Dwarf rhododendrons and azaleas

They will only succeed in a lime-free soil that preferably has had peat or leafmould added to it. (Do not add old peat-based potting compost as this often contains lime.) If there is any sign of the leaves turning yellow during growth water with Sequestrene.

If you have the right soil then these beautiful plants will delight you with their dazzling colours in spring and be no bother to you the rest of the year.

JAPANESE AZALEAS. Evergreen or semi-evergreen depending on climate					
'Blue Danube'. Violet-blue medium-sized flowers.	E	5		2	2
'Hinomayo'. Clear pink blooms on spreading branches.	E	4/5		2	1
'Johanna'. Carmine-red flowers and dark green foliage.	E	5		2	2
DECIDUOUS AZALEAS. Knap Hill Hybrids					
'Berryrose'. Scented rose-pink flowers and copper and green leaves.		5/6		2	2
'Gibraltar'. Orange red buds open to frilled orange flowers.		5/6		2	2
'Hotspur'. Flame-red with deeper markings.		5/6		2	2
RHODODENDRONS. DWARF EVERGREEN HYBRIDS					
'Chikor'. Masses of yellow flowers in May.	E	5		1½	3
'Elizabeth'. Spreading bush with rich scarlet flowers.	E	4	◐	2	1
'Linda'. Bright pink flowers. The new foliage starts as chocolate colour turning to dark green in late spring.	E	5		1½	4

UP THE WALL

Some shrubs are ideal for clothing walls and will, in time, mask ugly buildings and garden eyesores. They can give a plain walled house a nicely clothed look.

Many will thrive in quite inhospitable corners provided you ensure they have good soil round their roots.

NO VISIBLE MEANS OF SUPPORT

Many so-called climbing shrubs need support, so let me first mention a few that need little or none and will do quite nicely by themselves as long as you guide them in the right direction when they are young and give them just a little support when they get on a bit.

Cotoneaster horizontalis will grow quite happily up to about 6 ft tall flat against a wall with its spreading herring-bone branches clothed in small green leaves in summer and masses of red berries in autumn. It's no trouble as long as you just prune off the occasional shoot that wants to go in the wrong direction and give the occasional bit of support once the plant really gets going.

Cotoneaster microphyllus is similar to *horizontalis*. It is a pretty evergreen but as it is not quite as hardy it is more suitable for the milder parts of the country.

Hedera (ivy). The ivies are decorative and easy evergreens for clothing dull walls, tree stumps and almost everything else you don't like the look of. They thrive in almost any soil or environment. I'll just mention two.

Hedera colchica 'Dentata variegata' has large green leaves edged with yellow that create an almost tropical effect.

Hedera helix 'Goldheart' has a central splash of yellow in its green leaves which make it look equally attractive.

Hydrangea petiolaris is a self-clinging climbing form of this well-known shrub which will thrive in sun or shade – on walls or up a tree.

Parquia tricuspidata 'Veitchii', sometimes called Boston ivy, gives a dense wall cover which turns crimson and scarlet in autumn.

WITH SUPPORT

Some beautiful wall coverers do need support either from galvanized or plastic coated wires stretched between screw eyes at intervals along the wall

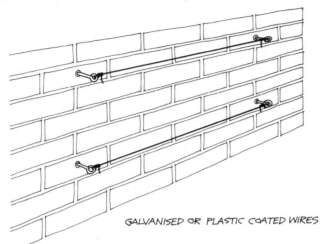

GALVANISED OR PLASTIC COATED WIRES

or from plastic coated metal mesh fixed to the wall

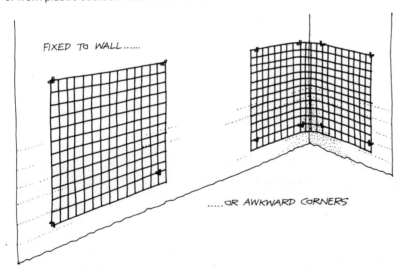

FIXED TO WALL......

.....OR AWKWARD CORNERS

or a wide mesh semi-rigid plastic netting is good for supporting subjects like clematis in awkward corners.
If you are willing to offer this kind of support it's worth considering the following.

Clematis. A vast and showy range of plants with flowers of great beauty. The plants need a soil rich in compost so that it is moisture retentive but well drained. The roots like to be in the cool and, with most varieties, the leaves and flowers in the sun. You can achieve the former with flat slabs or stones laid on the soil round the base of the plant.
     Most clematis need to be pruned each year but the following are quite happy without this time-consuming chore.

Clematis alpina. There are varieties with various colours. Flower in April.

Clematis chrysocoma. Pink and white varieties. Flower in May.

Clematis montana varieties come in white, pink and rose. Flower in May and June.

The *montanas* are fairly rampant and can be used to grow through trees with delightful effect and are happy on a north wall or fence.

Other well-known climbers are:

Jasminum nudiflorum (winter jasmine) has bright yellow flowers on the naked green stems in the winter.

Jasminum officinale is a semi-evergreen climber with fragrant white flowers from June to September.

Parthenocissus quinquefolia, the well known Virginia creeper, has beautiful maple-shaped leaves which turn to a magnificent crimson in the autumn.

Wisteria sinensis is a beautiful deciduous climber. If grown against a wall it will need wire supports and must be kept in shape by pruning back all the side shoots to three buds in the winter. An easier way is to grow it through an old tree and leave it to its own devices with just the occasional tidyup.

CHOOSING, PLANTING AND AFTERCARE

Choosing

Trees and shrubs may be field grown and dug up for sale in the dormant months or they may be grown in containers and available the whole year round. I would recommend container-grown plants for the reluctant gardener as they are so much easier to deal with. But do ensure that the plants have been grown in the containers and not just placed in them a few weeks earlier. If you gently pick up a 'container grown' tree by the stem and it starts to part company from the compost you may suspect that they haven't been long together.

Don't just take the first plant offered you but have a good look round and choose one that is a well-balanced shape with the branches and main stem undamaged.

Time of planting

Container-grown stock may be planted at any time of the year as long as they are kept well watered after planting in dry weather. Don't try to plant them if the ground is frozen. You needn't worry about a slight frost where there is just a thin crust of frozen soil – this can be skimmed off and moved to one side before taking out the hole. If the weather is very severe don't leave the container outside to get frozen either but keep it in a frost-free place till the weather improves – not indoors in the warm.

Plants not grown in containers should only be planted in the dormant season for the particular plant you have selected – from late autumn to early spring.

Depth of planting

Many plants suffer from being planted too deeply and fail to do well. The aim must be to end up with the tree or shrub being planted at much the same depth as it was in the nursery. So if it is a field-grown, or bare-root, plant look for the previous soil mark on the stem and replant to that depth.

Container-grown plants should end up with virtually no additional soil on top. Where a tree has been bottom grafted on to a dwarfing rootstock a few inches above the soil level then the graft must *stay* above the soil level, otherwise you may end up with a large tree and not the small one you expected.

Roots like what they are used to

If a container-grown plant is in a peat-based compost and gets planted into a heavy soil the roots may well refuse to venture out but stay where they are in their ball of peat, preferring to go round and round rather than push their way out into the cold hard world of the soil. As a result the plant may sit and sulk and fail to thrive.

So you must persuade those roots to do the right thing by adding some peat to the soil in the planting hole. The roots will then venture out from the peat compost into the part-peat soil and then from the part-peat soil into the pure soil. Get them to do this more readily by slightly untangling the container grown roots when planting and pointing them in the diretion that they need to grow, but make sure they don't get dry while you are doing it. The same applies to bare-root trees, never leave the roots exposed to the sun or to drying winds but keep them covered with wet sacks or wet newspaper while they are waiting to be planted.

Taking out the hole

The hole must be wider than the maximum spread of roots so that they may be well spaced out with room to spare. Provided you do this then if you are, say, planting in the lawn the hole can be whatever shape you like. A square one may be easier to mow round but a round one is easier to mark out and, I think, looks better. Push a stick into the lawn just where you want the tree to be. Tie one end of a piece of string to it and the other end of the string to a pointed stick. By keeping the string taut you can mark out a perfect circle on the turf with the point of the stick.

Before commencing operations spread some plastic sheeting over the lawn just next to where the hole is to be so that you can put the freshly dug soil and turf on it. Cut round the circumference of the circle with a sharp spade or edging-iron, skim off the turf to a depth of about 2 in and place this on the sheeting. Dig out the hole to the required depth, also placing the soil on the sheeting. Keep the dark topsoil separate from any lighter subsoil.

Break up the soil at the bottom of the hole with a fork. This will help drainage. Also break into the sides of the wall of soil round the inside of the hole with the fork so that the roots can more easily penetrate into it as they grow. Chop up the turf and place this upside down in the bottom of the hole.

Prepare the soil for filling

Preferably use just the topsoil. Add a liberal quantity of peat – say a bucketful for a tree or a large shrub – and some well-rotted compost if you have it. Sprinkle with 4 oz of Growmore or bone meal and mix it all together.

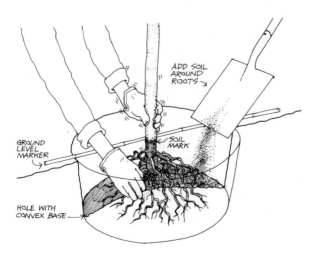

ADD SOIL AROUND ROOTS

GROUND LEVEL MARKER

SOIL MARK

HOLE WITH CONVEX BASE

PLANTING

Planting both shrubs and trees is more easily done by two people, one to hold the plant and one to fill the hole.

If you are planting a tree it will need the support of a stout tree stake and a couple of proper tree ties. The stake is best put in before the tree, although if the tree has been grown in a large container one sometimes has no alternative but to place the tree in position first and then drive the stake cleanly through the container compost – otherwise one can't get the stake near enough to the tree. The stake must be well and evenly pointed so that it goes in easily. One person should hold the stake and the other should hammer it home with a sledge or lump hammer from the top of a pair of steps or other stable support. The stake must go far enough in to be really rock solid. This may be as much as 2 ft.

Now inspect the tree. There will tend to be a front and back to it and one side will fit more snugly against the stake than the other. Place the tree (or shrub) in position with one person holding it upright and the other adding the soil – after of course removing the container, which these days is usually made of black plastic sheeting.

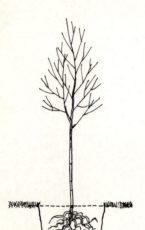

Water the plant well before removing the container, which is best done by slitting it right across the bottom before you place the plant in position and then continuing the slits up the sides after it is in position so that you can remove the container completely. Then fill the hole with a peat and soil mixture – say 3 parts soil to 1 of peat, gently treading as you go. If the plant is a bare-root one make sure you get the soil nicely in among the roots and not just on top of them. A bit of gentle joggling up and down with the tree will help and certainly don't be shy about using your hands. When the soil is all round and among the roots firm it down with the feet and then add some more soil and more firming until the soil is up to the previous soil mark on the plant. The tree and stake must be the right distance apart to fit the tree ties properly – just a couple of inches. Inspect the tree ties regularly after planting so that they are never so tight as to restrict the flow of sap.

Trees planted in a border rather than in individual holes in the lawn will tend to make more rapid growth as they have a freer root run, and there is certainly no reason why trees should not be planted first and the grass sown afterwards, but it takes a bit more trouble to ensure the soil ends up at the right level round the tree.

AFTERCARE

Keep newly planted stock well watered in dry weather.

Don't let trees and shrubs rock about in windy weather. Make sure they are firmly planted or staked.

Each kind of shrub has its own pruning requirements. I have in the main selected those that can be left to their own devices but a few general rules can be taken as a guide.

Never cut back a tree or shrub just for the sake of it. Some people are trigger happy when it comes to secateurs and often do more harm than good. If in doubt don't cut it out. If a shrub is outgrowing its allotted space either thin the branches when the plant is dormant in the winter, perhaps removing some completely, or move it to a place where is can grow to its full size.

Dead or diseased branches can be cut right back – preferably in winter. Smooth large cuts with sandpaper and leave them alone to heal over. Painting them is not necessary and may even be harmful. Evergreens may be trimmed in the spring.

Otherwise if your shrubs and trees are growing happily and healthily get back to your armchair and leave them alone.

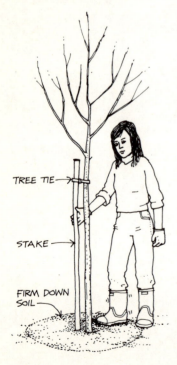

TREE TIE

STAKE

FIRM DOWN SOIL

19 THE FLOWER GARDEN

We have already discussed many plants that could turn your plot into a place of beauty – heathers, fuchsias, roses, bulbs, trees and shrubs – but there is still a vast variety of plants that could suit the reluctant gardener in his quest for easy-care plants for what most of us simply call 'the flower garden'.

The plant kingdom is so vast and there are so many different classifications of plants that the amateur is often confused. This confusion is sometimes caused by the fact that plants are not only described by which type they are but also by how they can be used in the garden. As we said in Chapter 11 'The Name Game', although an antirrhinum is a perennial and will flower year after year (if it survives the winter) it is usually treated as an annual and raised afresh from seed year after year to maintain a supply of healthy vigorous plants. So although it is a perennial it is treated as an annual.

For the sake of clarity I will, in this chapter, treat flowering plants by the way we use them rather than, strictly speaking, by what types they are.

HARDY BORDER PLANTS

These can be called perennial plants or herbaceous plants but we mean those plants which, once established, will come up again year after year.

They can almost all be raised from seed, some can be raised from cuttings and others from dividing up existing plants. The trouble with raising them from seed is that some will not come true to the parent plant and may well have inferior colour or habit so people tend to acquire most of their hardy border plants by buying them from garden centres, sending for them through the post from specialist nurseries, or begging bits of plants from friends. If one has to buy them all it can be an expensive business so we must certainly consider which ones can easily be raised from seed with reliable results.

However, let us first consider whether hardy border plants are suitable ones for the reluctant gardener. On the face of it, as they come up year after year, they sound ideal but there are a few snags – or should I say considerations.

As these plants stay in place and do not get turfed out each year, removing perennial weeds from amongst them can be a problem as the roots of the weeds can get inextricably mixed up with the roots of the plants. So if your border is infested with couch grass, bindweed, mares tail, ground elder or any other nasty pernicious weeds, give hardy border plants a miss until you are sure you have cleared out all the weeds and their persistent root systems by digging over the plot for a few years and doing a cleaning operation – you could go in for bedding plants instead.

The fact that the plants come up year after year does not mean there is no work to do. In spring and summer you will need to dig out or hoe off any weeds between the plants and in summer and autumn you will need to clear away the dead plant tops to the compost heap.

Some border plants are very invasive. They can spread and spread and take up more space than you meant so you may have to keep some of them in check usually by digging them up every couple of years, dividing them up, and replanting the healthiest bits. Michaelmas daisies are a case in point –

marvellous plants but they do really need digging up and dividing every year.

Of course it may be that you would welcome invasive plants – those that take over and don't give the weeds much chance – but do remember that they may not give some of your other prize specimens much chance of survival either so only use them where you don't mind them being invasive.

Some border plant varieties are very tall and need to be staked to prevent them blowing about in the wind and the rain. Unless you enjoy the chore of putting in supports I suggest you always select the shorter varieties of plants that will stand up by themselves.

However, in spite of those few problems there are some very good hardy plants that will give you a marvellous display year after year if you give them their ration of compost – just spread it on top of the soil each autumn or early spring – and are very well suited to the reluctant gardener.

My selection of hardy border plants for the reluctant gardener would include the following. Months mentioned are the flowering period.

1 *Achillea* (yarrow) 'Moonshine'. Bright yellow, silver foliage. June-Oct., 2 ft.
2 *Ajuga* (bugle) *reptans Atropurpurea*. Low-growing ground cover. Bronze leaves, blue flowers. May-June, 6 in.
3 *Anaphalis triplinervis*. Good silver foliage, 15 in
4 *Anemone japonica*. Various. Tall but will stand up. July-Oct. Pink and white, 2-3 ft.
5 *Aquilegia* (columbine). Various. Different colours. May-Aug., 2 ft.
6 *Armeria* (thrift) *formosa*. Long stemmed. Pink, rose and white. June-Aug., $1\frac{1}{2}$ ft.
7 *Armeria maritima*. (dwarf sea pinks). Lilac, pink, rose. May-July, 6 in.
8 *Asters* (Michaelmas daisies). Dwarf hybrids of various colours. Sept-Oct., 9-15 in.
9 *Aubrietia* (rock cress). Various in pinks and purples. April-May, 3-6 in.
10 *Bergenia* (elephants' ears). Various. Pink and rose red. April-May, 1 ft.
11 *Centaurea* (cornflower). Various. May-Aug. Pink or yellow, 2-3 ft.
12 *Ceratostigma plumbaginoides*. Cobalt blue. Aug.-Dec., 6 in.
13 *Coreopsis*. Various. Yellow. May-Sept., 9 in to 2 ft.
14 *Delphiniums*. Many varieties. 3-6 ft but choose the shorter ones. Blue. June-Sept.
15 *Dianthus* (pinks). Various. Pink, white, rose or red. June onwards, 6-12 in.
16 *Dicentra spectabilis* (bleeding heart). Red and pink. May-June, 2 ft.
17 *Erigeron* (fleabane). Various. Mauve, pink or blue. June-Sept., 2 ft.
18 *Euphorbia* (spurge) *polychroma*. Sulphur yellow. April-May, $1\frac{1}{2}$ ft.
19 *Gentiana* (gentian) *septemfida latifolia*. Bright blue. June-Aug. 9 in.
20 *Geranium* (the border kind). Various. 9 in to $2\frac{1}{2}$ ft. Choose the shorter. Pinks and blues. June-Sept.
21 *Geum* 'Mrs J Bradshaw'. Crimson. May-Oct., $2\frac{1}{2}$ ft.
22 *Hemerocallis* (daylilies). Various. A wide range of colours in yellows, pinks and reds. July-Sept., 2-$3\frac{1}{2}$ ft.
23 *Heuchera* (coral flower). Various. Coral, crimson and red. May-July, $1\frac{1}{2}$ to $2\frac{1}{2}$ ft.
24 *Hosta*. Various. Good foliage plants that also have flowers. Lilac and purple. 1-3 ft. Choose the shorter. June-Aug.
25 *Lavandula* (lavender). Various. Blue. 1-2 ft. July-Sept.
26 *Liatris* (gay feather) *callilepsis*. Deep lilac. Up to 3 ft. July-Sept.
27 *Lupinus* (lupin). Various. Pink, white, yellow, blue, purple. May-July. Choose the shorter varieties. 2-4 ft.
28 *Phlox decussata*. Whites, pinks, reds and crimsons. 2-$3\frac{1}{2}$ ft but choose the shorter varieties. July-Oct. Need good drainage.
29 *Polyanthus*. Various. almost all colours. Up to 15 in. March-May.
30 *Pyrethrum* (red ox-eye daisy). Various. Pink, crimson, white. June-Oct., 2 ft. Very good cut flowers.
31 *Rudbeckia newmanni*. Yellow, black centre. July-Sept., 2 ft.
32 *Salvia*. Various. Violet, blue and white. $1\frac{1}{2}$-3 ft. Choose the shorter varieties. June-Sept.
33 *Sedum*. Various. Rose red and ruby. 9 in-2 ft., Aug.-Oct.

34 *Stachys lanata* 'Silver Carpet'. Silver foliage for ground cover. 4 in.
35 *Tradescantia*. Various. Pink, white or blue. 1½-2 ft., June-Oct.

A BORDER OR AN ISLAND BED?

Basically you have the choice of growing hardy plants in a border backed by a fence or a hedge or in an island bed surrounded by lawn or paving.

The great advantage of an island bed is that the plants get plenty of all-round light and air to encourage strong stems and so reduce the need for staking. You also have the pleasure of viewing the bed from many different angles.

However, not every garden lends itself to island beds and the traditional one-sided border is often the only kind that will fit sensibly into the smaller garden. A path between the border and the fence or hedge will often ensure that the plants are not in dense shade or robbed of too much nutrient. Certainly the site should be away from overhanging trees. The soil should be clear of weeds, endowed with a good ration of compost or well-rotted manure and deeply dug.

Most herbaceous plants look better in groups of two or more plants to give a bold effect rather than as single specimens but, of course, this will depend on how much space you have.

As well as living in their own special bed herbaceous plants are often used to fill in pockets of space in the shrub border.

MARKING OUT THE PLAN

This can be a tricky operation and many articles on the subject give the gardener a complex plan of meandering shapes and advise him, or her, to mark out the areas for each variety with a sprinkled line of lime. But you need to be a bit of a geometrical genius to transfer these meandering shapes from a small drawing to a large garden bed. I have therefore simplified matters as much as possible by giving you shapes that are rather more regular and are fairly easy to scratch out with a stick on level raked soil. But by all means vary the shapes if the fancy takes you to have a more natural effect and have more plants of one variety and less of another.

Although the areas on the plans look rather symmetrical the varying shapes and habits of the plants will give a far less regimented final effect. And, of course, as the plants grow they will spread to fill up the gaps and soften the whole look of the thing.

THE BORDER PLAN

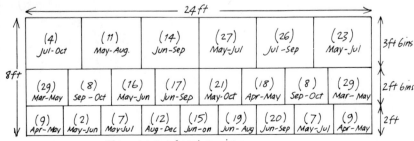

Four plants of each variety

This can be adapted to suit your own needs. It can be made longer or wider by adding more groups of plants or by using more plants in each group and it can be made narrower or shorter by missing out groups of plants. If you do add or take away groups of plants try to ensure that you are left with a good mix of colours and that you have something in bloom all summer long.

The numbers refer to those in the list of suggested plants but you may well wish to vary them to suit your own tastes. I suggest four plants of each variety if you wish to stick exactly to the dimensions of the plan but there is no reason why you should not enlarge one group to have five or more plants and reduce other groups to say three plants. (Use graph paper for accuracy.)

THE ISLAND BED

If you have the space an island bed is perhaps the ideal way to grow hardy border plants. The island could be a small one with just a few varieties or a larger one with say thirty or more varieties of plants.

In both plans I have repeated some of the varieties to give a balanced effect in the bed but you may prefer to have more varieties with only one group of each.

A small island might look like this with one plant of each variety in the outer circle and three plants of each in the four middle sections.

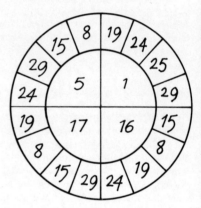

The numbers on the plan refer to the varieties on the plant list. 3 plans of each variety round the outside. 4 plants of each variety in all the inner areas.

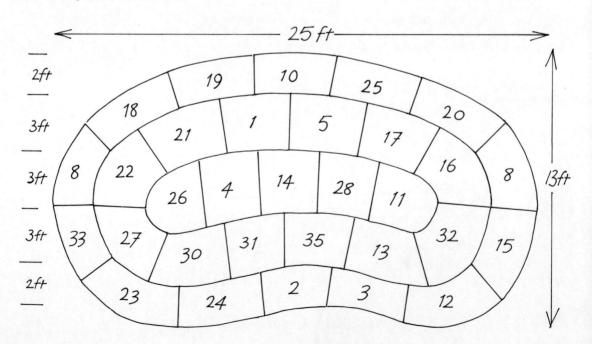

PLANTING

The best time for planting is the early autumn from late September to the beginning of November at a time when the dew is on the ground, there are fairly frequent showers, the chill of winter has not yet gripped the soil and the plants have a chance to make root growth before the cold sets in.

If the weather is mild carry on planting up to the end of November, spend December to February in your armchair and use March and early April as the alternative planting period. This is just a general guide as so much depends on where you live and how severe the winter is, but do at all costs avoid planting when the ground is frozen or waterlogged.

There are some plants for which spring planting is better than autumn planting. These include delphiniums and pyrethrums and those plants that flower late in the summer – say from August onwards – where there is plenty of time for them to put on growth before their flowering period starts.

Container-grown plants

Container-grown plants, which are sometimes in flower when you buy them, may be planted at any time unless the ground is frozen. First of all water the plant in the container well, then take out a hole with a trowel or a small border spade, carefully remove the plants from their containers trying not to disturb the roots and plant them in the border at about the same depth that they were in the pots. Water again and if the weather is dry keep them watered until they are well established.

Plants not grown in containers

A still, overcast day is the best time for planting these as the tender roots may be damaged by drying winds or the heat of the sun. If you must plant on a sunny day keep the roots covered, or the whole plants if you like, with wet sacking or wet newspaper while they are waiting to be put in and make sure everything is ready before you start planting – have the bed dug over and raked level, the planting plan marked out on the soil, a board to stand on if the ground is damp and a supply of marking/labelling sticks.

Take out a hole that is wide enough for the roots to be comfortably spread right out and not bunched up or doubled back. Plants with fibrous roots should end up about half an inch below the surface of the soil with their roots going down several inches – so the best way to plant many of them is to form a mound of earth in the hole you have dug. Those with fleshy roots can go a couple of inches deeper. If there are any stems with leaves on then do, of course, let those stay above the surface. If the ground is heavy put a sprinkling of peat round the roots before replacing the soil and put a bit in the soil as well. Firm the soil round the plant – with your hands if it is a small plant and with your boot if it is a big one – and straightaway mark the spot with a stick or label before you forget what you have put where. Lightly fork over the soil between the plants where you have been treading to make it look shipshape and stand back to admire your handywork.

WEEDING

As the plants grow keep the border hoed regularly to remove any annual weed seedlings before they compete with the plants for nutriment or moisture. This is particularly important when the plants are small. Perennial weeds like dandelions or docks will need to be dug out to remove their total depth of root.

DEAD HEADING

It is certainly worth removing the dead flower heads of the early flowering plants like delphiniums and lupins as soon as possible, as this will almost certainly encourage them to give a second flush of flowers as well as keeping the garden tidy. Some plants have decorative seed heads which you may wish to leave on to mature for winter floral decoration.

DIVISION

With some plants, like Michaelmas daisies, there is a continual outward growth of the plant so that the clump gets bigger year by year with the best parts of the plant on the outside and the older part in the centre. Dig up such plants (yes, the whole clump) every couple of years or so and by putting two forks back to back in the centre of the clump force it apart into two; now divide each half up again so that you end up with several plants, discarding the old woody section in the centre. You now have several plants instead of one. Choose the best ones for replanting into good soil. By dividing up big clumps of plants in this way you will enable them to retain their vigour, otherwise they are likely to swamp other plants or slowly deteriorate.

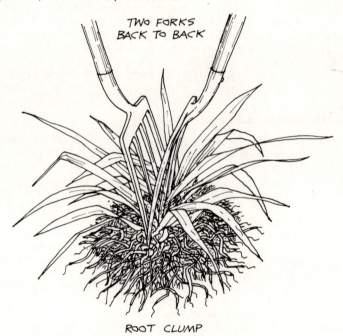

TWO FORKS BACK TO BACK

ROOT CLUMP

RAISING PERENNIAL FLOWERING PLANTS FROM SEED

Most of us gradually improve our collection of plants by buying a few at a time or begging bits from friends. If you are starting from scratch with a new bare plot the total cost of planting a whole garden or even a large border or island bed can be rather daunting.

So, if you are starting from scratch with a bare plot and the cost of plants is something you don't relish, or perhaps is the reason for your reluctance, then you may wish to consider using part of the garden in the first season to raise the perennial plants you need from seed – perhaps on a piece of land that will later become your vegetable plot.

May I suggest you arm yourself with a good seed catalogue and use it in conjunction with the following plan to select the quantity and range of plants you need. The plan covers a range of 23 different perennials and will produce ten or more plants of each in a plot 20 ft long by 10 ft wide. Obviously a shorter bed will give you fewer varieties and a narrower bed fewer plants of each.

I have chosen plants with varying heights and forms that will give a season of flowers from March to October that need little or no staking and can be raised without artificial heat in a normal garden bed. Most of them will not flower the year they are sown but will start to flower the second year – after they have been transferred.

The plot should be rough dug in late autumn or early winter incorporating some good garden compost or well-rotted manure if the soil is poor. In February test the acid/alkaline state of the soil and lime if necessary to achieve a pH of 5$\frac{1}{2}$ to 6.

In April or May, depending on where you live and the state of the weather, rake the soil to a fine tilth, take out the drills and thinly sow the seed. (see p. 71 for seed sowing.) Progressively thin the plants as soon as they are large enough to handle until they are the distance apart recommended on the seed packet. In the autumn water them well, take them up with a trowel or small fork with plenty of earth round the roots of each plant and transfer them to their permanent positions. It is obviously best to have the planting holes taken out ready to receive the plants before you dig them up.

Mark the position of the plants with sticks preferably with the names of the plants on. If you don't do this you may well forget where they are when their leaves die down and you may try to put something else in the same place.

Nursery bed for perennial flowering plants – 23 kinds of varying heights and forms with a season of flowers from March to October that need little or no support and can be raised without heat in a garden plot. pH reaction of soil to be 5$\frac{1}{2}$ to 6$\frac{1}{2}$.

10 ft		Height	Colour	Time of flowering
10 in	Coreopsis 'Golden Star'	1 ft 6 in	Yellow	Jul-Sep
	Lupinus (lupin) 'Dwarf Russell'	2 ft 0 in	Various	May-Sep
	Aubretia	4 in	Blue/violet	Mar-June
	Delphinium 'Blue Mountains'	2 ft 0 in	Various blues	Jul-Aug
	Alyssum 'Golden Globe'	6 in	Yellow	Apr-Jun
	Achillea(yarrow) ptarmica	2 ft 0 in	White	Jun-Oct
	Armeria (thrift)	9 in	Pink	Jun-Aug
	Agrostemma	2 ft 0 in	Crimson/silver	Jul-Aug
	Aster 'Subcoeruleus'	9 in	Blue	Jun-Jul
	Echinops (globe thistle)	3 ft 0 in	Lav. blue	Jun-Jul
	Heuchera (coral flower)	1 ft 6 in	Red	Jun-Aug
	Erigeron (fleabane)	2 ft 0 in	Pink	Jun-Aug
	Nepeta	1 ft 0 in	Lavender	May-Sept
	Gaillardia 'Burgundy'	1 ft 0 in	Copper red	Jun-Oct
	Doronicum (leopard's bane)	1 ft 6 in	Yellow	Mar-May
	Geum 'Mrs Bradshaw'	2 ft 0 in	Scarlet	Jun-Oct
	Physalis '(Chinese lantern, cape gooseberry)	1 ft 6 in	Orange	Jul-Oct
	Scabiosa	3 ft 0 in	Blue	Jun-Oct
	Platycodon	1 ft 3 in	Blue	Jun-Aug
	Pyrethrum	2 ft 0 in	Various	Jun-Oct
	Lavandula (lavender)	1 ft 6 in	Blue	Jun-Aug
	Veronica (speedwell)	1 ft 6 in	Blue	Jun-Aug
	Malva (mallow)	3 ft 0 in	Rose pink	Jul-Aug

BIENNIALS

Biennials have a two-year life. They are usually sown in spring, transplanted to their final positions in autumn and flower the following year. They are probably more time-consuming than other plants and many people don't bother with them. But if you like, say, wallflowers or sweet williams you may think they are worth the trouble. You can raise them in the same way as perennial plants or you can take the easy way out and buy plants from your garden centre in the autumn.

Some popular biennials

	Colour	Height	Flowers
Bellis (double daisies for edging and bedding)	Rose, red and white	6 in	Mar-May
Campanula medium (Canterbury Bell)	Pink, lavender and blue, etc.	$1\frac{1}{2}$-$2\frac{1}{2}$ ft	Jun-Jul
Cheiranthus (wallflower)	Scarlet, yellow, orange and many other colours	1-$1\frac{1}{2}$ ft	Mar-May
Dianthus barbatus (sweet william)	Pink, red, salmon, crimson, white and others	6 in-$1\frac{1}{2}$ ft	Jun-Jul
Dianthus (pink)	Pink, scarlet, salmon, rose, white and other colours	6-9 in	Jun-Oct
Digitalis (foxglove)	Pink, purple and white	3-5 ft	Jul-Aug
Lunaria (honesty)	Purple. Decorative seedpods	2 ft	May-Jul
Myosotis (forget-me-not)	Blue spring bedder	6 in-1 ft	Mar-Jun
Papaver (poppy Rose)	Cherry, pink, orange, scarlet	9 in-2 ft	May-Jul

HARDY ANNUALS

These are the easiest and cheapest of all flowers to grow. The seed is sown outdoors where the plants are to flower and they will stand cold spring conditions without any special treatment or early protection.

They soon come into flower and will bloom during summer and early autumn. You can get a really bold show from a few moderately priced packets of seed.

Time to sow

Sow the seed from March to early June – the earlier the better provided the soil is warming up and is not cold and wet.

Useful for spare space

If you have a bit of spare ground, perhaps an odd corner that you don't know yet what to do with, or even a whole plot that you haven't yet had time to develop, sowing with hardy annuals in the spring is one way of producing fairly instant colour. The job doesn't have to be too labour-intensive if you do it the rough and ready way.

Choose a clean spot. I certainly don't recommend growing annuals if the soil is full of weed seeds. The weeds will come up with the annuals and it will be a time-consuming job to sort one from the other. But if you've got a fairly clean bit of ground send for a seed catalogue, dig the ground if it needs it or hoe off any odd weeds if it doesn't and on a fine day in spring at a time recommended on the seed packet and when the soil is nice and crumbly break down the top couple of inches to get a good tilth. Get the soil nice and level, rake off any lumps or large stones and then carefully pull the rake through the soil in one direction to form rows of miniature seed drills. Get a long stick (to avoid treading on the bed) to mark out suitably shaped sowing areas for each variety and ensure that the taller types go to the back or to the middle if it is an island bed and the shorter ones at the front.

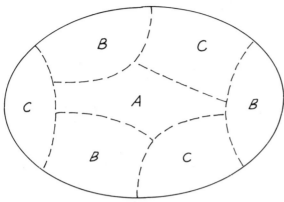

An island bed — say 12 ft × 6 ft

Some suggested varieties
A Cornflower
B *Linaria*
C Virginian stock
or, of course, you could have 7 quite separate varieties.

An island bed, say 12 ft × 6 ft (use graph paper, taking, say, 1 square = 1 ft)

Don't make the areas too small and fussy but tend instead to have bold clumps of plants.

Scatter the seed very thinly. Your aim should be to avoid having to bother with subsequent thinning so have those seeds no nearer than a couple of inches apart. That is not always easy as some seed is so fine and light that weight for weight it costs more than gold. So treat it as such and to help you spread it thinly mix it with a little fine dry sand and scatter the mixture.

After sowing carefully pull the rake all over the bed in the opposite direction so that the seed gets mixed with the top soil. Just one raking will do. The seeds won't be very deep but this is quite suitable for seeds with a recommended sowing depth of ¼ in. If deeper drills are needed make them with a piece of stick. After carefully raking the seed in pat the earth firm with the back of the rake (you may need to stand on the soil to do this) and then pray for some light steady rain.

PAT, PAT!

LIGHT, STEADY RAIN....

Some popular and easy to grow hardy annuals Flowering during the summer and early autumn

Anchusa. Like giant forget-me-nots. Blue. 9 in
Bartonia. Golden yellow. Long flowering. 1½-2 ft
Calendula (pot marigold). Orange, gold, yellow. 1-2 ft
Calliopsis. Yellow, crimson and yellow. 1-2 ft
Chrysanthemum (annual). Yellow, bronze, orange, white, scarlet. 1½-2 ft
Clarkia elegans. Salmon-pink, mauve, carmine, purple. 2 ft
Dimorphotheca (star of the veldt). Yellow, orange. 6 in-1 ft
Eschscholzia (californian poppy). Yellow, white, orange, red, pink. 6 in-1 ft
Godetia. Pink, salmon, crimson, carmine. 1-1½ ft
Helianthus (sunflower). Yellow, bronze-red. 2-8 ft
Iberis (candytuft). White, pink, carmine, lavender. 9-15 in
Larkspur. Rather like delphiniums. White, pink, violet, blue. 2½-4 ft
Lavatera (mallow). Bushy plants for back of border. Pink. 2 ft
Linaria. Like little antirrhinums. Many colours. 9 in-1 ft
Linum (flax). Scarlet, crimson. 1-1½ ft
Malcolmia maritima (Virginia stock). Yellow, white, red, lilac, rose. 9 in
Nasturtium. Good for poor soil. Gold, scarlet and many other colours. Some short, some climbing.
Nigella (love-in-a-mist). Blue, rose, pink, white. 1-1½ ft
Papaver (poppy). Scarlet and other colours. 1½-2½ ft
Salvia horminum (clary). Pink, blue, white. 1½ ft
Schizanthus (butterfly flower). Pink, carmine, white, purple, crimson. 1/1½ ft
Silene (cats fly). Rose-pink. 1 ft

Sweet sultan. Pink, lavender, purple, white, yellow. 1$\frac{1}{2}$ ft
Tropaeolum (canary creeper). Easy to grow climber. Canary-yellow.
Viscaria. Blue, lavender, pink, scarlet, white. 1 ft
Xeranthemum. Everlasting flower. Purple, rose, lilac, white. 2 ft

BEDDING PLANTS

These are the ones that save you all the bother of sowing, thinning and transplanting. You go to the garden centre in spring when the danger of frost is past with a wallet full of money and buy trays of plants to bed out in your garden. Most of them are half-hardy annuals which will have been raised under glass.

Some – like *Alyssum* and *Lobelia* – make good edging plants to go round the rose bed; others – say busy lizzie or bedding begonias – make a grand display planted out on their own or mixed with other bedding plants about 9 in apart each way. Or they can be used in tubs and window boxes. Others – like pansies or antirrhinums – can be used as dot plants to fill in gaps in the border. Most of them can be used in any of these ways just as the fancy takes you.

A few tips on planting

You will almost certainly buy bedding plants in plastic boxes or strips. First water the containers well – you can't really overdo this – and then take out holes in the garden with a trowel where the plants are to go. The holes should be big enough to accommodate the root ball of each plant and deep enough so that they end up a little deeper than they were in the box. There will be 30 or more plants in a full box, 15 in a half box and 6 or more in a strip. I have a friend who thought each strip was just one plant. He found bedding plants very expensive until he discovered the strip divided up into several plants. Although the plants may look a little lonely planted at, say, 9 in apart, they will soon grow to cover the intervening bare soil and most will end up touching each other when fully grown.

To get the plants out of the box lift it up nearly vertically on end and give the bottom end of the box a sharp tap on the ground to make the block of plants move down a bit and allow you to get your fingers in and under the plants to lift them out.

The whole job is really one for fingers and hands – perhaps with rubber gloves if you want to protect your lily-white skin. The plants are best gently pulled or broken apart by hand to leave as many roots as possible intact rather than being cut apart with a knife.

Pop the plants in their holes, cover the roots with soil and firm them down so that they are growing at much the same height as they were in the boxes. Water them and keep them watered for at least the first week until they are properly established.

...IT'S ALWAYS SPRING TIME ON THIS PLANTING BED....

Many are in bloom when you buy them, most have a long season of flower in summer and autumn and some, like *Alyssum*, will go on till the first frosts
Alyssum. Very popular as an edging plant. White. 6 in
Antirrhinum (snapdragon). A whole range of colours. 6 in-3 ft
Asters. A whole range of colours. 6 in-2 ft
Begonia semperflorens. Unbeatable for summer bedding. White, pink, red. 6-8 in
Cineraria (silver leaves). A silver foliage plant. 9 in-1 ft
Geranium. For pots, summer bedding and for baskets. A whole range of colours and types.
Helichrysum. Everlasting flower that will attract butterflies. Many colours. 1-4 ft
Lobelia. Often planted with alyssum as an edging plant. All shades of blue. 6 in
African marigolds. A whole range of types and sizes in golds and yellows. 10 in-3 ft
Dwarf French marigolds. Very easy to grow. Many types. Gold, yellow, bronze. 4 in-1 ft
Mesembryanthemum (Livingstone daisy). Brilliant glowing colours for dry places. 3 in
Nicotiana (flowering tobacco). Beautifully scented. Pink, red, rose, white. 1-2$\frac{1}{2}$ ft
Petunias. A whole range of very popular bedders in all colours. 9 in-1$\frac{1}{2}$ ft
Phlox Drummondii. Very reliable. Pink, rose, salmon, crimson, violet-blue. 6 in-1$\frac{1}{2}$ ft
Salvia. Free flowering in fiery scarlet and other colours. 1 ft
Sweetly scented stocks. Many types. Beautiful for scent and colour. 1-1$\frac{1}{2}$ ft
Tagetes. Like a small African marigold. Covered in yellow and golden flowers. 9-15 in
Verbena. For bedding, edging and window boxes. Pink, salmon, violet, crimson. 6 in-1$\frac{1}{2}$ ft

PAEONIES, PELARGONIUMS AND DAHLIAS

Each of these groups of plants has something special to offer the reluctant gardener.

PAEONIES

There are probably no other plants that give such a marvellous display of colour for so little effort. Paeonies will grow in almost any soil as long as it is not waterlogged and in almost any part of the garden. They will stand cold winters and hot dry summers.

There is a space for the paeony in every garden from lightly shaded woodland to open sunny situation. They will grow in beds, borders, between shrubs, in front of shrubs, in walled town gardens and in open country ones. Provided they are allowed to settle down without disturbance they may flower for as long as fifty years. Some are scented and almost all make marvellous cut flowers for the house.

Their only drawback is that their season of flowering is relatively short. Some varieties flower in May but most display their magnificence in just the month of June and early July. But when the flowering has finished that is not the end of the story. Their foliage will still lend an attractive feature to the garden and with some varieties the added bonus of rich autumn colouring before they die down for the winter rest.

Culture

As with almost all plants those grown in an open situation will have the strongest stems so if your garden is in any way shaded it is probably best to choose the shorter growing varieties with single flowers so that there is no heavy weight of blooms to weigh down the more slender stems in the wind and the rain.

Paeonies will do well on chalk as well as in acid soils and while they will do best in a heavy loamy soil they will certainly grow well enough in light soil especially if you improve it with compost, peat, leafmould or well-rotted manure. Just put it on top of the soil and fork it into the top couple of inches whenever you have some to spare.

Planting

Paeonies may be planted from October right up to Christmas as long as the weather allows.

Take out a hole deep enough to accommodate the roots in comfort so that with light soils the top growth point of the plant – called the 'crown' – is just 2 in under the surface by the time the soil has settled down and only 1 in below if the soil is heavy. If you plant them deeper than this they may fail to flower. Many have long roots so the holes will probably have to be as much as 1½ or even 2 ft deep.

Plant them not less than 3 ft apart and preferably up to 4 ft. Make sure the spaces between the roots are filled with soil and after planting tread in firmly and water well.

Clear away the foliage once it has died down in autumn and add a top dressing of compost or other organic manure.

A small special selection

There are many to choose from. I have selected just a few which will do equally well for you in either a small or large garden.

Flowering in May

Byzantine. Single. Maroon-red. 2 ft tall
Mollis. Single. Dark purple. 1½ ft
Officinalis 'Alba Plena'. Semi-double. Pure white. 2½ ft
Officinalis 'Rosea Plena'. Double. Bright rose. 2½ ft
Officinalis 'Rubra Plena'. Double. Crimson. 2½ ft

Flowering in June and early July

Single with coloured autumn foliage
'Dresden' Blush white. 2½ ft
'Gay Ladye' Deep rose. 3 ft. Fragrant.
'Kestrel' Rosy purple. 3 ft
'Lord Kitchener' Maroon-red. 3 ft
'Nymph' Flesh pink. 2 ft
'Pink Delight' Light pink. 2½ ft. Fragrant
'Red Flag' Scarlet-maroon. 2½ ft. Fragrant
'Silver Flare' Carmine with silver edge. 3 ft. Fragrant
'Sir E Elgar' Chocolate-crimson. 2½ ft
'White Wings' White 2½ ft. Fragrant
'Wilbur Wright' Black-red. 3 ft

Double – with autumn coloured foliage. All more or less fragrant
'Albert Crousse' Shell pink. 3 ft
'Auguste Dessert' Salmon-rose edged silver. 2½ ft
'Ballerina' Lilac pink turning white. 3 ft
'Carmen' Cherry-rose. 3 ft
'Chestine Gowdy' Pink and creamy white. 3 ft
'Edith Cavell' White and yellow with red stain. 3 ft

'Flamingo' Pale salmon-pink. 3 ft
'Inspecteur Lavergne' Crimson-tipped silver. $2^1{}_2$ ft
'Kelway's Supreme' Blush turning white. 3 ft
'L'Eclatante' Dark rosy-red. $2^1{}_2$ ft
'Magic Orb' Rose and cream. 3 ft
'Miss Eckhardt' Silvery-rose. $2^1{}_2$ ft
'President Poincare' Ruby-crimson. 3 ft
'Solange' Amber with buff centre. $2^1{}_2$ ft

Imperial paeonies

These are rather like water lilies with shell-shaped guard petals round the outside and tightly packed petaloids in the centre.

The first colour is the outer one and the second the inner one.
'Aureole' Carmine-cherry/cream $2^1{}_2$ ft
'Barrymore' White/gold 3 ft
'Bowl of Beauty' Pale pink/cream 3 ft
'Calypso' Light carmine/gold 3 ft
'Crimson Glory' Ruby-red/gold and red 3 ft
'Dominion' Soft pink/peach and gold 2 ft
'Emperor of India' Dark red/gold 3 ft
'Globe of Light' Rose pink/yellow 3 ft

Tree paeony

Tree paeonies are hard wooded deciduous shrubby plants that grow up to 5 ft high. The plants themselves are not particularly beautiful but the flowers can be very striking. Tree paeonies grow in much the same conditions as herbaceous paeonies but as they send out their shoots somewhat earlier they can suffer from late spring frosts.

They are not perhaps the ideal plants for the reluctant gardener but no doubt you will have a go if the fancy takes you.

A few titles:

'Countess of Crewe' Pale pink
'Duchess of Kent' Bright rose
'Duchess of Marlborough' Deep rose
'Lord Selbourne' Pale salmon-pink
'Superb' Cherry-red
'Souvenir Du Maxime Cornu' Golden yellow edged pale carmine.

PELARGONIUMS OR 'GERANIUMS'

The common zonal pelargoniums are frequently called geraniums. Just to clear up any confusion: zonal pelargoniums are tender evergreen plants suitable for growing in the greenhouse, for summer bedding or as house plants and they will rarely survive frosts whereas geraniums are, strictly speaking, hardy herbaceous perennials that will. They both belong to the same plant family *geraniaceae*.

It is the tender ones we are talking about here. They are called zonal pelargoniums because their pale to mid-green leaves have a conscpicuous zone of darker green, bronze or maroon on them.

The great thing about zonal pelargoniums is that if you keep the dead flowers picked off they will give a display of colour all summer long. There are hundreds of varieties in shades of red, pink, white and orange. Some are grown solely for their foliage and have fairly inconspicuous flowers. Perhaps the most famous are 'Paul Crampel' and 'Gustav Emich', both brilliant scarlet. One sometimes suspects that somewhat inferior strains are sold under these famous names.

Other well-known named varieties include:

'Del Greco', an F_1 hybrid seed strain in various pinks, salmons and scarlet

'Carefree' seed strain with white, light pink, salmon and scarlet
'Delight' vermilion red
'Hermione' double white flowers
'Mrs Henry Cox' orange red

The 'Irene' strain which includes 'Electra' crimson, 'Irene Springtime' salmon-pink, and 'Irene Treasure Chest' orange scarlet – all semi-double.

Outstanding foliage varieties include 'Caroline Schmidt' silver leaves, 'Golden Harry Hieover' golden leaves, 'Henry Cox' variegated leaves of maroon, red, cream and green, and 'Mrs Quilter' golden-bronze leaves. But the great thing about zonal pelargoniums is that you can go to a garden centre or nursery and see them in flower and leaf and make your choice on the spot of those that you like.

Cultivation

Pelargoniums will do well in almost any well-drained garden soil. Don't make it too rich or you may encourage the plants to produce leaves at the expense of flowers.

From late May onwards, when the danger of frost has gone, plant them in full sun in a bed of their own, or use them to brighten up any dull spots in the garden or, perhaps most popular of all, plant them in pots, tubs, urns and window boxes.

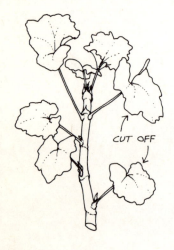

CUT OFF

Overwintering

The drawback with pelargoniums is that they will not survive the winter frosts so you must dig up the plants in October, pot them up in potting compost and put them in a frost-free cool room or greenhouse for the winter. In late May cut back the stems to sturdy growth and replant outside. If they are in pots you can, of course, just move the whole pots into a frost-free place for the winter.

Propagation

These older plants will in time get too big and leggy. So maintain a supply of healthy new plants by taking cuttings from the old ones in August and early September.

You can very simply just cut off 4 to 6 in lengths of stem, trim off the flower stalk if there is one and all the leaves except the top two or three, make a hole in a pot of compost with your finger, pop the cutting in so that a couple of inches of stem are below the soil, firm the compost round the cutting and water in. Pop a plastic bag over the top until the cutting has rooted then overwinter away from frosts. You will know when a cutting is well rooted because the white roots will appear at the bottom of the pot – after about ten to fifteen days – if you pick it up and look.

If you can't be bothered to find pots and compost in August but would like to take some cuttings just pop the cuttings into the garden soil beside the 'mother' plant and later on pot up any that have taken. You will probably find that more than half of them have.

The professionals trim off the stem just below a leaf node and certainly more seem to take if you do this.

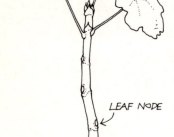

LEAF NODE

...ENDING UP WITH THIS

DAHLIAS

There are two main groups of dahlias: border dahlias which although suitable for mixed borders are really better grown on their own and bedding dahlias which are grown afresh each year from seed.

We are concerned with border dahlias.

They are another group of plants which will have strong appeal to the type of reluctant gardener who doesn't mind digging but wishes to avoid seed sowing, and the other delicate delights like pricking out and potting on. There is nothing fiddly about dahlias. They are easy. They will grow for anyone and will produce marvellous displays of flowers year after year after year.

There are two snags. The first is that nearly all of them grow so tall that they need support and the second is that they have a root system made up of a bunch of what are botanically speaking swollen underground stems, called tubers, which will die if they are frozen.

Cultivation

So each autumn a few days after the first frosts of the winter have blackened the foliage cut down the stems to 6 in above the ground. Loosen the soil all round about a foot from the plant with a spade and then carefully dig it up taking care not to damage the point where the tubers and the stem meet (the crown) and from where each year's new growth will come. Cut off any damaged tubers with a sharp knife and dust the cuts with flowers of sulphur to stop them rotting.

Store the tubers upside down under cover for a week to let any water drain from the hollow stems. Now store them the right way up in shallow boxes with damp (not wet) peat packed round the tubers but not over the crowns. This will keep the tubers nice and plump during the winter.

Store the boxes in a cool, dry, frost-free place – ideally about 40°F. It is a good idea to tie a label to each plant saying what variety or colour it is because you may not remember next year.

Check the tubers every few weeks during the winter. Discard any that are rotting or diseased. If any appear to be shrivelled pop them in a bucket of water overnight to plump them up. Dry them properly before replacing in the boxes. In mid April to May just replant them in the garden with 4 in of soil above the crowns. Work the soil carefully between the tubers as you plant and mark each plant with a stick. By August you will have a grand display of flowers that will go on until the first frosts and then suddenly one night the frosts will get them and they will be blackened.

I once had a neighbour who had enough of gardening at work, because that was his job, so he just planted the whole of his back garden with dahlias every single year. He worked hard in his garden in November and April, did very little in between, and had a very impressive display of flowers every year with plenty to pick for the house.

Propagation

The seed of most dahlias will not produce plants like the parent (they will not breed true) but will generally produce plants that are inferior. So to get more plants like the parent, the parent itself has to be divided up into two or more plants.

From March onwards make sure the peat round the plants is kept moist and then some time in April you will notice that the eyes, the new growth points, on the crowns of the tubers have started to swell.

Divide up the plants with a sharp knife ensuring that each division has at least one tuber and one undamaged eye. Dust the cut parts with flowers of sulphur and plant in the garden the same way as the others.

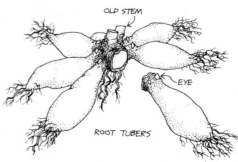

OLD STEM

EYE

ROOT TUBERS

Varieties

They come in a very wide range from enormous flowers up to a foot across which win prizes at local flower shows but which are only suitable for very large gardens to miniature ball and pompon flowers as small as 2 in across. The plants themselves range from about 1½ to 5 ft tall so most of them will need to be staked.

Perhaps the most popular dahlias for both the garden and for cut flowers are the medium and small decorative varieties. I will list the types and mention a couple of varieties in each one but the full list would run into hundreds.

Single-flowered 1½ to 2 ft. Blooms up to 4 in diameter. Planting distance 1½ to 2 ft. Single flowers.
'Nellie Geerlings' scarlet.
'Orangeade' orange flame.

Anemone-flowered 2 to 3½ ft. Blooms up to 4 in diameter. Planting distance 2 ft. Double flowers which have flat outer florets surrounding closely packed short tubular florets.
'Bridesmaid'. White outer petals. Yellow inner ones.
'Lucy'. Purple outer petals. Yellow inner ones.

Collerette 2½ to 4 ft. Blooms up to 4 in diameter. Planting distance 2 to 2½ ft. Blooms with a single ring of flat ray florets, an inner ring of smaller florets and a central disc.
'Can-can'. Pink petals. Yellow inner ring.
'Nonsense'. Creamy white petals. Orange inner ring.

Paeony flowered Up to 3 ft. Blooms up to 4 in diameter. Planting distance 2 ft. The blooms consist of two or more rings of flat ray florets with a central disc.
'Fascination'. Purple.
'Grenadier'. Scarlet.

Decorative The flowers are double with a central disc. They have broad flat-ray florets usually slightly twisted with blunt ends. there are five types of decorative dahlias according to the size of blooms.
Giant Blooms 10 in or more. 4 to 5 ft. Planting distance 4 ft.
'Playboy'. Yellow.
'Liberator'. Crimson.

Large Blooms 8 to 10 in. 3½ to 5 ft. Planting distance 4 ft.
'Enfield Salmon'. Pink.
'Silver City'. White.

Medium Blooms 6 to 8 in. 3½ to 4 ft. Planting distance 3 ft.
'Alloway Cottage'. Orange-yellow.
'Yellow Terpo'. Yellow.
'Breckland Joy'. Bronze.
'Evelyn Foster'. White.
'Mrs A. Woods'. Pinky mauve.

Small Blooms 4 to 6 in. 3½ to 4 ft. Planting distance 2½ ft.
'Nina Chester'. Lavender and white.
'Rothesay Robin'. Pink.
'Suffolk Snowball'. White.
'That's It'. Flame.

Miniature Blooms up to 4 in. 3 to 4 ft. Planting distance 2½ ft.
'David Howard'. Orange.
'Jo's Choice'. Scarlet.

Ball As the name implies they have ball-shaped flowers sometimes flattened on top. There are two types.

Small ball Blooms 4 to 6 in. 3 to 4 ft. Planting distance 2$\frac{1}{2}$ ft.
   'Charles Dickens'. Purple.
   'Opal'. White and pink.

Miniature ball Blooms up to 4 in. 3 to 4 ft. Planting distance 2$\frac{1}{2}$ ft.
   'Connoisseur's Choice'. Flame.
   'Dr John Grainger'. Orange.

Pompon The flowers are very much like ball dahlias but they are rounder and smaller with the florets curving inwards.
   'Andrew Lockwood'. Lilac.
   'Little Conn'. Dark red.

Cactus The blooms are double with pointed ray florets. These are rolled back and look like quills for about half their length. There are five types of cactus dahlias.

Giant Blooms 10 in or more. 4 to 5 ft. Planting distance 4 ft.
   'Candyman'. Pink.
   'Super'. Scarlet.

Large Blooms 8 to 10 in. 4 to 5 ft. Planting distance 4 ft.
   'Hallwood Quills'. Pink.
   'Royal Sceptre'. Orange and yellow.

Medium Blooms 6 to 8 in. 3$\frac{1}{2}$ to 4$\frac{1}{2}$ ft. Planting distance 3 ft.
   'Authority'. Orange and bronze.
   'Autumn fire'. Apricot yellow.
   'Banker'. Flame.
   'Eastwood Pinky'. Pink.
   'Suffolk Bride'. White
   'Sure Thing'. Red.

Small Blooms 4 to 6 in. 3$\frac{1}{2}$ to 4 ft. Planting distance 2$\frac{1}{2}$ ft.
   'Athalie'. Deep pink.
   'Doris Day'. Crimson.
   'Hoek's Yellow'. Yellow.
   'Pink Margie'. Pink.

Miniature Blooms up to 4 in. 3 to 4 ft. Planting distance 2$\frac{1}{2}$ ft.
   'Charmer'. Purple.
   'Poppet'. Yellow and salmon.

PLANTS FOR SUNNY, SHADY AND EXPOSED PLACES

All gardens have their difficult situations – those areas where some plants will be difficult to grow.

    The walls and fences may reflect sunlight and create hot dry conditions or conversely they may obscure the sun and give areas of shade. Those areas of shade will shift as the sun traverses its daily arc across the sky, rising higher in the summer and sinking lower in the winter.

    Many garden areas get a mixture of sun and shade which happily suits the vast majority of plants but there are some situations where the shade is dense all day and others where in the middle of summer the sun seems to give no respite.

    I have selected a few plants that are especially able to stand these different problem conditions. They are all easy to look after and are from the lists of plants already selected. For full details of the individual plants see the sections on Hardy Shrubs and Hardy Border Plants. Some are so good-natured that they will cope with more than one set of difficult conditions.

PLANTS FOR A DRY SUNNY SITE

Shrubs *Abelia Berberis Cotoneaster Euonymus Genista Hebe Potentilla Santolina Spirea Symphoricarpus*

Hardy Border Plants *Achillea Anaphalis Bergenia Ceratostigma Dianthus Geranium Sedum Stachys*

Hardy Annual Nasturtium This deserves a special mention as it is easy to grow from seed and will do especially well in a hot dry area transforming it into a blaze of colour.

PLANTS FOR SHADE

Almost no plants will thrive in really dense shade but the following will do quite well in partial shade, or dappled shade where the sun is filtered through a lightly leaved tree, or where there is only a limited amount of sunshine or reflected light.

Dry shade

Shrubs *Berberis* – deciduous varieties *Cotoneaster* – the lower-growing and ground-hugging ones *Euonymus fortunei Hedera Mahonia aquifolium Pachysandra terminalis Rubus tricolor Vinca*

Hardy Border Plants *Ajuga* (bugle) *Bergenia Salvia*

Moist shade

Shrubs *Gaultheria procumbens Hedera* (ivy) *Hydrangea Pachysandra terminalis Rubus tricolor Sarcococca humilis Symphoricarpus* (snowberry) *Vinca* (periwinkle)

Hardy Border Plant *Hosta* in its many varieties

SHRUBS FOR COLD EXPOSED INLAND PLACES

Berberis (will also do well by the sea) *Cotoneaster* – the medium to low-growing ones *Euonymus fortunei Pachysandra terminalis Potentilla Spirea*

20 THE GARDEN POOL

There is a magic about water that fascinates most of us. There is mystery and delight mixed with a little fear, the fun of watching fishy things and the call of the primordial element from which we evolved.

If it is well sited, properly made and well stocked a garden pool is great fun. It can be a horrible headache if it isn't.

THE CHOICES

There are five basic ways of forming a pool that will continue to contain the water that you put in it.
1 The simplest way is to sink a tank or barrel into the ground. Remember that if it is deep it may be a danger to small children.
2 Puddled clay was often used for lining canals and village ponds. It is a skilled hard task not recommended for the amateur gardener.
3 Ready formed artificial pools made from plastic or fibre glass are not too difficult to install if they are small but they usually continue to look highly artificial.
4 Concrete-lined pools are excellent but entail a great deal of hard work and some degree of skill.
5 Many modern pools are lined with PVC or butyl rubber sheeting.
I would recommend the last method as being the best for most of us. Pools with liners are easier to construct, they can stand up to the pressures imposed by ice and they are easier to move if you decide that you want to dispose of your pool or move it to another place.

THINK IT OUT

The rule of good gardening 'if you want to save time in the long run you had best do things properly in the first place' applies to garden pools as much as to anything else.

Take a good long look at your garden to decide on a suitable site and do some planning on paper before you do anything else. Garden pools are expensive. As a result of your paper planning you will be able to make enquiries about the costs of the main items – the liner, paving, sand, rocks, plants and possibly a fountain. You can see if they suit your pocket before you get out your spade.

SITING YOUR POOL

Water plants love the sun. They need it to grow strongly and flower freely. Rotting leaves can easily pollute a pool giving off foul gases and killing the fish. So site your pool right out in the open and not under or too close to trees. Most gardens have a fair number of leaves blowing about them in autumn but you can stop them getting in the pool by stretching a large flat net over it – weighed down with stones at the edges.

An informal pool is best sited where it would be in nature – at the lower level of the garden, while a formal pool will look quite at home on a raised patio or other paved areas.

Make sure you can get a hose to your pool to fill it and think about where you will empty it if you ever want to clean it out – which you may need to do every few years if any amount of debris or rotted leaves has built up at the bottom. But certainly don't empty it for the sake of doing so.

SIZE AND DEPTH

Very shallow pools can freeze solid in winter killing the fish. If the depth is 1 ft 3 in or more you will almost certainly avoid this and you will also be able to grow water lilies – the aristocrats of the water garden.

Otherwise the size will depend on your garden, your pocket and the kind of fish and plants you wish to have. A few small goldfish will be quite happy in a pool, say, 3 ft square but I wouldn't like to see large fish like golden orfe in anything less than 8 ft long.

MATERIALS AND CONSTRUCTION

Formal pools

These could be made from a tank or half barrel sunk to its rim in the ground with paving protruding an inch or so over the edge to camouflage the rim.
Or from a section of concrete sewer pipe sunk in the same way with a concrete floor added and painted with bitumen to seal the joint.
Formal pools can be constructed from concrete. The floor is laid first and then timber shuttering installed for the concrete walls. Larger formal pools would need metal reinforcing bars set in the concrete.
A shallow area at the edge of the pool would allow marginal plants to be grown.

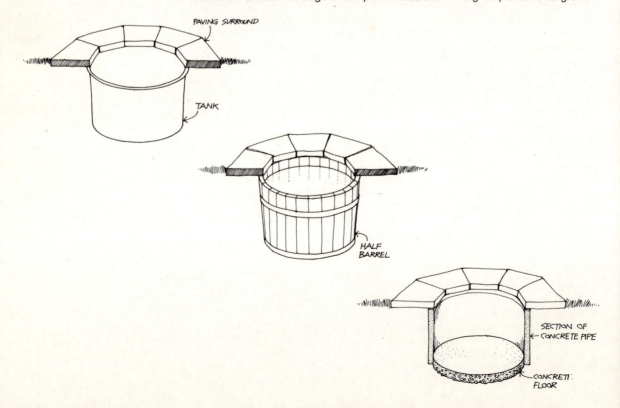

PAVING SURROUND

TANK

HALF BARREL

SECTION OF CONCRETE PIPE

CONCRETE FLOOR

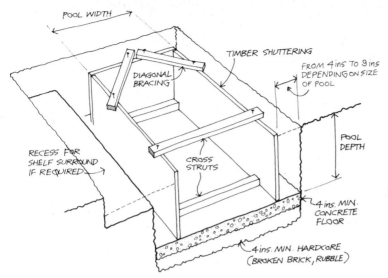

POOL WIDTH

TIMBER SHUTTERING

DIAGONAL BRACING

FROM 4 ins TO 9 ins DEPENDING ON SIZE OF POOL

POOL DEPTH

RECESS FOR SHELF SURROUND IF REQUIRED

CROSS STRUTS

4 ins. MIN. CONCRETE FLOOR

4 ins. MIN. HARDCORE (BROKEN BRICK, RUBBLE)

Informal pools

These are probably the most popular. They lend scope for imaginative design and are much easier to construct, especially for the non-professional. The basic system is that a hole is dug with smoothly shelving sides. A flat sheet of plastic or butyl rubber is laid over it and water poured on it which makes the sheeting take up the shape of the pool. There will be some folds in the fabric but they will cease to show after a few weeks.

PVC or butyl rubber?

Many garden pools have been found wanting because they have been made from thin polythene sheeting which has been punctured by garden tools, birds' beaks and children poking with sticks. Special reinforced sheeting made specifically for pools is better but the best of all is butyl rubber sheeting. It is certainly the most expensive but bearing in mind the time and trouble a pool takes to make it is best in the long run if you can afford it.

Plants in plastic containers

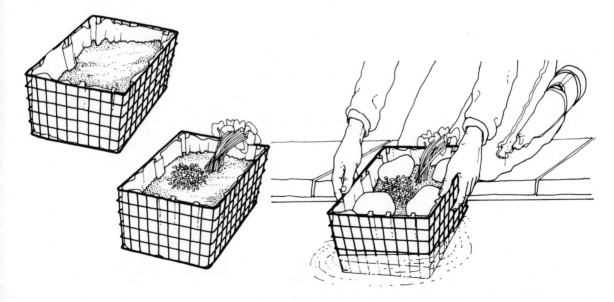

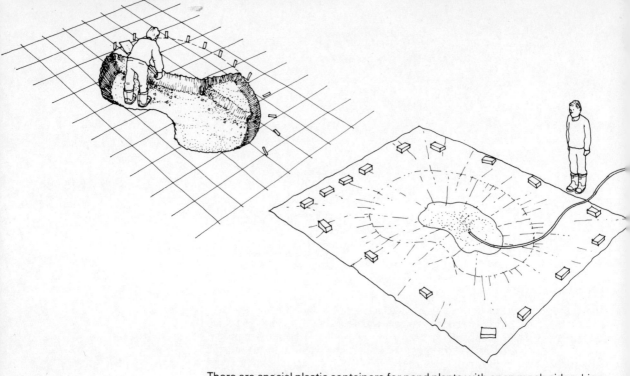

There are special plastic containers for pond plants with open mesh sides. Line them with an old bit of rag or sacking, fill with a mixture of good topsoil and compost, put in the plant and then cover the surface of the compost with stones to stop it washing away. Lower gently into the pool.

The containers are ideal as they can be moved around, allow you to take the plant out of the pond to divide it up if necessary and make cleaning out the pool that much easier if it ever has to be done.

THE SHAPE OF THE POOL

Allow some slope on the sides so that when the water freezes expanding ice will slide upwards rather than exert presure sideways. Have some shallow areas at the edges of the pool on which to put containers of marginal plants and have the pool deep enough (1 ft 3 in or more) to grow lilies if you want to and to stop the water freezing solid in winter so killing any fish.

The pool should be of such a size that it can take a standard size sheet of butyl rubber, otherwise you may waste some of your money or have a tricky join. So check sizes with your supplier first.

Don't make the shape too fussy or it will be difficult to construct with too many folds in the material. If you want a rock outcrop or waterfall at one point you will probably find it easier to build the main pool first and add the other effects afterwards – although you will no doubt plan it all to start with. The sheet liner will need to be weighed down or anchored in place at the edges. This can be done by growing grass over it, but it really is best to have paving of some kind around the sides of the pool to avoid lawn mowings or earth from flower beds getting into the water. In any case an access area round the pool makes it easier to look after plants and inspect the pond life.

A kind of fat kidney shape is a very good one for the informal garden pool.

A combination of drawing out the pool on graph paper and pegging it out on site should ensure that you get what you want where you want it. You must also decide where you are going to put the topsoil and the subsoil that you dig out.

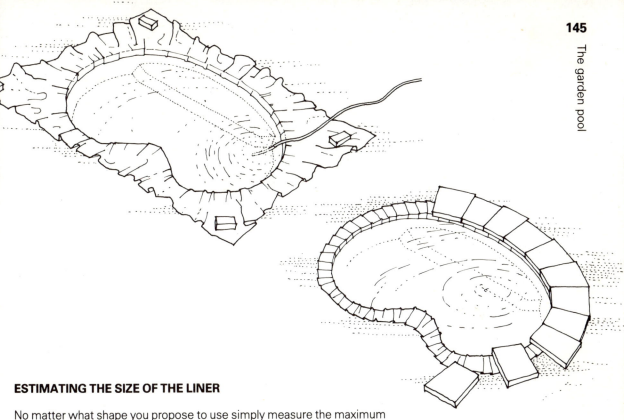

ESTIMATING THE SIZE OF THE LINER

No matter what shape you propose to use simply measure the maximum length of the pool and add twice the depth, then measure the maximum width and add twice the depth to that also. As the pool will have sloping sides this should give sufficient length and width to give an overlap all round of about 6 in. If in doubt measure the contours of the pool with a flexible tape measure.

MAKING THE POOL

Carefully mark out the site then dig the pool with smoothly sloping sides. Remove all sharp stones, firm the earth, then cover it with a 1 in layer of soft sand to give a smooth bed for the liner to lay on.
Carefully position the liner over the pool so that there is an equal overlap all round and weigh down the edges with bricks.
As you fill the pool from a hose the weight of water will pull the liner and bricks in towards the pool firmly and gently moulding the liner into position.
Remove the bricks and cut off the surplus leaving about a 6 in wide overlap of liner all round. Tuck this flat against the earth and pave over it.

THE TOTAL PLAN AND THE PLANTS

As well as making the pool deep enough for lilies it is advisable to have shelves round part of the sides to allow marginal plants like irises to be grown. Many plants are happy in about 6 in of water. Some prefer more and some less. For those that prefer less it is quite simple to put a slate or brick under the container to raise it up.

The design on p. 146 shows a fairly large pool of 12 ft × 9 ft that can accommodate quite a variety of plants. You can easily scale it down, or scale it up. There are shelves for marginal plants that need shallow water but there are also areas where one can get right to the water's edge to feed the fish and peer into the depths.

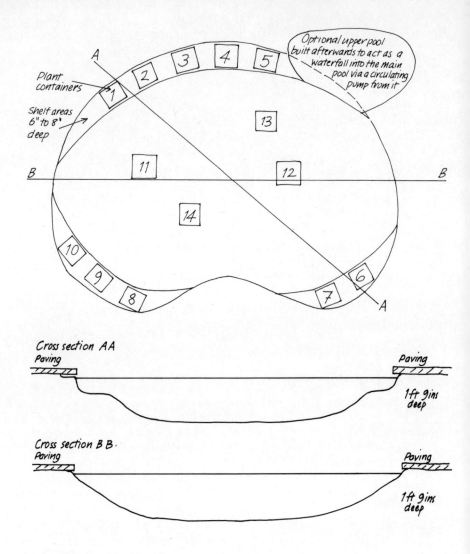

Plant containers

Shelf areas 6" to 8" deep

Optional upper pool built afterwards to act as a waterfall into the main pool via a circulating pump from it

Cross section AA
Paving

Paving

1ft 9ins deep

Cross section B B.
Paving

Paving

1ft 9ins deep

WHEN TO PLANT OR DIVIDE?

Most pond plants die down in late autumn and are dormant in winter. They are best planted in April or May when the water is warming up and the days are getting longer but while there is still plenty of time for them to make good growth before flowering.

Most water plants are propagated by division so April/May is the best time to do that too. Always choose a wet or humid day for dividing or transplanting and cover the containers with wet sacks while they are out of the water as a few minutes in the strong sunshine can do a lot of damage to tender new growths. It is advisable to wear rubber gloves for this operation as some plants, like waterlily roots, can stain the hands quite markedly.

SOURCES OF SUPPLY

Many large garden centres can supply all your aquatic needs and Yellow Pages list aquarium and pond suppliers. Please do not take plants from ponds in the wild or for that matter do not take any plants from the wild. They should be left for the enjoyment of all. Many plants are protected by law.

SOME SUGGESTED PLANTS

In designing your pool due consideration must be given to the depth of water that various plants need. Some are happy in just a few inches and others – like lilies – need much deeper water.

You must also consider the angle from which the pool will normally be viewed so that the taller plants tend to be where they look most natural. The beauty of having plants in containers is that they can be moved around to get the best effect.

In my plan I have put the taller plants at the back in containers 1 to 5. All the plants in containers 1 to 10 can cope with water 5 to 8 in deep, thus allowing for some evaporation in summer, but the plants in containers 1 and 7 really prefer slightly more shallow water so I will put a brick under each of those. The lilies in 11 and 12 have been chosen for the total depth of the pool so they will sit on the bottom. So will the aerating plants – which help to keep the water clear and supply oxygen to the pool.

My selection

With approximate heights out of the water.

Container (in some containers there are 2 plants)

1 *Pontederia cordata* 1½ ft
2 *Lythrum salicaria* 2-3 ft
  Iris laevigata 1½ ft
3 *Iris pseudacorus variegatus* 2 ft
4 *Iris versicolor* 1½ ft
  Iris 'Shirley Queen' 2 ft
5 *Acorus calamus variegatus* 2½ ft
6 *Orontium aquaticum* 9 ins
7 *Myosotis palustris* 1 ft
8 *Mentha aquatica* 1½ ft
  Mimulus luteus 1 ft
9 *Caltha palustris plena* 9 in
10 *Menyanthes trifoliata* 9 in
11 Water lily 'James Brydon' Leaves and flowers will float.
12 Water lily 'Rose Arey' Leaves and flowers will float.
13 (Aerating plant to supply oxygen) *Ceratophyllum demersum*. Will grow under water

14 *Hottonia palustris.* A floating plant that you just put in the water

N.B. Some of the taller plants would not be suitable for a small pool so you would need to choose smaller species or types.

LIVESTOCK AND AFTERCARE

Much animal life will arrive of its own accord. This may include pond-skaters, whirligig beetles, frogs, toads and newts.

As tadpoles are such good scavengers it is worth putting in some frogspawn if none appears spontaneously. At one stage tadpoles eat minute plants like algae that discolour the water. The curly ramshorn snails help in this way as well. I am not keen on chemical cleaners and would rather leave the job to these watery friends. By the way the long pointed water snails eat plant leaves so they are best avoided if you want to keep your choice plants intact.

Aftercare consists of keeping the pool topped up with water (have a permanent hose laid handy), and keeping rubbish and leaves out so cover with a large strong net in the autumn. Use a small fishing net to clear the surface when the need arises in the summer.

Don't put in rampant plants like *mimulus guttatus* which is sometimes included in 'bargain bundles' or 'beginners' collections' but can do a right takeover and don't let lawn mowings get in the water.

Divide up any plants that take up too much space and pull out any blanket weed by hand. It looks like a cloudy patch in the water and the long hair-like green threads which combine into a solid mat can choke other plants and small fish.

Use floating pellets to feed the fish so that you know you are only giving them as much as they can eat within a few minutes and there is none left over to rot. The fish won't need feeding at all in cold weather.

If the pool freezes over in winter don't try to crack the ice with a hammer and give the fish concussion but make holes at each end by standing saucepans of hot water on the ice. This will allow gases to escape and keep the water fit for the fish.

A better way is to float a couple of blocks of wood in the water before winter sets in. When the ice is $\frac{1}{2}$ in thick – or thick enough to bear its own weight – remove the blocks of wood by pouring boiling water over them to free them and remove an inch of water from the pond. Cover the holes with planks of wood or thick material and you have created a double-glazing effect. When the thaw sets in top up the pool and start the process again.

KEEP IT CLEAN

Murky water is basically due to mineral salts being released into the water from rotting vegetation or too much organic material in the pool which encourages the growth of algae. So don't put too much rich compost in the containers. Most water plants don't need it or will become too lush with too few flowers. The exception is lilies and their diet can be topped up from special slow-release sachets which are slipped in the container and renewed annually. Keep leaves, lawn mowings and fertilizers out of the pool.

Many pools become quite well balanced and need no cleaning out but if you ever need to do so early spring is the best time. Put the plant containers in buckets of water or cover with wet sacks. Carefully net the fish and other pond life and put these in containers too – large enough for them to turn round. Keep them in the shade to avoid violent fluctuations of temperature. The murky water, rotting vegetation and silt will then have to be pumped out, siphoned out or baled out. So if your pool is not too far from a drain so much the better.

The whole job is best done with bare legs and feet so that you don't make your clothes smell or damage the pool liner with your boots. Refill the pool and return the plants and livestock as soon as possible and head for a nice hot bath.

Great ramshorn

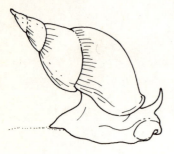

Great pond snail

21 PATHS, PATIOS AND FENCES

If you are a reluctant gardener you may also be a reluctant handyman but I don't see how you can completely escape some construction work unless your resources and inclinations are such that you can call in a contractor for every job.

    If you decide to do the work yourself then don't rush at it – easy does it to start with. In fact the first thing to do is nothing. Do nothing at all until you are absolutely sure of just what you want to do. Perhaps another reading of Chapter 10 on Garden Plans will help you form a clearer idea of just how you want your finished garden to look and give you a legitimate reason for getting out your pencil for a bit rather than your spade.

SO MAKE HASTE SLOWLY

Don't build any paths, patios or fences until you have cleared the whole site, decided on an overall plan and worked out the various finished levels you want in the garden – otherwise you may subsequently find that you need to bury the bottom half of some timber fencing to get the levels right, which will do it no good at all, or you may have to completely relay a path because you have got a border in the wrong place.

    So, nice and easy does it to start with. You can delay the work just a little longer by having a look round all the garden centres you know to see how various types of materials look 'in the flesh'. Quite a number of centres have built-up sample sections of paving and fences for your edification and temptation. Work out how much money you can spare, do a few calculations and decide on your order of priorities. The main path down the garden will probably take precedence over most other things so that you can move around the place in bad weather without stepping in the mire, perhaps followed by some fencing for privacy.

BE A GOOD BUYER

Shop around to get the best prices. If you are buying in quantity you may well find that a builder's merchant will give you a better deal than a garden centre.

CONCRETE, MORTAR AND WOODROT

Funny bedfellows but I put them together because they are three things you need to think about. You need to have some rudimentary knowledge of all three if you are going to do any kind of construction.

    You will need odd quantities of concrete in all kinds of places, perhaps to fill in odd spots that can't easily be paved, to dollop round the base of fence posts so that they stay upright and as a sure and certain foundation for walls. You will need mortar to stick blocks or bricks together and to pop under paving slabs.

    You will need woodrot like you need a 'flu virus, so take steps to avoid it.

Woodrot

The same rotting processes that take place in the compost heap will more slowly take place in any wooden structures in the garden unless you take steps to avoid them.

The simple rules are: don't have painted fences unless you intend to repaint them regularly. It is better to use the type of preservatives that soak into the wood and which are much easier to apply – creosote if there is no danger of damage to plants or special proprietary brands of preservative if there is. You will need to apply most preservatives every few years so make sure fences and other structures are easy to get at.

It is best not to put timber uprights in the soil. Even if they have been treated with preservative under pressure they will rot at some tiime. Instead use full-length concrete posts or shorter concrete 'godfathers' to which timber posts are bolted. Replacing timber uprights that have rotted in the soil is a hell of a slog. Slotting new fence panels into tall concrete posts is a doddle. Fixing new timber uprights to 'godfathers' is an acceptable compromise.

Don't buy the cheapest types of fence panels – poor quality interwoven ones with no overlap in the horizontal members are bound to cause you problems in the long run. So get the better type of interwoven or overlapped panels – more expensive to start with but cheaper in the long run.

CONCRETE AND MORTAR – FIRST A FEW TIPS

Watch the weather. If rain or frost is forecast put off any work that calls for concrete or mortar. Heavy rain will get them in a right mess and frost will destroy their bonding properties if it catches them before they are set.

Don't mix up more mortar or concrete that you can comfortably cope with in one operation. It's funny stuff to know what to do with if you have got some over although I put spare concrete into seed trays to make mini paving slabs – quite useful for very narrow paths or stepping stones.

Make sure you have a firm clear area to mix on – perhaps the garage floor if it is a concrete one but do clean up properly afterwards. A little layer of mix left behind on each occasion will slowly but surely take the floor nearer to the ceiling.

Basic tools you will need

Rubber gloves	Wheelbarrow
Bucket	Tamping beam – perhaps with handles
Watering can	Wooden or steel float
Shovel or spade	Steel tape measure
Straight edge	Trowel
Spirit level	Lump hammer or mallet
Line and pins	Small block of wood

Concrete

Concrete is a mixture of aggregate (gravel or crushed stone), sand, cement powder and water and is often used over a layer of broken bricks, rocks or other 'hard-core' to build up the bulk and keep down the cost. Concrete is used for foundations, supporting fence posts, floors, drives, steps and paths – although paving slabs are usually more popular for the latter.

A typical all-purpose mix of concrete would be 3 parts of gravel (say shovelfuls) to 2 parts of sand and 1 of cement. Sometimes the sand and gravel come ready mixed as 'aggregate'.

The right consistency

A handful of mixed-up concrete, when squeezed, should stay together. If it oozes out of your hand it is too wet and if it falls apart when you open your fingers it is too dry. Too dry a mix is difficult to lay and too wet a one is difficult to transport and gives a weak end result as cement tends to separate out if there is too much water present. Always use clean water – it makes a stronger end product.

Using a mixer

Concrete could be made in a concrete mixer by shovelling in 3 parts of gravel, 2 of sand and 1 of cement repeatedly until the machine is fully loaded or you have enough mix for the job, letting the machine turn it over thoroughly until it is a uniform grey colour and then adding water a little at a time.

Mixing by hand

On to a clean dry base repeatedly shovel 3 parts of gravel, 2 of sand and 1 of cement into a heap until you have enough for the job or that you can use in one go. Then take shovelfuls of the dry mix and dump them down into a new heap a few feet away until the whole heap has changed places. If the shovelfuls are taken from the *outside* of each heap but dumped down on *top* of each new heap the materials will mix together. Carry out the operation three times and you will have a well-mixed heap.

Now arrange the heap so that you open up the middle to form a crater and pour enough water into it to form a shallow pool. Work round and round the outside of the heap taking up small shovelfuls of dry mix and spreading them into the water. As the water gets fully absorbed add some more and carry on with the shovelling in. If you end up with too dry a mix you may have to make a new crater and repeat the operation using some more water. Finally turn over the whole heap a couple of times until all is well mixed together.

Mortar

Mortar is a mixture of sand and cement that is used for bonding blocks or bricks together, for laying paving slabs on or for filling in the gaps between them.

An all-purpose mix would be 4 parts of sand to 1 of cement – about 12 shovelfuls of sand and 3 of cement being enough to mix up in one go. Adding a plasticizer will make the mortar easier to handle – what the professionals call 'fatty'. The plasticizer may either be a proprietary one with the instructions on the container or it could be an eggcup full of neat washing-up liquid per mix. This will give much the same result.

Mortar is mixed in much the same way as concrete. Great care should be taken to use a really clean mixing place so that you avoid any small chippings or stones getting into the mix. These can be a right pest if they get between a couple of blocks or bricks that you are trying to get neatly tucked up together.

If the mortar mix is too wet it will not stay put but will ooze out from the place you put it and if it is too dry it will be too stubborn. To test it trowel some mortar on to a block or brick and place another one on top. If the mortar supports the top brick but allows you to tap it down into place it is just right. If the mortar runs out down the brickwork it is too wet and if you can't tap down the brick it is obviously too dry.

What about ready-mixed concrete – the wet kind?

For a large amount it is certainly the easiest answer.

Once you have worked out how much concrete you need (you buy it in cubic yards) decide whether it is worth mixing your own or whether you would like it all ready mixed and wet ready for laying. Get a few prices and compare them. For quantities of 3 cubic yards or over you should certainly consider the saving in labour of a ready-mixed load.

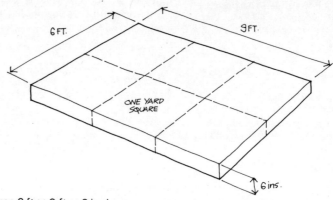

An area 6 ft × 9 ft × 6 in deep
would represent 1 cu yd.

But if you do buy ready-mixed you must have the site completely ready
for when the lorry arrives. The formwork to retain the concrete must be in place
(see p. 153) You must either be able to get the lorry right on to the site or have
wheelbarrows and helpers ready to transport the concrete to just where you
want it. It is not the kind of delivery that can be delayed.

One cubic yard of ready mixed concrete weighs about 2 tons – which
represents about 30 wheelbarrow loads.

What about dry mix?

You can buy dry mixed concrete and mortar in bags. All you have to do is add
the water. It is an expensive way of buying concrete or mortar but a very handy
one if you just want a small quantity. A 1 cwt bag will make up into just under 1
cu ft of finished material.

TERRACES AND PATHS

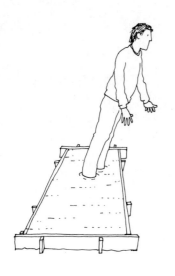

These can have a practical and decorative function. Certainly a solid surface
immediately round the house will give a clean approach to doorways. Most
builders now lay concrete or tarmac paths in the immediate vicinity of new
houses and usually lay the driveways as well.

How much solid or paved area you have will naturally depend on the
layout of the house, the size of the garden, your own inclinations and perhaps
your bank balance. A patio or terrace can be a handy way of incorporating
unsightly features such as manholes or of dealing with different levels round
the house by building steps or slopes.

Whatever kind of terrace, patio or paths you have do construct
adequate foundations. These may vary from a 6 in layer of vibrated or rammed
hardcore laid on a properly excavated site for a load-bearing drive to a layer of
sharp sand as a bed for paving slabs which are usually locked into place with
spots of mortar – one for each corner of the slab and one for the middle.
Certainly the paving slab and mortar spot technique is the quickest and easiest
way for the amateur to lay terraces or paths for pedestrian use, but concrete is
more suitable for heavy weight-bearing paths or drives.

LAYING CONCRETE

I am not suggesting that you will want to lay much concrete. It is quite a slog.
But you will almost certainly want to lay some at some time or other so let us
look at the basic principles.

If the soil where you want to lay a path or drive is soft or loose carefully remove it without digging downwards further than absolutely necessary. Put on a layer of rubble or stones and compact it with a roller. If the soil is really solid and firm then lay the concrete slab (with its hardcore filling) straight on to it but do skim off any weeds without disturbing the soil and roll the ground to make it even more solid.

Under the concrete you will need a 3 in layer of hardcore for drives but just 1 or 2 in will do for paths. Cover the rubble with clean sand and then lay the concrete on top. Leave a space between the hardcore and the formwork to give solid concrete sides.

You will need the timber formwork to hold the concrete until it has set. Make this from any kind of old timber or floor boards about 1 in thick and wide enough for the depth of hardcore plus concrete you need. Support the formwork with stout timber stakes about 18 in long driven into the ground on the other side of the boards from where the concrete will be poured. Have the formwork slightly lower on one side so that any water drains off the finished slab, making sure that the slope is away from any buildings. Check this with a spirit level and a length of wood. The formwork must be rigid and able to withstand the pressure of the compacted concrete. The stakes should not be further than 3 ft apart, preferably closer.

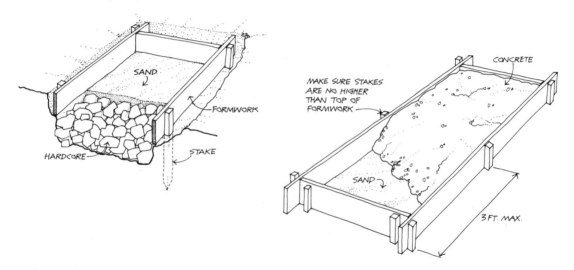

Set up the formwork and check the levels. Put the hardcore in place. If you can't tip in the concrete from the side a plank laid temporarily on top of the hardcore will give you easier access for the wheelbarrow. Pour in the concrete so that it ends up just above the level of the formwork. Use a tamping beam – a heavy plank on its edge – to compact the concrete down to a level surface. This is more easily done by two people than just one. Keep lifting and dropping the tamping beam just a few inches to firm the concrete down advancing just half the width of the beam at a time. With one person at each end of the beam you can develop a rhythmic chopping action. When you get to the end go back to the beginning to remove any excess concrete by sliding the beam backwards and forwards with a sawing motion slowly advancing along the slab and forcing any surplus concrete along to the end. If you want a smooth surface finish with a timber float or for an even smoother one with a metal float. Just gently smooth the surface with long, straight strokes. These very smooth surfaces can be rather slippery in frosty weather, so if you prefer a textured surface with more grip, use a stiff broom to brush across the slab (after the concrete has lost any sloppiness but while it is still pliable: in most cases this operation can normally follow straight on after the levelling and smoothing). Brush in one direction only to give a professional look. Cover the slab with plastic sheeting or damp sacks for a couple of days. This will stop it drying out too fast in dry

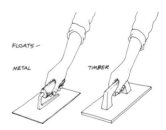

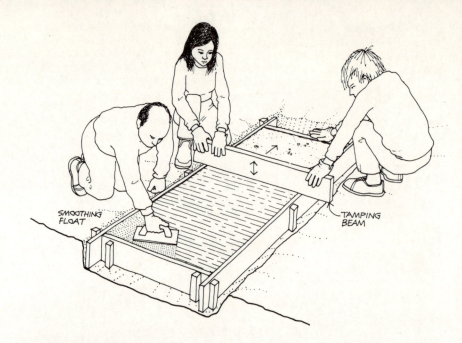

SMOOTHING
FLOAT

TAMPING
BEAM

weather or being rained on in wet weather. Then carefully remove the
formwork. The concrete will continue to strengthen over the ensuing weeks
and months. Treat it carefully to begin with.

Do not lay concrete in frosty weather unless you add a special anti-
freeze available from your supplier otherwise frozen water particles will destroy
the concrete's setting properties. Ideally I think it is best to avoid frosty
weather altogether.

LAYING STANDARD CONCRETE SLABS OR THOSE MADE FROM REFORMED STONE

Laying concrete slabs is quicker and easier than laying concrete. The slabs are
available in various colours, sizes and shapes.

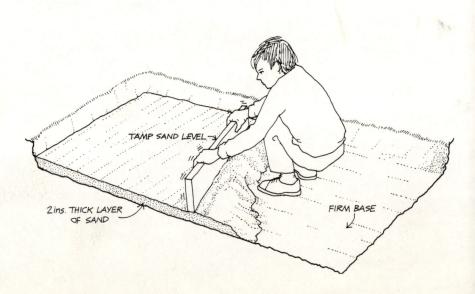

TAMP SAND LEVEL

2 ins. THICK LAYER
OF SAND

FIRM BASE

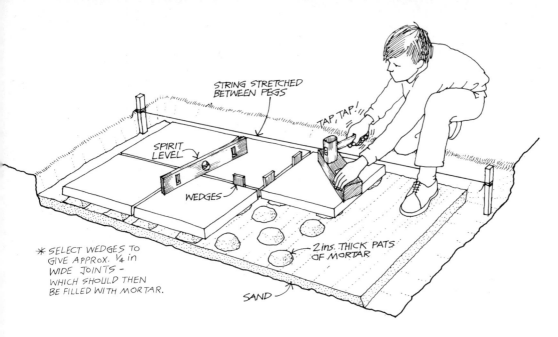

STRING STRETCHED BETWEEN PEGS

TAP, TAP!

SPIRIT LEVEL

WEDGES

2 ins. THICK PATS OF MORTAR

*SELECT WEDGES TO GIVE APPROX. ¼ in WIDE JOINTS – WHICH SHOULD THEN BE FILLED WITH MORTAR.

SAND

Make sure you have a firm foundation. It is best to remove the top 3 to 4 in of soil and if the soil is soft roll in a layer of stones or rubble to make a firm base. Mark one edge of the path with string stretched between pegs to ensure that the finished path is straight.

Put down a 2 in thick layer of sharp sand. Bed each slab on to 5 pats of fairly stiff mortar (3 parts sand to one of cement) on top of the sand with one pat in the middle of where the slab will go and one just inside each of the corners.

Tap down each slab into place with a block of wood under a hammer making sure each slab is level with adjacent slabs and is in line with any necessary slope. Check with a spirit level.

THE TEMPORARY SLAB PATH

If you are not entirely sure about the final position of the path just bed the slabs straight down on the sand with no mortar. If the sand is level you will get a fairly level path but not quite so spot-on as it would be with the mortar. But it will then be easier to move at a later date or it won't be too herculean a task to lift the slabs and add the mortar pats if you decide to leave the path where it is.

ERECTING A FENCE

Fences can be of many kinds – close boarded either vertically or horizontally, rustic, chain link, wattle hurdles or trellis work, but the easiest to erect and the least troublesome to maintain for the reluctant gardener is probably the lapped or interwoven panel supported between concrete posts.

The panels can, of course, be supported between timber posts but concrete ones will save you trouble in the long run because almost all timber posts will start to rot at some stage, especially where they enter the soil even though their life can be considerably extended with preservatives applied before erecting.

The panels should be good quality ones – the kind where the horizontal boards overlap each other. Those that don't overlap tend to twist and deteriorate far too quickly.

If you don't like the look of white posts the concrete can easily be stained with the preservative you are using for the fence. There won't be a perfect take-up of colour but you will lose the dead white look.

Concrete posts will certainly take more time to erect than timber ones and will probably be about twice the price but they are certainly a good investment and will act as a permanent support structure for your fence allowing you to fairly easily replace any panels that suffer the ravages of time.

Erection

The fence can be erected in one straight line.

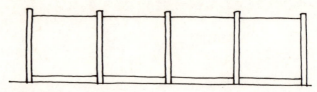

Or stepped to cope with slopes.

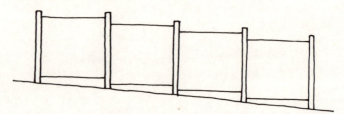

The posts are slotted to receive the panels and concrete gravel boards which can be used at the base to keep the wooden panels well away from the soil. If the gravel boards are partly buried in the ground at the base they can be used to retain a modest depth of soil and act as a pet-proof enclosure.

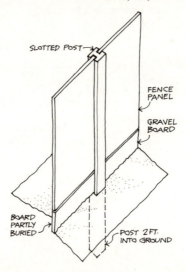

Sizes

The panels come in standard sizes 3 ft to 6 ft high by 6 ft long. You may need a mixture of lengths to fill the available space. When calculating the total length of the fence don't forget to make allowance for the width of each of the posts as well as the panels and allow for one post at each end.

At least 2 ft of each post should be in the ground to give a firm anchorage. They will need to be concreted in the soil.

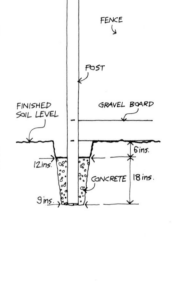

What you will need

As well as the panels, posts and preservative you will need:

Spade
Line and spirit level
Wheelbarrow
A rammer – a length of timber post about 3 in in diameter to ram the concrete into place
Two people – the posts and gravel boards are heavy to handle
Some lengths of timber battens to act as supports while waiting for the concrete foundations to set
Some odd bits of wood the same width as the slots in the posts to fix these supports to.

Method

Clear the whole line of the garden where the fence is to go of all obstructions and weeds and level the soil. Stretch a line the length of the fence and take out a very shallow trench – say a couple or more inches deep – so that the gravel boards can be let into the soil. Remember that your fence panels can only be erected exactly at right angles to the soil – so the fence will need to be stepped to cope with slopes.

Handle with care

Concrete posts can get chipped or cracked if dropped so treat them with care.

Mark the posts

Decide how much post, if any, you wish to protrude above the panels and mark each post with chalk to show the final erected position of each panel and gravel board.

Post holes

These should be 2 ft deep overall. Set the post on a stone or brick (if necessary) to ensure that top of the post is level with the next one. Level up the posts in this way before the concrete is poured in.
Erect the first post. Make sure it is absolutely upright in both directions. Take out the next hole according to the next length of fence panel and then position the first gravel board.
Swing the second post into position against the gravel board and make sure it is square and in line with the first post before adding the concrete.

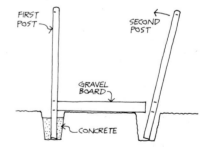

Support the supports

You can help the posts to stand up while the concrete is setting by ramming some hardcore round the base before you pour the concrete in, but as the posts do need to be exactly upright in all directions it is best to give them some support for a couple of days with some timber (or metal) props while the concrete is setting.

Jam some short lengths of wood into the slots in the posts to which you can nail these supports and then prop up the posts as you proceed. Use a spirit level to check that the posts really are upright. The props can be long or short ones depending on the timber available – the longer ones giving a more secure hold and making a spot on result more easy to obtain.

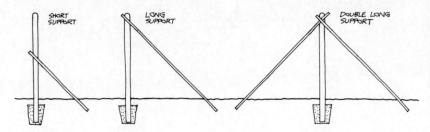

Slotting in the panels

It is best to slot the panels in after the concrete has set, otherwise a high wind may give the fence a list to leeward. This is best done by two people and you will each need something to stand on if the fence is 6 ft high. Again, this job is best not done in a high wind.

You may get the odd panel that is slightly out of square so be prepared to do a bit of planing to the sides of the panels if necessary to ensure an easy fit. Apply some preservative to such planed places.

22 A HEDGE AGAINST INFLATION

A hedge has one great advantage over a fence. It filters the wind.

Fences act as solid barriers but the wind outsmarts them and goes whistling up over the top and down the other side to cause swirling eddies of moving air. If there are any gaps the wind will go searching through them and to be really mean it will sometimes blow the fences over.

Whereas a hedge will court the wind and play with it. It will allow some of the wind through to give a flow of air that will help to counteract any downward draught from over the top of the hedge.

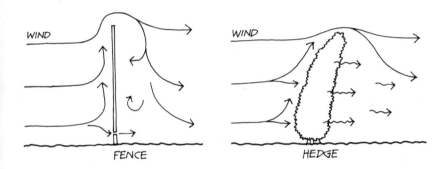

Hedges may get buffeted by the wind but they are hardly ever blown over. They bend and sway with it and when the wind has gone they stand up again – provided they have been properly planted in the first place.

But that is not to say that hedges are ideal for every situatiion. If space is limited they may take up a disproportionate amount of room and some hedges need a lot of time spent on them. You should not only give thought to whether you have enough room for a hedge but also what demands the various kinds of hedging plants will make on your time.

HEDGES HAVE SOME DISADVANTAGES

Their roots may rob surrounding plants of water and nutrients.

They can get broken with the weight of winter snow if they have not been cut to the right kind of shape.

They can look a little bare in winter if they are deciduous.

As we have said they can take up room.

They take time to grow – probably five or six years to reach as many feet in height.

They need trimming.

Can these drawbacks be avoided? Not entirely but we can certainly minimize some of them.

STOPPING THEM ROBBING OTHER PLANTS

You can keep this problem to an acceptable level by putting a path between the hedge and the border, and then once a year sliding the spade down the side of the path away from the hedge to cut through any invading roots. A stainless steel spade is best for this job as it has a thin edge to cut through any roots and it easily slides through the soil.

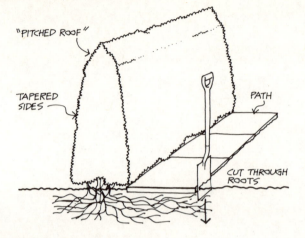

SHEDDING THE SNOW

If you taper the hedge as it grows so that it is broad at the base and narrow at the top and then shape the top like the sharp pitch of a roof you will have little trouble with snow building up on top of the hedge and breaking it down with its weight.

HEDGES TAKE UP ROOM

There is no way round this one. A hedge must have enough room to develop properly. If you haven't got the room then don't have a hedge. A 6 ft high hedge will need to be at least 2 ft wide – preferably 2 ft 6 in or more – at the base.

CHOOSING THE RIGHT KIND OF PLANTS

What your hedge is grown from should depend on what you want it to do for you and not just what are the cheapest or the easiest plants to come by.

If you need a hedge as a barrier against four-legged or two-legged invaders then you will need something that is just a little bit uncomfortable.

THE BARRIER HEDGE

Three types of plants are ideal.

1 Hawthorn (*Crataegus monogyna*) or one of its more expensive relatives. Its disadvantages are that as it is deciduous it is bare in the winter time and that ideally it needs clipping twice a year. But it makes an acceptable hedge and it is cheap.

2 *Berberis*. Several members of this prickly family of plants make good hedges including *Berberis darwinii* (evergreen – 6 ft or more tall) and *Berberis thunbergii* (deciduous – 4 ft or more) but probably one of the best for a formal hedge is the evergreen *Berberis* × *stenophylla* (6 ft or more). It will stand

clipping right to the ground without going bare at the bottom. It should be lightly trimmed after flowering each year.

3 Common holly (*Ilex aquifolium*). It is rather slow growing in the first few years but it eventually makes a good evergreen barrier hedge 6 ft or more tall. Variegated forms can give added interest but can be rather expensive.
All three, hawthorn, berberis and holly, make good barrier hedges but they are prickly customers to deal with and stout gloves are recommended at planting time and trimming time.

THE TALL FORMAL HEDGE

There are many plants to choose from and the gardening advertisements make all kinds of claims but for a good background hedge for the reluctant gardener – and other gardeners – there is nothing to beat yew.

Yew (*Taxus baccata*) is a slow growing evergreen with small mat-green leaves which act as a good background to other plants. If the soil and other conditions are good it will grow at about 1 ft a year to give a respectable hedge in five or six years.

You may be tempted by quicker growing plants such as *Cupressus macrocarpa*, *Thuja plicata* or Leyland cypress. Their quick growth is a boon in the first few years but a nuisance later on and if left unclipped they will really reach for the sky. So while they all make good hedges I would recommend yew to you as the ideal hedge for both the enthusiastic gardener as well as the reluctant one. Yew needs clipping just once a year and will give you a hedge to be proud of.

...MUST BE A BIT OF LEYLAND CYPRESS IN THERE ....

There are also two deciduous plants that make good hedges: beech (*Fagus sylvatica*) and hornbeam (*Carpinus betulus*) grow to 6 ft or more tall and give some privacy in the winter as they retain their brown leaves until the new growth starts in the spring. They make attractive hedges, are long-lived and only need clipping once a year. They present more variety during the year than an evergreen hedge as they change from the fresh green spring growth to the darker green of summer and then the russet of autumn but they do not give the complete privacy in winter that an evergreen hedge does.

There is also one popular hedge that deserves mention as it has had so much loving care bestowed on it by so many British gardeners. Oval leaved privet (*Ligustrum ovalifolium*) is cheap, it grows quickly and it makes an attractive hedge but it is a hungry feeder robbing the soil of nutrients so that other plants have a rough time, and it needs clipping several times a year. I don't think it is the right kind of hedge for the reluctant gardener.

SUMMING UP THE CHOICES

For the adventurous gardener with time to spare there are all kinds of plants that can be used for hedges but for most of us my choice would be hawthorn, berberis or holly if you definitely need a barrier hedge, otherwise I would strongly recommend yew for an evergreen hedge and beech or hornbeam for a decidous one.

PUTTING THE HEDGE IN THE RIGHT PLACE

Your neighbour will have the right to cut the hedge back to the boundary as it grows over on to his land, if he so wishes. So do plant the hedge on your side of the boundary if you want to be in control of it. If you intend the hedge to be, say, 2 ft 6 in wide overall then you will need to plant it 1 ft 3 in from the boundary.

It is worth taking a bit of trouble to get the plants the right distance from the boundary and the right distance apart in a straight line. Securely peg out a

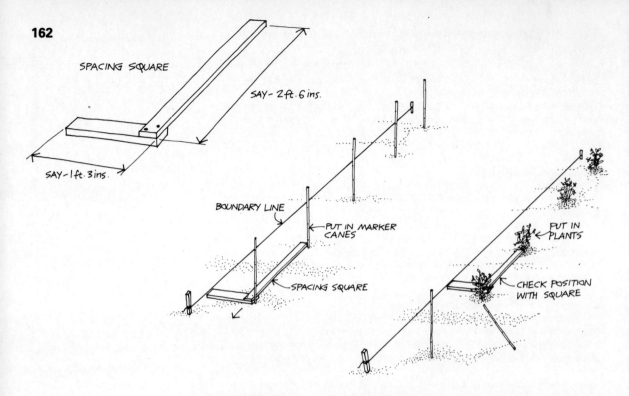

SPACING SQUARE

SAY - 2 ft. 6 ins.

SAY - 1 ft. 3 ins.

BOUNDARY LINE

PUT IN MARKER CANES

SPACING SQUARE

PUT IN PLANTS

CHECK POSITION WITH SQUARE

line directly on the boundary and then use a simple spacing square made from a couple of pieces of wood to enable you to put in a cane exactly where each plant is to go. Check that the canes are all in line and that you have the right number of plants. Then after you have dug out each hole use the spacing square again to recheck the position as you put in each plant.

If you want a good hedge it is worth spending a bit of time to ensure that every plant is properly planted and will have a good start in life. See the chapter on Trees and Shrubs, 'Choosing, planting and after care', p. 120.

HOW FAR APART?

Sometimes a double row of plants is recommended but for a normal garden hedge this really is rather a waste of money and time. A single row of plants properly put in will make a very satisfactory hedge. Some of the cheaper kinds of plants sometimes advertised in the gardening press may have to be planted as close as 1 ft apart but good quality plants of yew and cypress may be planted 2 ft 6 in apart with hawthorn, hornbeam, beech, berberis and holly a little closer at 1 ft 6 in to 2 ft.

WHAT SIZE PLANTS?

It can be very tempting (and expensive) to put in big plants with the hope of a quicker hedge. In fact middle-sized plants – say 2 to 3 ft tall – suffer less from replanting and will usually catch up and overtake bigger plants.

TO STAKE OR NOT TO STAKE?

The quicker growing varieties with a lot of top weight, like *Leylandii*, need supporting with stakes against the winter winds. Slow growing or bushy plants like hawthorn or berberis can manage without.

See 'Trees and shrubs', p. 121.

TRIMMING

Most hedges will need one initial trim towards the end of the first summer after planting. Cut back the leading shoots by half the growth they have made that year and trim off any straggling side shoots. Use secateurs or sharp shears for the first few years and only use a mechanical cutter after the hedge is firmly established.

If you want a smooth-faced hedge then this can only be achieved by regular and careful cutting several times a season, perhaps as often as once a month in the growing season. But if you are willing to accept a certain fuzziness of line then a minimum trim could be once in the late summer for yew, cypress, beech and hornbeam, twice a year in June and September for holly and hawthorn, and once a year after flowering for berberis.

Remember that the hedge needs to be wider at the base than the top. Many gardeners find this difficult to achieve and some hedges even end up wider at the top than the bottom with consequent damage from snow loading. So, unless you have a very good eye for levels it pays to use a line to ensure that as your hedge grows it is kept wide at the bottom and narrow at the top with an acute angled ridge to shed the snow. Stretch a line (strong string will do tied to sticks at each end pushed into the ground) along the bottom of the hedge and trim to it. Try not to cut the string. Then stretch a line tied to tall bamboo sticks the height of the hedge and trim to that to get the top edge straight and where you want it. Finally trim between the top and the bottom of the hedge.

23 SOMETHING TO EAT

Many reluctant gardeners do not want to be bothered with vegetables. Unfortunately most vegetables are annuals and so there is a fair amount of repetitive work to do each year. Yet there is something so satisfying about eating something you have grown yourself that I cannot resist tempting you to try. Why not grow a few vegetables among the flowers or have your own tomatoes growing by the kitchen door?

But isn't growing vegetables a complicated business? Isn't there a lot of digging and manuring and raking and seed sowing and something called rotation of crops? Yes, there is. What is more, vegetable growing needs planning. But it is all very worth while because if you grow your own crops you can have varieties with a flavour that you can seldom buy – varieties like Little Gem lettuce, Gardener's Delight tomatoes and Little Marvel peas. Vegetables that really are worth the effort.

So let me give you a few wrinkles, a few basic rules and explanations, and if you are still interested perhaps you will have a try.

Rule 1 Don't try to grow vegetables in the shade. They must be right out in full sun.

Rule 2 Don't try to grow vegetables in poor soil. It will get poorer still and so will the crops. If the soil is starved and thin you will need to add plenty of compost or manure.

Rule 3 Don't try to grow vegetables cheek by jowl with other plants. They need room. Almost all vegetables are hungry feeders and do not like competition close up against them.

Rule 4 Don't try to grow vegetables in very acid or very alkaline soils. If your garden is knee-deep in leafmould it will almost certainly be acid and you will need to add lime to correct this. If your garden is based on a bed of chalk it will be very alkaline and you will need to add plenty of peat to the areas where the vegetables are to grow. A pH of 6.5 is a good average for most vegetables (see p. 10). It's best to buy a simple soil-testing kit from your plant centre – it will tell you how to test and correct your soil.

Rule 5 Don't try to grow tender vegetable plants outdoors until all danger of frost has passed. Tender plants include tomatoes, peppers, aubergines, marrows and courgettes, melons, runner beans and French beans. The first week in June is the safe planting time for tender crops for most areas but be guided by local conditions.

Rule 6 You must rotate your crops. This means growing crops in a particular sequence to avoid exhausting or contaminating the soil.

Plants belong to families and a disease which affects one member of a family will almost certainly infect another member of that family but may have no effect at all on another plant family. Clubroot, a serious disease of cabbages, is passed on *through the soil* to other members of the family, say from Brussels sprouts to turnips, but will have no effect on potatoes. And potato blight which can seriously effect tomatoes (a close relative) has no effect on lettuces. So by knowing the families to which plants belong we can work out a rotation system to ensure that no member of any plant family is grown in the same position more than once in three or preferably four years (see p. 34).

Rule 7 Water well. All vegetables need supplies of water deep down at their roots. It is better to give them a really good soaking once or twice a week than a modest sprinkling every day.

So much for the rules, now for a few wrinkles.

CROP ROTATION

The easiest way to help you keep to rule 6 is to give you the list of families to which vegetables belong. This is at the end of the chapter. You may not want to bother to try to pronounce the family names but do avoid putting members of any single family in the same place more than once in four years.

VEGETABLES AMONG THE FLOWERS

There is no reason why vegetables should not be grown in the flower beds if you haven't enough space to have a special vegetable plot – some vegetables are quite handsome in their own right. Carrot tops look like decorative ferns and runner beans are a pretty red-flowered climber.

HAVE FOUR OR MORE VEGETABLE AREAS

Allocate four or more separate areas to crop growing and grow different things in each one. There is no reason why you shouldn't have more than one plant family in any single area as long as no plant family is in the same area more than one year in four. (Or if you only have room for one area just follow the same basic principle and have different things each year.) Note: keep a record of what you grow and where or you will forget before next year. Then each year change the plants round so that they are growing in different areas and by year five are back where they started – then start the rotation dance all over again. This will help to avoid the build-up of those soilborne pests and diseases. And you will get better crops.

VEGETABLES HAVE A HABIT OF GROWING

Many vegetables will make some sort of growth even if you don't treat them right, but with a little bit of love and attention they will do so much better. Understanding their individual needs and growth habits will help you to get a good return for your efforts.

So let us look at a few fairly easy to grow crops and see how they should be treated.

But first please read the section Planting and Sowing on p. 69.

Carrots

They are such attractive plants that if they didn't exist we would have to invent them.

There are some simple but essential rules for growing carrots successfully. They can be ruined by carrot-fly maggots which burrow into the carrots and which hatch from eggs laid by carrot flies in the summer. The flies are attracted to the plants by their smell so the rule is to try not to brush against their leaves which if you do give off that carroty smell; also sow the seed far enough apart to completely avoid having to thin the plants. This should be no closer than $\frac{1}{2}$ in apart in drills $\frac{1}{4}$ in deep and 1 ft apart.

If you sow an early and a late variety you can have a longer season of supply, and I would strongly advise pulling them from July onwards when they are no bigger than your finger. They are such delicious vegetables when very young and if you pull them early you may beat any carrot-fly maggots to it. Progressively thin the plants to a final distance of 6 in apart if you want to leave some to grow big – using the thinnings to eat.

Carrots need a rich, deeply dug soil – but no fresh manure should be added as this tends to make the carrots fork instead of growing straight and true. A soil manured for a previous crop is ideal.

Chicory (sugar loaf)

Sugar loaf chicory is a relative of the blanched chicory that you can buy as a winter salad food which has been grown in the dark to keep it from being too bitter. Sugar loaf does not have to be blanched and is used straight from the garden. It is like a big cos lettuce that grows towards the end of the season and that will stand fresh in the garden for a long time and will then keep well in the bottom of the fridge. It tastes like a cos lettuce with just a hint of bitterness in its flavour.

Sow in June or July $\frac{1}{2}$ in deep in rows 1 ft apart – only one seed to the inch – and progressively thin to 10-12 in apart. Or you can sow a few seeds in a group, 1 ft apart. Sugar loaf chicory needs a fairly fertile soil to grow well.

The plants begin to be usable by the end of October. They can stand a little frost and if the weather is mild can be left outdoors all winter. Otherwise they can be cut, with all the leaves intact, and stored in a fridge or a cool shed or cellar for many weeks. Then take off the outer leaves and use the crisp solid centres as you would lettuce.

Corn salad or lamb's lettuce

Another useful substitute for lettuce which can be sown in spring for summer use or sown in late summer for winter use. It will do well in any reasonable soil.

Sow in April/May or in late August/September $\frac{1}{2}$ in deep in drills 6 in apart or sow in a group. Thin the plants to 6 in apart (see p. 76) as soon as they are large enough to handle.

The spring sowings will be ready from August onwards and the later sowings from Christmas onwards. You can either gather the leaves one at a time or pull up the whole plant. The leaves need to be well washed as, being low growing, they get splashed with soil. In winter protect the plants with straw or bracken cuddled up round them or cover them with cloches.

Courgettes See Marrows

Cucumber – outdoor. See Marrows

Garlic

Garlic is easy to grow.

A bulb of garlic is made up of a dozen or more individual 'cloves'. Take a bulb apart, leaving each clove with its own skin and its bit of base intact, and from March to May plant the cloves upright in a nice warm spot with their tips just below the surface of the soil, with 9 in between each plant. They can, of course, either be in a row or a group or even just one by itself. Each clove of garlic will grow into one full bulb.

Lift and dry the bulbs in late summer by laying them out on a concrete or paved surface in full sun for a couple of days and then store in a dry frost-proof place.

Lettuce

Most shop lettuce really is quite dreary, some of it like tasteless thin green paper. If you grow your own you have the choice of a whole range of flavours and textures and you can pick and eat them within the hour when they are at their best. But do make sure that you eat them at the peak of their perfection. When they are solid and crisp. If you eat them too young they won't have much flavour and if they have started to 'bolt' (to start growing upwards ready to flower and seed) they will taste bitter.

Many people think that the variety 'Little Gem' is the best of all and I am inclined to agree with them. But flavour is such an individual thing it is fortunate that the range of varieties is so large.

To get a long season of supply either grow different varieties or sow a few seeds every couple of weeks.

Sow thinly, just two seeds to the inch, in a drill $\frac{1}{2}$ in deep from March onwards depending on the variety. Progressively thin so that no seedling touches its neighbour until they are at their final distances from 6 in to 12 ft apart depending on the variety. Seedling lettuce will transplant quite easily if you water them well first. You can do this as soon as they are big enough to be able to be handled and preferably before they are more than about a inch across. Take up each seedling with plenty of soil round it and then water it well in afterwards. I find an old dessertspoon a useful tool for this job. Cover the early sowings with cloches if you want to bring them on more quickly.

Lettuce need a good soil rich in organic matter. They need it for nourishment and they need it for its water-retaining properties. Keep lettuce well watered in the dry summer months.

Pull up the whole plant when they are ready to be picked, putting the roots and any discarded leaves on the compost heap. Use half a row at a time and immediately the soil is clear rake it level and sow some more, right up to mid August.

Marrows and outdoor cucumbers

Courgettes are varieties of marrows picked young – about 6 in long – and cucumbers belong to the same plant family so they can all be treated in much the same way.

The simplest way to grow any of them is to buy ready-grown plants for putting out in early June but if you want to bring them on from seed then you can either do this indoors to get early plants or you can sow them outdoors for later crops.

If sowing indoors, then in mid April put two seeds $\frac{3}{4}$ in deep on their edge in each $2\frac{1}{2}$ or 3 in pot of potting compost. Water well and allow to drain. Cover the top of the pot with plastic film or put it into a plastic bag and keep in a warm dark place, the airing cupboard will do, until they come up. Inspect them daily and directly they are up remove the plastic and bring into full light either in a greenhouse or on a south-facing window sill in a warm room. If both seeds come up remove the weaker one.

As the plants develop keep them well watered and pot on into larger pots if the leaves start to get at all pale. Plant out in early June, when the frosts have gone, 2 ft apart each way for bush plants and 3 ft for trailing plants. Or sow the seed outdoors at a depth of $\frac{3}{4}$ in from May to June – again putting two seeds at each station and thinning down (see p. 76) to the best plant.

They all need a deeply dug, well-manured soil and plenty of water in the summer. Or they can be grown in growing bags – say two plants in each bag. A growing bag is a black plastic bag about 3 ft long and 1 ft wide that has been filled with potting compost and all the correct nutrients and sealed at either end so that it is easy to transport. It is put in place and then slit open with scissors or a knife according to the instructions on it so that it can be planted up with all manner of plants. It is like a transportable plastic window box.

Keep the marrows cut when they are young and tender to get a long cropping season – at 6 in if you want them as courgettes. Closely wrapped in plastic film, cucumbers and courgettes will keep in the bottom of the fridge for up to a couple of weeks. At the end of the season any mature marrows can be left on the plants to let their skins harden and then brought indoors before the first frosts to be stored on a shelf or hung up in a net in a cool, frost-proof place. Marrows do best in a nice sunny position although I must say the modern varieties seem to do well even in quite dull summers.

Mint

Most people like to grow a bit of mint in the garden but they don't like the way its roots can spread and do a takeover bid of the surrounding soil.

You can contain mint's activities by growing it in a bucket which has been riddled with drainage holes and sunk to its rim in the soil – preferably near the kitchen door. Use a plastic bucket by all means, carefully making the holes with a hot poker.

Dig up the mint and replenish the soil every few years to keep the mint growing well. You can either get a plant from a garden centre or beg a bit from some one else but make sure it's a healthy specimen that produces good mint.

Onions – spring

The well-known salad crop. Easy to grow on good soil.

Sow the seed in March just three to the inch in a drill $\frac{1}{4}$ in deep. Thin (see p. 76) directly they are large enough to start eating. If you try to pull them when the soil is dry you will often leave the bottom of the onion in the soil, so water well first and hold the onion right at the base to get it out intact.

Onions – Welsh

The Welsh onion is sometimes called the perpetual onion. It grows to the size of a spring onion but each single onion that is planted spreads into a clump of thirty or more onions. You just dig up a bit of the clump when you need a few spring onions and start off another group in a new place every few years when you think the soil is getting flogged.

They can be eaten raw or used for cooking.

Parsley

An essential herb to many cooks which is much better fresh from the garden.

Sow from March to June in a drill $\frac{1}{2}$ in deep with three seeds to the inch.

Parsley seed can take up to five weeks to germinate. To shock it into growth pour a kettle of boiling water along the row after the seed has been planted and covered over – it softens the outer skin of the seed. Thin (see p. 76) to 3 in apart when they come up and finally to 6 in.

Parsley likes a rich, moist soil and will grow quite well in partial shade. Pick off the sprigs as you need them leaving the plant to grow. If you take off any flower heads it will encourage the plant to produce leaves instead of going to seed.

Parsley is a biennial so it needs resowing every second year and preferably every year to keep a continuous supply.

Potatoes

I doubt whether you will want to go in for maincrop potatoes (those that are dug up in the autumn for use right through the winter) but as the taste of new potatoes straight from the garden when the skin virtually comes off in your hands is one of the real rewards of gardening you may like to grow a few, or even just one plant by itself in the flower garden. Potato plants are grown from potatoes but don't plant those you have bought for cooking – they will tend to produce poor quality diseased plants. Buy proper 'seed' potatoes that have

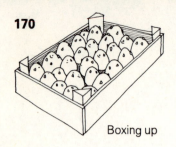

Boxing up

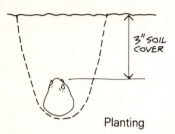

Planting

Earthing up

been specially grown for the purpose and are certified free from disease. You can get them from garden centres and seed merchants in early spring.

The soil. Potatoes will grow on most soils but a well-drained, deeply dug soil is what they really like. They do not like lime.

Boxing up. Seed potatoes should be set up in shallow boxes or seed trays as soon as you get them. The rose end – where most of the eyes are – should be uppermost. Keep them in an airy, frost-free place in full light. When the shoots start to grow rub off the weak ones leaving just the best two on each potato. Make sure the shoots don't get knocked off during planting – they are the vital growth points.

Planting. Early potatoes should be planted 1 ft apart in rows 1 ft 9 in apart during the middle of March in the south through to the middle of April in the north.

There should be about 3 in of soil over the top of each tuber after planting. The easiest way is to take out individual planting holes for each potato with a large trowel or small spade. Plant them with the shoots uppermost.

Earthing up. Sunlight causes potatoes to turn green in which state they are not only unpalatable but poisonous. Potato plants are normally earthed up as they grow to keep the light off the potatoes and to improve the yield. The soil is drawn up to form ridges over the roots. It is a bit of a chore getting in among the plants to do this. You can, of course, not bother to earth them up at all and just discard any green potatoes as you dig them but you will get a smaller crop. One way to beat the system is to plant them in shallow trenches and then fill in the trenches as the plants grow. Earthing down is much easier than earthing up.

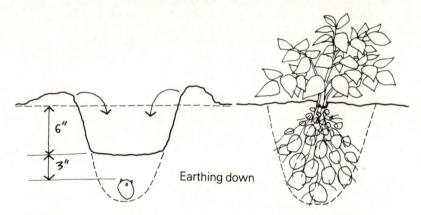

Earthing down

Harvesting. You can test if your potatoes are ready by digging up a root when the plants are in flower – the first indication they may be ready, although it varies from variety to variety, and having an exploratory dig is the normal way to find out. If they are too small leave them for another couple of weeks and try again. If you only have a few plants you may prefer to just carefully remove some soil to see what size the potatoes are before putting in the fork.

They are certainly best straight from the soil, so dig them as you need them.

Radishes

Probably the first thing you can gather at the beginning of the year are some tender crisp radishes – how welcome after the long winter wait. Early varieties can be ready for pulling in 6 to 8 weeks from a sowing in early March and they can be sown right through to August, though the later sowings won't produce such crisp roots.

Sow in short drills ¹₂ in deep just a few at a time and at regular intervals. They have a high rate of germination so really the best thing is to sow just one seed every inch so that you don't have to bother to do any thinning.

Keep them well watered so that they grow quickly. Pull them, wash them and eat them within the hour to have them at their best.

Runner beans

Just a few. If you want to grow just a few runner beans for fun, perhaps in the flower garden, the easy way is up a 'wigwam' of poles or canes about 7 or 8 ft tall. Put up the poles first.

You can either put in seed about 2 in deep outdoors in mid May or you can buy plants to be put out the first week in June after the frosts have gone. Buy the plants in May if you wish and harden them off by putting the pots outside during the day and taking them in at night.

It is normal to have just one plant growing up each pole but have two if it makes you feel happier.

More than a few. The traditional way to grow a bigger crop of runner beans is up a framework of poles anything from say 6 ft to 10 ft tall and anything from 3 ft to a mile long – depending on your needs and the space you have.

Put up the framework first with a double row of poles 1 ft 3 in apart and 9 in to 1 ft between each pole so that a bean or plant may be sown at each one. Push the poles into the ground in an upright position and then pull each opposing pair together near the top, cross them over and lay another pole in the V formed. Tie the canes together with string.

If you can't get a large number of poles you can have strands of string stretched from poles fixed to the top and bottom of a support structure.

Soil and harvesting. Grow runner beans in deep rich soil, pick them while they are young and tender before any 'strings' have formed down the sides and try to grow them in a different place each year.

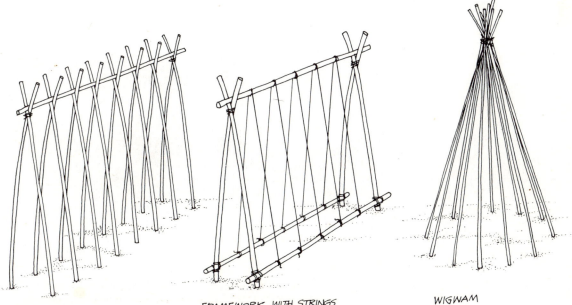

TRADITIONAL   FRAMEWORK WITH STRINGS   WIGWAM

Shallots

These are one of the easiest vegetables to grow. They are useful in cooking and a pickled shallot has a more nutty flavour than a pickled onion. Shallots can be obtained from seed merchants or garden centres. Plant one shallot and it grows and divides to form a cluster of six to twenty shallots.

As soon as the soil is dry enough to get on in February or March take out small holes 1 in deep and 9 in apart with an old spoon. Put in a shallot, pull the earth round it and firm it into position with your fingers so that the top half of the shallot is left above the soil.

Shallots can be grown in rows, in squares or in small groups, perhaps in the flower garden, 9 in apart each way. They like well manured, well drained soil.

When the tops turn brown in July, pull up the shallots and dry them off for several days in the sun before storing them in open boxes or in nets in a cool, dry, frost-proof place.

Seakale beet

Seakale beet will look quite well in the flower garden and it is easy to cultivate. It is grown for its leaves and not for its root. The green part of the leaf is cooked like spinach and the white mid-rib like asparagus, or both may be cooked together.

If the outer leaves are picked off as required complete with stem right down to the base the plants will keep producing more leaves right through to autumn.

Sow in 1 in deep drills with one seed every 2 in or so. They are cluster seeds so thin down to one seedling in each cluster when they come up and then progressively thin to a final distance of 1 ft apart.

This vegetable will do well in most soils, although it will produce a better crop if the soil has been deeply dug and well manured.

Tomatoes

There was a time not so many years ago when outdoor tomato growing was a very risky business. After a lot of staking, tying, stopping and feeding most people ended up with loads of green tomatoes and very few red ones. There was more green tomato chutney in the land than marmalade. All that has changed now that there are many varieties that ripen well in our sometimes sunless climate.

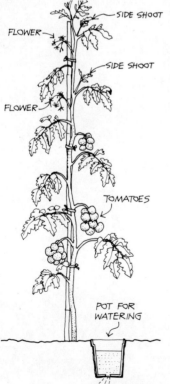

SIDE SHOOT
FLOWER
SIDE SHOOT
FLOWER
TOMATOES
POT FOR WATERING

PINCH OUT SIDE SHOOTS

The very easy way. There are now several very good strains of outdoor *bush* tomatoes that are sold by garden centres as plants in May and June and that ask no more than that they should be planted out in the garden or in growing bags in June when all danger of frost has passed about 1½ to 2 ft apart and that they should be kept watered in dry weather.

Make the hole slightly deeper than the pot so that the rootball is covered with about an inch of soil. Always hold the plant by the rootball, being careful not to damage the stem.

To get the plant out of the pot turn it upside down supporting the rootball with one hand by having the plant upside down between the fingers and then tap the edge of the pot sharply against something hard like the edge of a table to release it from the pot. Place the rootball in the hole, replace the soil and then water. If you then sink the empty pot in the ground about 6 to 9 in from the plant and keep it topped up with water in dry weather the water will get through to the lower roots.

Tomatoes will do best if you plant them in a sunny situation and don't have the soil too rich. Too much nourishment in the early stages tends to produce leaves at the expense of fruit. Wait till several trusses of small fruit have set and then water with liquid tomato fertilizer if you feel you must.

The fairly easy way. If you want to grow the upright variety there is slightly more work but not so far to stoop to pick the fruit. Put a strong 6 ft stake at each position and plant close up to it following the instructions above.

Tie the plants loosely to their stakes with soft string, making sure the stem has room to swell. Tie at intervals as the plants grow.

Remove any side shoots that develop from where each leaf joins the main stem (see illustration) otherwise the plants will produce too many stems and become bushy and unmanageable and the final crop will be less. Do this while the shoots are still small (do not pick out these shoots on bush varieties). Be careful that you do not pick off the flower shoots by mistake. They come from the stem *between* one leaf and another and not where a leaf joins the stem.

Harvesting. You can leave the fruit on the plants until they are red or you can pick them after they have started to change colour and let them finish ripening at normal room temperature indoors.

At the end of the season, before the frosts come, pick off all the green fruit as well as any that have started to change colour and store in a cool, dry, frost-proof place. As the fruits start to change colour take them indoors into normal room temperatures to ripen off. They may shrivel if you take them into the warmth while they are still green.

If you find vegetable growing enjoyable and wish to know more about it, then there are many good books available on the subject, among which is my own *Planned Vegetable Garden* (Dent, 1979).

THE BOTANICAL FAMILIES TO WHICH VEGETABLES BELONG

Chenopodiaceae

Beetroot. Spinach beet. Seakale beet. Spinach.

Compositae

Lettuce. Chicory and endive. Globe artichoke. Jerusalem artichoke. Salsify (vegetable oyster) and scorzonera.

Cruciferae

Cabbage. Kohl rabi. Broccoli. Cauliflowers. Kale. Brussels sprouts. Radish. Turnip. Swede. Cress. Coleworts (collards). Chinese cabbage.

Cucurbitaceae
Marrow. Courgette. Cucumber. Melon.

Gramineae
Sweet corn.

Leguminosae
Peas. Runner beans. French beans. Broad beans. Haricot beans.

Liliaceae
Onions. Welsh or perpetual onions. Leeks. Shallots. Garlic. Chives. Asparagus.

Solanaceae
Potatoes. Tomatoes. Capsicum (sweet peppers). Aubergines (egg plants).

Umbelliferae
Parsley. Celery and celeriac. Parsnip. Carrot.

Valerianaceae
Corn salad (lambs lettuce).

Fruit growing is not really for the reluctant gardener. It can be a complex, time-consuming operation – but there is something so satisfying about seeing fruit growing in the garden and something so pleasurable about gathering it and eating it that most of us cannot resist the temptation to try. There is also the advantage that the plants are perennial.

So let us look at some of the complexities involved and see if we can grow some fruit and still leave time for other things.

TYPES OF FRUIT

Tree fruit is usually called 'top fruit' – apples, pears, plums, etc. Cane, bush and plant fruit is called 'soft fruit' – raspberries, blackcurrants, strawberries, etc.

But be careful about that word 'bush'. It can be used to describe bush trees as well as currant bushes.

WHAT SHALL WE GROW AND WHERE?

If you have a very large garden you could devote a part of it specifically to fruit; if you have a medium-sized garden you may want to incorporate it into the total plan because fruit is not necessarily just a utility crop – many types of fruit can be used as decorative features adding interest and colour to the garden in the spring when the blossom is out and in the autumn as well with mellow fruitfulness. If your garden is small you may just like to grow a little soft fruit like raspberries or strawberries, or have an apple tree.

There is one basic rule. Unless you have a very large garden, avoid standard and half standard trees (see pp. 108 and 109). A standard Bramley cooker can, for instance, grow to more than 25 ft across – which would quite dominate many gardens (see Trees and Shrubs p. 107).

Get trees grown on dwarfing root stocks (see p. 109) such as bush trees, cordons, pyramids or other trained forms.

THE BIRDS AND THE BEES

They can both have a profound effect on your crop.

Some birds, like bullfinches, will peck out the young growth buds of many top fruits and soft fruits in the spring just as they are coming into growth and then in the autumn the blackbirds will finish off the villainy by pinching what little fruit has managed to form. In some districts the only answer is to put cages over the smaller fruit bushes and throw nets over the larger ones – another reason for keeping to the smaller forms of tree is that it can be very difficult to net a large tree.

Bees and many other flying insects are, on the other hand, very welcome in the fruit garden. The transfer of pollen from one fruit flower to another is essential for fertilization and this is mainly done by the bees and other insects.

With apples, pears, cherries and plums there is an added complication. Only a few varieties will set fruit with their own pollen. They have to be fertilized by the pollen from a different variety flowering at the same time and even then some varieties are incompatible. Variety A, for instance, may well pollinate B but B may not pollinate A so C has to be grown to fertilize A. It is all to do with whether their chromosomes are diploid, triploid, tetraploid or hexaploid.

So don't be tempted to buy just one apple or pear tree and plant it on its own. Unless there are other trees of the right kind in the vicinity it probably won't bear fruit.

In the fruit garden plans that are included further on in this section I have selected varieties that will pollinate each other so if you change the plans in any way, or just select a few of them, do check with your nurseryman that your selection will pollinate each other.

THE WEATHER

The wrong kind of weather can also result in a poor crop. Don't try to grow fruit in frost hollows. The danger period is when the flowers are open – the frost doesn't seem to damage tightly closed buds or small set fruit in the same way. High winds or heavy rain at flowering time can also result in a poor set.

THE RIGHT KIND OF SOIL

Most fruits prefer a slightly acid soil. A pH of 6.0 is a good average, going up a bit to pH 6.5 for stone fruits like peaches, plums and cherries. You won't get good results on chalky soils unless you add large amounts of compost, manure or peat.

TOP FRUIT

Types of trees

Most fruit trees are grafted on to different root stocks which have the effect of reducing the vigour of the tree and therefore its size and shape, because most of us haven't got room in our gardens for large standard trees. In any case we would rather have a small crop of several different varieties than a lot of just one variety.

A bush tree is probably the most easily managed form of fruit tree in that if you don't want to bother to do anything else you can keep it in order by just taking out those branches, if any, that are keeping the light and air from the others aiming to have an open-centre tree. One problem with a bush tree is that if you grow it in the lawn it is rather difficult to mow under so it is perhaps best planted in one of the beds.

Other trained trees need to be carefully pruned to achieve the ultimate shape but as they can become quite handsome garden features some people think it is worth the trouble.

The most common forms are:

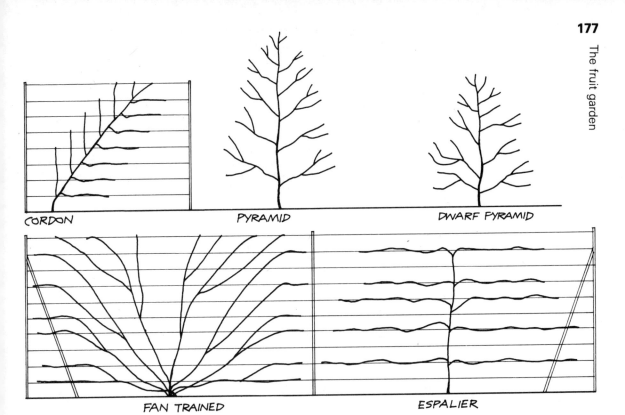

CORDON PYRAMID DWARF PYRAMID

FAN TRAINED ESPALIER

Planting

The normal time to plant fruit trees, bushes and canes is in the dormant season from December to early March but if the plants are container grown they can, of course, be planted at any time of the year – see the sections Choosing, Planting and Aftercare of trees and shrubs on pp. 120-122.

Many garden centres stock fruit trees and bushes but you may have to order in advance to get the varieties you want. Or buy one of the popular gardening magazines in autumn or early winter and you will see plenty of advertisements from specialist growers.

Pruning – general principles

Pruning is normally carried out in the dormant season from late December to the end of February or even early March if the winter is long. The main reasons for pruning are:

1 To train the tree into the required shape.
2 To encourage the formation of fruit buds – those that contain the embryo blossom. They are the round plump ones as opposed to the slim pointed growth buds.
3 To remove overcrowded growth so that sunlight and air can get to all parts of the tree.

Is is essential to have the tree on the right kind of rootstock for the ultimate tree form.

Initial pruning. On year-old trees, called maidens, the single straight stems are cut back to produce side growths to build up the basic framework for the tree's ultimate shape and the tree is then pruned each year to get it to form that shape.

Pruning is based on the principle that terminal buds, the ones at the ends of the shoots, when left unpruned, inhibit the development of lateral or side shoots and vice versa. So if you want a side shoot to develop you will need to prune back the terminal shoot at that point. But I think the reluctant gardener would be well advised to purchase trees up to three years old where the basic shaping has been done by the nurseryman.

Subsequent pruning. The fruit bearing habit of the particular variety, the type of rootstock on which it is growing and the desired shape of the tree all need to be taken into account.

Apples and pears produce fruiting buds on short spurs which develop on wood that is more than one year old. Some apples and a few pears are tip bearers and have most of their fruit buds at or near the ends of two-year-old shoots. So although pruning to regulate new growth may have to be done, giving a fruit tree a close trim every year is much worse than doing nothing at all because you may well be cutting off many of the fruit buds.

If in doubt just thin out the branches to remove any overcrowded and crossing growth. This especially applies to the plum family. Once plum trees are established all that should be done is the removal of dead wood and crossing branches. And this is best done in early spring just as the sap is rising and growth is starting. Autumn or winter pruning might give rise to infection by silver leaf disease.

Pruning of other fruit trees is normally carried out in winter with just a little summer pruning of thin new growths to prevent overcrowding.

Types of top fruit

Apples. These can be grown in almost any form – bush, cordon, pyramid or espalier. A single cordon can yield 4 to 8 lb of fruit. Cross-pollination is essential as most varieties will not set fruit with their own pollen. See p. 182 for good varieties.

Pears. They flower earlier than apples so can get damaged by frosts. They can be grown in the same form as apples and cross-pollination is again important. Even so-called self-fertile varieties like Conference will set a better crop with a mate. See p. 182 for good varieties

Plums, damsons and gages. Like pears their early flowers are at risk from frosts so plant them in a sheltered position. They are best grown as bush, pyramid or fan trained and don't do well as cordons. Many varieties are self-sterile and need a mate. Very acid soils should be improved by sprinkling a few ounces of lime per square yard in the spring. See p. 182 for good varieties.

Sweet cherries. They are delightful fruits but growing them is not to be recommended. No dwarfing stocks are available, they need a pollinator, they take a long time to come into bearing and the birds will probably get any fruit that there is before you get a chance to.

If you have a really large warm wall you could try training a sweet cherry as a very large fan on a semi-vigorous rootstock called Colt, but do protect it from the birds. **Good variety**: Stella. No pollinator needed.

Acid cherries (for cooking). A much happier story – the birds tend to leave them alone. They can be grown as bush trees or fan trained against a wall. Morello or Kentish Red will set a crop with their own pollen so they can be planted singly.

Figs. As they need a warm situation they are best grown as fans on a sunny wall. Or if you have a really warm spot where two walls meet that would be ideal.

Figs are grown on their own roots as no rootstocks are available. In their natural habitat figs are used to growing in poor dry soils. In our richer and

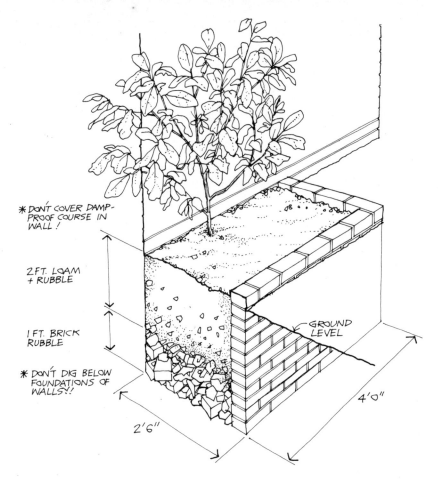

* DON'T COVER DAMP-
PROOF COURSE IN
WALL !

2 FT. LOAM
+ RUBBLE

1 FT. BRICK
RUBBLE

* DON'T DIG BELOW
FOUNDATIONS OF
WALLS!!

GROUND
LEVEL

4'0"

2'6"

wetter soils their roots must be restricted or the tree will make a lot of growth
but set little fruit.

So plant in a brick or concrete trough sunk into, or built into, the soil
with no base to it but tightly packed at the bottom with brick rubble about 1 ft
deep. Fill the trough with good loam mixed with a couple of bucketfuls of old
mortar rubble.

Figs will fruit by themselves – no pollinator is needed. **Good varieties:**
Brown Turkey, White Marseilles.

SOFT FRUITS

There are no pollination problems but soft fruit often needs to be caged unless
you can grow enough for both the birds and yourself.

Strawberries

Personally I don't think it's worth the bother of growing strawberries. They also
have to be protected from birds, so I prefer to pick my own at a local fruit farm –
but there is no doubt that this is the fruit that gives the quickest crop and many
people enjoy growing theirs.

Those planted half way through one year will be cropping the next.
Some can be planted as late as the autumn. The plants send out runners with
new young plants on them. These should be removed to retain the vigour of
the parent plant unless you want to expand your stock or to replace the old
parent plants which should be done every three years or so.

When planting take out a shallow hole wide enough and deep enough to spread out and bury the roots but to leave the plant just sitting on top of the soil. Strawberries need good soil with plenty of compost and should be planted 1 ft 6 in apart in rows 2 ft 6 in apart. Pick off some of the flowers if you want big fruit.

Select the best runners to increase your stock. Leave them attached to the parent plant but peg them down so that they are in contact with the soil, pick off any flowers so that the strength goes into building up the plants. Sever from the parent plant when they are well rooted and transplant to where they are needed. **Good varieties:** Cambridge Prizewinner, Cambridge Vigour, Royal Sovereign.

Raspberries

A very popular fruit that gives a good return for the amount of space occupied, but they have to be protected from birds with nets or in cages. Grow them 1 ft 6 in apart in single rows 6 ft apart. Train them up horizontal wires stretched between stout posts which are set 2 ft into the ground and are 6 ft above it with the wires at 2 ft 3½ ft and 5 ft or more from the ground. Each year cut out the old canes that have fruited right down to the ground and tie in the best two or three new canes of each plant which will fruit the following year.

Once they are well established after a couple of years, raspberries send up several canes from the same plant and additional canes will come up from the roots away from the main clump so if you need to expand your stock carefully dig up individual canes with some root attached, replant, cut the cane down by half, pick off any flower buds the first year to direct all the growth into the new cane that will grow from the base. **Good varieties**: Malling Promise, Malling Delight, Glen Cova.

Black, red and white currants, gooseberries and worcesterberries

The are all related. They will accept a wide range of soil as long as it is well drained and contains plenty of compost. They will all tolerate partial shade but do best in an open sunny situation.

They are all normally grown as bushes 5 to 6 ft apart each way although gooseberries are sometimes grown fan-tailed or as cordons supported by posts or wires.

Birds can do a lot of damage to their buds and pinch the fruit – especially gooseberries and worcesterberries – so they are best caged.

Good varieties: Blackcurrants: Wellington XXX, Malvern Cross   Redcurrants: Laxton No 1, Stanza   White currant: White Versailles   Gooseberries: Keepsake, Careless   Worcesterberry: Just order as such.

Planting. See section on Shrubs.

Pruning. These bush fruits normally only come into full bearing after 2 to 3 years and pruning must take the following into account.

Blackcurrants produce their best fruit on one-year-old wood. White and red currants produce their fruit on short spurs on old wood and in clusters at the base of one-year-old growths. There may also be a few fruits further along this new wood.

So blackcurrants can be cut back after fruiting to produce some new growths, but don't overdo it, while white and red currants are best just trimmed into shape or to encourage some new growth to replace some very old growth.

Gooseberries and worcesterberries will fruit on both old and new wood. The bushes get a bit straggly after a while so every few years some vigorous new growths should be allowed to replace some old growths which should be cut out.

This pruning is all best done in the winter.

Blackberries, loganberries and other hybrid berries

They will grow in partial shade and a variety of soils but will do best in good soil in full sun.

They can all be trained along boundary fences, over arches and other structures and against fences and walls, but as they nearly all fruit on the previous year's growth whilst they are also sending up new canes for the next year's fruit perhaps the easiest way to train them is to have the fruiting growth trained to one side and the new shoots to the other. At the end of the fruiting season the old growth is cut off right down to the ground and the new growths securely tied in.

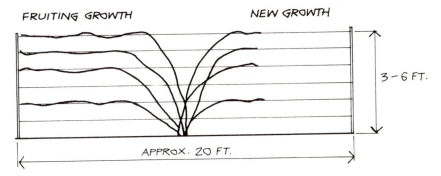

FRUITING GROWTH   NEW GROWTH   3 – 6 FT.   APPROX. 20 FT.

Training and picking are much less painful if you grow the thornless varieties.

Planting. If they come in containers carefully take off the container and plant with another inch or so of soil over the top. If they are bare root spread out the roots and plant a couple of inches deeper than they were in the nursery. Don't let the roots get dry while planting – cover them over.

Good varieties: Blackberries: Merton Thornless, Oregon Thornless Loganberry: Just order as such   Hybrid berries: Tayberry, Thornless Boysenberry

Grapes

Although you can let grape vines wander where they will perhaps to clothe a pergola or some other structure they do need a rather complex system of pruning to encourage a worthwhile crop.

Grapes are not produced on old wood but only on the current season's growth, so each season's new growth is cut back to the basic framework of the vine that has been allowed to develop – unless you wish to enlarge this framework. Rub off unwanted buds at the start of the season to limit the number of branches and then also limit the number of bunches of grapes by pinching some of them off directly they appear. Then pinch off the growth two leaves past each bunch of grapes so that the grapes are encourged to grow and not more leaves.

Planting. Grape vines are best planted in the spring. Plant the same depth they were in the nursery or just a bit deeper.

Good outdoor varieties: Muller Thurgau, Madeleine Sylvaner. Both white.

Good varieties of apples, pears and plums

Most varieties do need a mate and will not have a good set of fruit unless there is a suitable partner in the vicinity that flowers at the same time and is compatible.

I have selected some top quality varieties which are not too vigorous and I have also suggested some suitable partners.

My choice of apples – dessert

Variety	When to pick	Ready to eat	A good pollinator
Discovery	Aug	Aug/Sept	Greensleeves or Cox's Orange Pippin
Greensleeves	End Sept	Oct/Nov	Cox or Discovery
Worcester Pearmain	Mid Sept	Sept/Oct	Cox or Greensleeves
Cox's Orange Pippin	Late Sept	Nov/Feb	Discovery or Greensleeves
Spartan	Early Oct	Nov/Jan	Greensleeves, Discovery or Cox
Gavin	Mid Sept	Oct/Dec	Greensleeves or Discovery
Red Charles Ross	Mid Oct	Oct/Dec	Greensleeves, Discovery or Gavin

Cooking apples

Grenadier	Aug/Sept	Aug/Sept	Greensleeves or Discovery
Lanes Prince Albert	Early Oct	Oct/Feb	Greensleeves or Discovery

My choice of pears

Williams bon Chrétien	Aug 30th	Sept/Oct	Conference or Onward
Onward	Late Sept	Oct/Nov	Conference or Williams
Louise Bonne de Jersey	Late Sept	Oct	Conference
Conference	Early Oct	Oct/Nov	Louise Bonne de Jersey
Doyenné du Comice	Mid Oct	Nov	Conference or Onward

My choice of plums

	Pick and Eat	
Victoria	Late Aug/early Sept	None needed
Czar	Early Aug	None needed
Kirkes Blue	Mid Sept	Victoria

ESPALIER TREES AS A GARDEN DIVIDER

A rustic screen with espalier trees on wires makes a handsome divider between say the flower and vegetable garden. The trees suggested are compatible, flower in the same period and give a long season of supply.

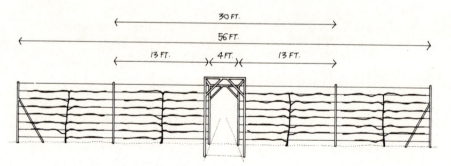

For a 56 ft wide screen have either

4 pears

Williams Bon Chrétien	Conference		Louise Bonne de Jersey	Doyenné du Comice

or 4 apples

Red Charles Ross	Greensleeves		Cox's Orange Pippin	Discovery

or 2 apples and 2 pears

Discovery	Cox's Orange Pippin		Conference	Louise Bonne de Jersey

For a screen 30 ft wide have either

2 pears	Conference	Louise Bonne de Jersey
or 2 apples	Discovery	Cox's Orange Pippin

Or carry out the same idea using cordons to give more variety.

A decorative pergola

If you have a walk running north/south that gets plenty of sunshine and you have some skill and plenty of patience you could use espaliers or cordons to make a delightful feature. (Made of metal.)

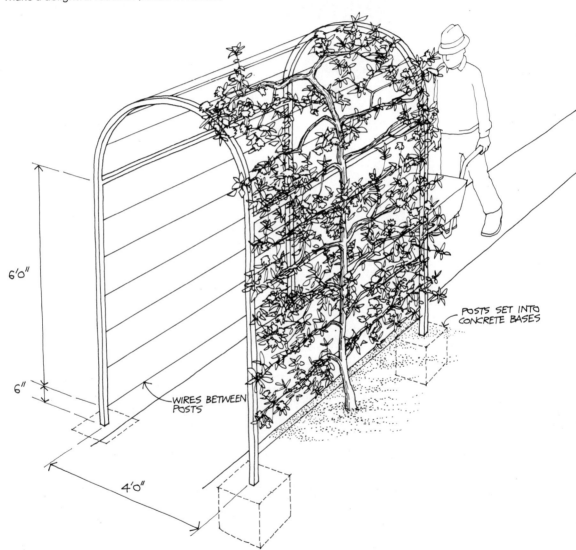

6'0"

6"

POSTS SET INTO CONCRETE BASES

WIRES BETWEEN POSTS

4'0"

Rhubarb

If you have good deep soil rhubarb is easy to grow and is very welcome at the beginning of the season when there is not much else in the garden to pick.

Although rhubarb can be grown from seed the offspring will not breed true to the parent plant and will be inferior. Rhubarb is therefore usually propagated by dividing up existing clumps which divisions will all, of course, be like the parent because they are part of it.

Rhubarb has long thick tap roots and when you buy a plant make sure the root or roots are intact and not broken and that there is a good plump sound bud at the top.

Where and when to plant. Plant in either October or March. Although rhubarb prefers to be right out in the sun it will stand partial shade but not dense shade. Its roots like to be well fed, cool and moist but well drained. As the plants will be in the same place for a number of years dig the site deeply and incorporate plenty of compost or manure and after planting put a 2 in deep layer of compost on top of the soil each year in January or February – the worms will take it down.

The roots should be planted with the tops just 1 in below the soil level and there should be 2 ft 6 in between plants each way if you have more than one. Do make the hole deep enough and wide enough to take the root(s) in comfort.

Harvesting. Don't pull any sticks the first year or you will weaken the plant as it is trying to get itself established. Be sparing what you pull the second year. If you want some pale pink sticks early in the season then cover your plants, or just some of them, with large upturned boxes to exclude the light – a small dustbin will do but remove the covers by May after pulling the early crop and then leave the plant alone for at least a month to allow it to recover. By the way 'pull' the rhubarb to remove the whole stick – don't just cut it off; stop pulling altogether by the end of July so that the plant can re-establish itself before the winter rest.

Recommended varieties. Hawke's Champagne. Timperley Early. The Sutton.

APPENDIX A

A SUMMARY OF TIME-SAVING TIPS

If things are easy to do they are more likely to get done. Here is a miscellany of thoughts that may save you time.

Compost collecting. Make compost easy to collect. Have a compost colander in the kitchen right by the sink and a covered compost bucket by the back door to be emptied on the compost heap just once a week.

Diseases. Choose varieties of plants that are specified as being resistant to diseases. Those that are prone to diseases are great time-wasters if you try to cure them, so turn them out and replace them with disease-resistant types.

Floppy plants. Avoid tall floppy plants that need supporting – ones like the taller Michaelmas daisies – go for the dwarf varieties that can stand up for themselves.

Geranium cuttings. The quick way to take outdoor geranium cuttings in the summer to increase your stock is just to break off 4 to 6 inch lengths of stem whenever the fancy takes you and do no more than just push them in the soil - right by the parent plant if you wish. Many will take and can be potted up later to be taken indoors for the winter ready to plant out the next year.

Ground cover. Use ground cover plants under and around shrubs to smother weeds. See p. 114.

Hedges. Don't plant fast growing types. They are fine for the first few years but endless work to keep cut once they have grown up. Go for the slower growers – like yew – that require less work in the long run.

Hedges. Have paths alongside hedges; they make cutting and clearing up much easier.

Hoes. Use a Dutch hoe all round the garden once a week in the summer whether the weeds are showing or not. That way you will kill off the seedlings before they emerge and save time in the long run.

Hose. Have a hose permanently laid all round the garden – tucked under the hedge or against the fence – with junctions at intervals to make it easy to water any area as the need arises.

Lawn shapes. Give lawns continuous curves to make mowing easier. Avoid dead ends or sharp corners.

Manure, muck and compost make the soil easier to manage. They hold moisture too so there is less watering necessary for well manured soils.

Mint. Have some mint or other herbs handy by the back door. Mint has a spreading habit, so contain it by planting it in some good soil in a sunken bucket with some drainage holes put in it.

Paths. Paving slab paths in the vegetable garden make it easy to measure distances between rows of plants and are easy to keep tidy.

Plan on paper. Planning your garden layout on paper first saves a lot of time and quite a few mistakes. Paper planning is easy to put right.

Potatoes. If you plant in trenches you can fill in the trenches as the plants grow and save yourself the bother of 'earthing up'. See p. 170.

Protecting fences. Use creosote or other wood preservatives of that type to take care of your fences. They are easier and quicker to apply than paints. But do keep them off the plants.

Prunings for burning. Always cut up any prunings for the bonfire nice and small – they burn better that way.

Raised beds. Raised beds can save stooping – helpful if you are disabled or have a few aches and pains.

Seed sowing. Mix dark coloured seed with a little talcum powder shaken up in the seed packet. You will then see where you are sowing as the seeds will stand out against the soil.

Seed sowing. Mix very fine seed with fine dry sand to make it easier to sow thinly and evenly.

Seed sowing. Sow thinly. It is a bore but it saves a lot of thinning later on – a bigger bore.

Soil. Think twice about buying a house with heavy clay soil.

Soil. Carefully conserve your top-soil and make sure it stays at the top. Top-soil is so much easier to handle and grow things in than sandy, chalky or clayey sub-soil.

Tools. Clean your tools before you put them away. I know it is a bind but it will save you time and effort in the long run. Shiny tools slide through the soil so much easier than dirty ones. Keep an oily rag hanging up where the tools are stored so that you can give them a wipe over when they are put away to keep the rust away. If you have got the money go in for stainless steel tools – they take a lot of effort out of gardening.

Tools where they are wanted. Keep tools nearest to where they will be used. If a tool is not handy a job will often not get done. If you have a long garden it is worth keeping a Dutch hoe and perhaps a fork at each end so that you aren't faced with a long walk any time some weeds need dealing with.

Water. Have an outside tap for ease of watering in summer but have an inside stop-cock to shut it off in winter so that it doesn't get damaged by frost.

Wheelbarrow wisdom. Before you load up point your wheelbarrow in the direction that you intend to go – it may save a muscle-pulling manoeuvre.

APPENDIX B

THE GODFREY BOX

If you can get a supply of rustic poles about 3 in in diameter and up to 7 ft 6 in long you can build a compost box fit for a king with virtually no carpentry – ideal for the reluctant handyman. It will be good to look at and will produce connoisseurs' compost.

For a double box with total outer measurements of 6 ft long by 4 ft 3 in wide you will need:

Rustic poles (About 3 in in diameter)

Uprights	10 @ 5 ft 6 in	
	3 @ 6 ft 6 in	Treat all timbers with
	2 @ 7 ft 6 in	preservative. This is especially
Back rails	12 @ 6 ft 0 in	necessary for the uprights
Side rails	36 @ 4 ft 0 in	which will be set 2 ft in the
Roof support rails	2 @ 7 ft 0 in	ground

Front boards Use any planks of wood about 2 ft 4 in long to drop in behind the front uprights and retain the compost as the boxes are filled.

Housebricks 36 in number. To be laid on the ground to give an air space under the compost.

Weldmesh 2 sheets of galvanized weldmesh about 2 ft 4 in wide by 4 ft long to lay on top of the bricks to support the compost. Measure the exact sizes after you have built the bins. Weldmesh comes in various thicknesses and sizes of mesh. A 3 in by 1 in mesh of 10 gauge material does very well.

Corrugated sheets Enough to make a sloping roof approximately 7 ft by 4 ft 6 in.

Method of construction

Build on a level site of bare earth.

Take out holes for the uprights and set them 2 ft in the ground with just enough space between each pair to take the thickness of the back and side rails. The plan assumes this is 3 in.

Set out the bricks in the pattern shown. Drop in the horizontal back rails and then the side rails. Lay in the weldmesh floor, cutting the corners to fit snugly round the uprights. Fix the roof support rails to the uprights.

If the corrugated roof is fitted in such a way that it is removable it will be easier to empty the bins – but you may need to put weights on it to hold it down in windy weather.

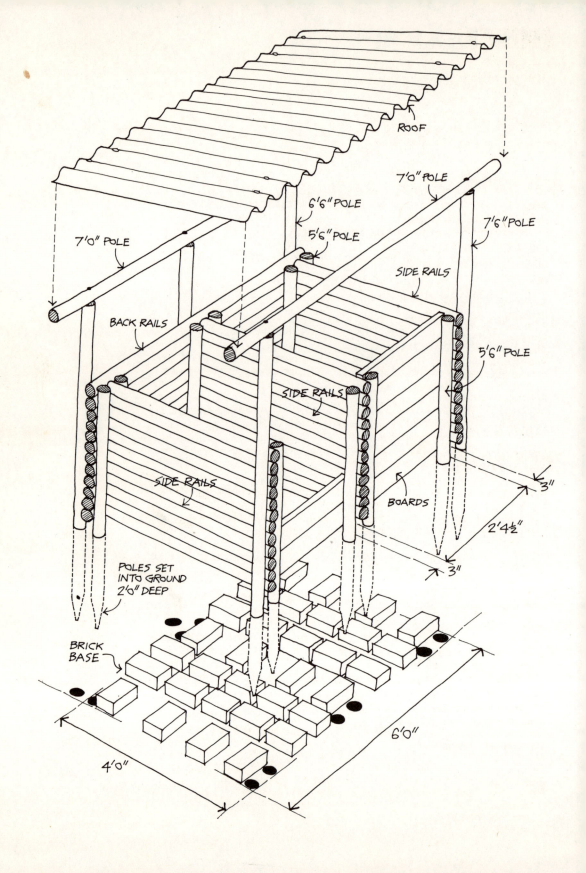

ROOF

7'0" POLE

6'6" POLE

5'6" POLE

7'0" POLE

7'6" POLE

SIDE RAILS

BACK RAILS

SIDE RAILS

5'6" POLE

SIDE RAILS

BOARDS

3"

2'4½"

3"

POLES SET
INTO GROUND
2'0" DEEP

BRICK
BASE

6'0"

4'0"

INDEX